Solution-Focused Therapy with Children and Adolescents

Solution-Focused Therapy with Children and Adolescents offers mental health professionals an integration of creative and playful approaches and solution-focused therapy. The author presents developmentally appropriate and expressive alternatives to oral communication including sandtray, writing, puppetry, drawing and coloring, photography, and music. The text presents an overview of strength-based and creative approaches with a focused examination of the philosophy and process of solution-focused therapy, then divides chapters into specific stages of therapy—beginnings, searching for treasure, setting goals, and ending the session—with creative techniques offered in each section. The final chapter addresses working with children and adolescents in solution-focused groups, including how to set up groups and progress through different group stages, presenting specific techniques and activities focused on each stage of the group process.

Elizabeth R. Taylor, PhD, LPC-S, LMFT, RPT-S, teaches counseling at Texas Christian University. As a licensed counselor and play therapist, she has presented workshops on solution-focused therapy, play therapy, and resiliency at state, national, and international conferences.

Solution-Focused Therapy with Children and Adolescents

Creative and Play-Based Approaches

Elizabeth R. Taylor

Routledge
Taylor & Francis Group

NEW YORK AND LONDON

First published 2019
by Routledge
52 Vanderbilt Avenue, New York, NY 10017

and by Routledge
2 Park Square, Milton Park, Abingdon, Oxon, OX14 4RN

Routledge is an imprint of the Taylor & Francis Group, an informa business

Library of Congress Cataloging-in-Publication Data
Names: Taylor, Elizabeth, 1970- author.
Title: Solution-focused therapy with children and adolescents : creative
    and play-based approaches / Elizabeth R. Taylor.
Description: New York, NY : Routledge, 2019. | Includes bibliographical
    references and index.
Identifiers: LCCN 2018056694 (print) | LCCN 2018057585 (ebook) |
    ISBN 9781315166674 (E-book) | ISBN 9781138054547 (hardback) |
    ISBN 9781138054554 (pbk.) | ISBN 9781315166674 (ebk.)
Subjects: | MESH: Psychotherapy, Brief—methods | Sensory Art
    Therapies | Child | Adolescent
Classification: LCC RC480.5 (ebook) | LCC RC480.5 (print) | NLM WS
    350.2 | DDC 616.89/14—dc23
LC record available at https://lccn.loc.gov/2018056694

ISBN: 978-1-138-05454-7 (hbk)
ISBN: 978-1-138-05455-4 (pbk)
ISBN: 978-1-315-16667-4 (ebk)

Typeset in Minion
by Swales & Willis Ltd, Exeter, Devon, UK

Dedication

To my parents, L.G. and Edna Taylor, who always encouraged me in my physical, spiritual, emotional, and educational development—who demonstrated the true meaning of sacrifice and unconditional love.

To my nieces and nephews: Taylor, Kenzie, Joe, Kaitlyn, Emma, Kathryn, Reagan, and Olivia. Words cannot express how much they mean to me! They taught me about the amazing and complex world of children but also about my own capacity to love unconditionally.

To their parents, Tommy and Dayna, and Tenna and Mike, who support me by giving me a soft place to land—who make me feel at home in their homes and give me space and time to love their awesome children.

Contents

Illustrations

Figures

Tables

CHAPTER 1

Introduction

Elizabeth R. Taylor

Historically, the field of psychotherapy viewed the client through a deficit lens, examining and assessing what was wrong with the client, what the client did to continue to have problems, and how the client behaved that negatively affected others. However, over the past few years, therapeutic approaches gradually moved from a problem-focused view of the client to one that views the client as capable with personal strengths, resiliencies, and coping skills. New approaches to therapy, primarily considered brief therapies, emphasized "what" and "how" in the here and now rather than dwelling on the why and past problems and symptoms. One of the more recent fields of psychotherapy, solution-focused therapy, views the client as an expert on his or her problems and solutions, not the therapist; uses language to envision a new future that client and therapist co-construct; and focuses on challenges, strengths, and solutions from the client's perspective.

Solution-Focused (SF) therapy provides a hopeful, positive approach to help clients realize their strengths, focus their energies, and realize their goals. The SF therapy approach matches with what we know about effective therapy. Researchers (Duncan, Miller & Sparks, 2004) believe that the success of therapy is related to four different factors: client factors (40%), relationship factors (30%), techniques and methods (15%), and hope and expectancy (15%). Solution-focused therapy encompasses each of these factors.

The SF therapist focuses on client factors, gaining the client's perspective, focusing on client resources, and uncovering client strengths. The therapist asks questions out of curiosity and respect for the knowledge clients have about themselves, their problems, and solutions. By focusing on what clients want from therapy the therapist assumes clients have the resources they need to solve their problems (client factors). The therapist treats the client with respect by building rapport, asking questions out of curiosity for the client's perspective, and collaborating with the client rather than working from a top-down position (relationship factors). In SF therapy, techniques serve to highlight and reinforce client strengths, resources, and solutions and enable clients to realize goals they create (techniques). By focusing on strengths and not on deficits and problems, the therapist builds hope throughout the process. Further, the therapist asks questions using language that assumes positive change. Rather than expecting problems, the therapist continues to believe the best of the client and the client's strengths and resources (hope and expectancy factors).

However, therapy can be challenging with children and adolescents, and even with some adults, when working from primarily a verbal approach. Sometimes, verbal approaches miss developmentally appropriate ways to address children and adolescents who do not have the verbal skills to communicate with the therapist, those who may have cognitive deficits, or those who have such emotionally charged concerns that words cannot address the visceral pain young clients carry. Most mainstream therapies (person-centered, psychodynamic, cognitive-behavioral, and many family therapies, including solution-focused) tend to rely on verbalization skills to assess and address client problems and challenges. Not only are these not always appropriate for children, they may not be the most effective for adults.

Therapists require effective approaches that address children and adolescents at appropriate developmental stages in tangible, brief, and impactful ways to positively impact client outcomes. Reliance on words in talk therapy limits the range of effectiveness with various populations. For example, some clients may not have the maturity to understand or express themselves verbally, have language and learning differences, struggle with speech impediments, or have experienced traumatic or shameful histories that preclude the ability to use words. For those who have suffered neglect and abuse, accessing the cognitive skills needed for verbal expression may not be possible until lower levels of brain functioning are first addressed, including those areas responsible for self-regulation, impulsivity, and attention (Perry, 2006, 2008). To work with the SF model, the therapist needs to be flexible and open to other modalities and approaches that make therapy more understandable and developmentally appropriate (Selekman, 1997).

Solution-focused therapy offers several advantages in working with children and adolescents. Instead of focusing on what children do wrong and their weaknesses, SF therapists work with children to uncover their strengths and talents, empowering them to meet their challenges. Sklare (2005) provides a good example of the effect SF therapy can have on children:

> After 3 weeks of using SFBC with at-risk middle school students, the school secretary reported that she had asked these students the same two questions. The first was, "Do you want to come back and see the counselor again?" They enthusiastically responded, "Yes, I would like to do that." And the follow-up question was, "Do you think (the counselor) wants to see you?" They emphatically responded, "He sure does!"
>
> (p. 13)

Solution-focused therapists do not grill children regarding their motives—the "why" questions—but ask details regarding "how," "what," "when," and "where."

Therapists engage the child's imagination by using some unusual questions, such as the miracle question, scaling questions, and relationship questions. They respect the child or adolescent's opinion regarding what the problem is and possible solutions (Lethem, 2002).

Children's natural and preferred form of communication in learning (or therapy) involves creating, activity, and play (Johnson, 2006); therefore, it makes sense to find ways to adapt SF therapy techniques to younger populations. Berg and Steiner (2003) state,

> We recognize that since children do not have fully developed language skills, they communicate with body movements, looks, imagination, fantasy, and many other creative ways that adults knew once but have forgotten. Therefore, working with children requires different ways of observing and listening.
>
> (p. 14)

In *Children's Solution Work* (2003), Berg and Steiner describe different ways to adapt SF therapy when working with children and adolescents. Inspired by their text, I build on their suggestions by providing a variety of approaches that employ the senses and embody learning.

The need to use creative and playful approaches also applies to many adolescents. Often, therapists assume that youth in the adolescent stages of development possess higher level cognitive skills and vocabulary. However, we must be cautious in assuming that, because adolescents talk like adults, they function at higher cognitive levels, particularly those who miss school frequently, who have histories of serving time in jail or detention centers, or have histories of mental illness or abuse. Disabilities, trauma, or a lack of formal education may delay reasoning skills and emotional development. Alternative approaches in communication provide other avenues for communication, highlight strengths, and minimize learning differences.

Using more tangible, physical, and expressive approaches to communicate thoughts, feelings, and behaviors offer many advantages:

a   Clients prefer it. It is creative and fun. As a result, clients more fully engage in the counseling process.

b   Young children's natural mode of communication is through play and expressive approaches. "Children do not have the cognitive and verbal maturity to communicate in counseling in the manner as adults' converse. Children communicate through play" (Homeyer & Sweeney, 2011, p. 1).

c   Tangible and expressive approaches utilize embodied learning. By using techniques that include the senses and physical movement, clients experience a better understanding of the changes they desire and how these might occur.

d   Using expressive approaches removes the problem from the client and projects it onto paper, clay, and other materials, so that the problem is externalized, thus shifting the role of the client from being a victim of cir-cumstances to one with some control over problems and adversity.

e   By using tactual and expressive materials, clients use multiple modali-ties to envision hoped-for outcomes and progress they make toward their goals.

f   Using creativity and play in counseling opens new dimensions and pos-sibilities by allowing the client to "expand outwardly and inwardly" (Gladding, 2005, p. 9).

g   Having expressive materials available allows clients to select how they want to communicate, giving them choice in the therapy process.

h   Children with disabilities in language or for whom English is a second language may lack adequate words or expressive skills to communicate. By offering visual and tangible approaches, clients can select their preferred method of communicating or experiment with a different approach.

i   Art and play are common expressive modalities across cultures.

j   "Repetitive and reward-driven activities including art making and crafts" (Malchiodi, 2011, pp. 23–24) rewire the brain and reduce depression and anxiety (Lambert, 2010).

k   Those who have experienced trauma may not have the words to express their traumatic memories, so that clients overgeneralize threats at the sen-sory level. By using sensory materials, clients can express thoughts and feelings that do not have words attached to them but hold meaning for the client. The therapist works with the client, moving the client from the sen-sory areas of the brain to the cortical area, so that clients can give words to their experiences and capitalize on their strengths and ability to cope (see Perry, 2006; Perry & Hambrick, 2008).

Overview of This Book

Each chapter of this text begins with a case study taken from many of our experiences in the field. Many of the stories presented provide a background of where the "rubber meets the road" and the different types of challenges chil-dren face. Names and identifying information have been removed and many of the details of the cases have been changed to protect client identities.

Chapter 2 provides background information on strength-based approaches, including Werner and Smith's resiliency studies, Garmezy and Masten's Project Competence, and Martin Seligman's Positive Psychology. A brief summary of constructivist approaches, including Narrative and Solution-Focused therapy, provide a backdrop to the approaches and techniques provided in the text.

Chapter 3 provides background information on many of the creative and playful approaches (play therapy, sandtray, art therapy, music therapy, and others), including basic information needed about materials and guidelines. Chapter 4 provides information on working with special populations, those diagnosed with a disability or serious health concerns. Suggestions for the therapy office, process of therapy, and working with families provide information that the therapist might consider when working with clients who have special needs.

Chapter 5 provides a deeper look at SF therapy, the principles and process on which it is based, research supporting the use of SF therapy, and how SF therapy has been integrated with other creative and playful approaches. Chapter 6 provides the reader with information about how to engage different types of clients according to their motivation for attending therapy.

Chapters 7–10 provide more detailed information about SF therapy and contain many different creative and playful approaches that can be used with children and adolescents. Chapter 7 discusses building rapport and getting to know who and what are important to the client. "Digging for Treasure," Chapter 8, looks at working with clients to identify their strengths, using compliments, encouragement, and affirmation, relationship questions, and scaling questions. Chapter 9 explores goal setting using the miracle question and other goal-setting techniques, and provides information on how to help the client break goals down into smaller attainable goals. Chapter 10 explores ending the session and provides discussion on how to decide which suggestions to give.

Chapter 11 examines follow-up sessions using the EARS approach—looking for exceptions, amplifying, reinforcing, and starting over. Chapter 12 provides an overview of SF group therapy, therapeutic factors, stages of group, and useful activities and techniques to use when conducting group.

The purpose of this text, to provide creative and playful approaches when using SF therapy, focuses on the individual child. However, we recognize that for therapy to affect change significantly, parents, guardians, and other members of the child's larger system need to be involved. However, the approaches

Table 1.1 List of Materials.

Pencils, pens	Precut magazine pictures	Blank masks (commercial or made from card stock)
Crayons, pastels, watercolors	Sandtrays and miniatures (see Homeyer & Sweeney, 2011)	Blank CDs
Glue sticks	Instamatic camera & film	Variety of music according to ages
Index cards	Clay or play dough	Poster board
Tape (duct, masking, scotch)	Paper (8 × 10 white and different colors); construction paper; tagboard, poster board	Small nerf balls and bats
Matte board frames	Games (checkers, Uno, Jenga, playing cards)	Variety of household items: toilet paper and paper towel tubes, small cardboard boxes, scrapbook décor, sticks, string, stones, yarn

provided may be adapted to use with client systems, and we encourage the therapist to expand on the techniques to make it applicable.

Throughout this text, different activities are provided according to different phases and techniques in SF therapy. The basic materials for the activities and approaches suggested in this text are provided in Table 1.1. Appendix A provides a detailed list of activities for Chapters 7–12 and the necessary supplies to conduct each activity.

I hope that you will view the activities provided as a starting point for creating and tailoring SF therapy to youth and their families. These activities provide different levels of client engagement, are useful with different developmental levels, and may be useful with other SF techniques than those provided. This text aims to provide creative and playful approaches to enhance SF therapy so that those who do not or cannot communicate verbally may have a voice and participate fully in the therapy process.

References

Berg, I. K. & Steiner, T. (2003). *Children's solution work*. New York, NY: W. W. Norton.

Duncan, B. L., Miller, S. D. & Sparks, A. (2004). *The heroic client: A revolutionary way to improve effectiveness through client-directed, outcome-informed therapy*. San Francisco, CA: Jossey-Bass.

Gladding, S. T. (2005). *Counseling as an art* (3rd Ed.). Alexandria, VA: American Counseling Association.

Homeyer, L. E. & Sweeney, D. S. (2011). *Sandtray therapy* (2nd Ed.). New York, NY: Taylor & Francis.

Johnson, L. M. (2006). Elementary school students' learning preferences and the classroom learning environment: Implications for educational practice and policy. *Journal of Negro Education, 75*(3), 506–518.

Lambert, K. (2010). *Lifting depression: A neuroscientist's hands-on approach to activating your brain's healing power*. New York, NY: Basic Books.

Lethem, J. (2002). Brief solution focused therapy. *Child and Adolescent Mental Health, 7*(4), 189–192.

Malchiodi, C. (2011). Art therapy and the brain. In C. A. Malchiodi (Ed.) *Handbook of art therapy*, pp. 17–26. New York, NY: Guilford Press.

Perry, B. D. (2006). Applying principles of neurodevelopment to clinical work with maltreated and traumatized children. In N. B. Webb (Ed.), *Working with traumatized youth in child welfare*, pp. 27–52. New York, NY: Guilford Press.

Perry, B. D. & Hambrick, E. P. (2008). The neurosequential model of therapeutics. *Reclaiming Children and Youth, 17*(3), 38–43.

Selekman, M. D. (1997). *Solution-focused therapy with children*. New York, NY: Guilford Press.

Sklare, G. B. (2005). *Brief counseling that works* (2nd Ed.). Thousand Oaks, CA: Corwin Press.

CHAPTER 2

Strength-Based Approaches

Elizabeth R. Taylor

Recently, an international awards committee named Caylin Moore a Rhodes Scholar, one of just 32 named from the United States. Coming from a neighborhood plagued with gangs, violence, and a lack of resources, and a father in prison for life, his mother raised him as a single mother, whom he credits for his success. Caylin learned to excel at football, and it provided his way out of a life that could have ended in bloodshed, poverty, and early death. Instead, this young man has achieved the honor of becoming a Rhodes Scholar and attending Oxford. Although he didn't play football as much as he hoped due to injuries, he never failed to work and study hard. His comment to Lester Holt when interviewed about his remarkable story exemplified his resilient spirit: "I like to dream dreams that are so big, so unfathomable, so unimaginable that without divine intervention they are destined to fail." Of course, he didn't just dream dreams, he put forth great effort to make the most of his talents. Throughout, he continued to give back to others through mentoring, speaking, and acting as a role model (NBC News, 2017). He wasn't supposed to be a high achiever, to live his life on such a high level of accomplishment and integrity. He was supposed to fail, given the odds stack against him, but he didn't.

Caylin Moore provided an example of resiliency, of that ability to rise above difficult circumstances and thrive. At one time, researchers might not have been interested in Caylin's story except to examine his many risks. Clinicians would have spent much of their time discussing the problems he endured, his many difficulties, and how they handicapped his ability to achieve.

Today, however, many researchers and clinicians often focus on the ability of individuals and communities to withstand difficult circumstances, to use their strengths and resources to survive and thrive. This new focus encourages the examination of research on resiliency, positive psychology, and strength-focused interventions, including Narrative Therapy and Solution-Focused Therapy. This chapter examines research trends beginning in the 1950s that moved from focusing on risks, pathologies, and their causes to examining strengths, resiliencies, and interventions with those who face difficult challenges, trauma, and major stressors. These trends begin with a focus on resilience then move into the development of strength-based approaches focused on post-modern social constructivism, and then into the development of positive psychology, all part of the strength-based movement of the past 70 years. As this strength-based movement gains momentum, the number of articles on strength-based theory and approaches multiplies, so that new journals focused on strengths and resiliencies occupy many of the shelves beside those focusing on risk. Journals, such as *Journal of Happiness Studies, The Journal of Positive Psychology*, and the *Journal of Solution-Focused Brief Therapy*, address prevention and treatment approaches focusing on strengths people employ to overcome difficult circumstances and thrive in the face of them.

Kauai Longitudinal Resiliency Study

In 1955, Emmy Werner and colleagues conducted a landmark longitudinal study with the population of 698 children born in 1955 on the small island of Kauai, Hawaii. The researchers gathered information on a variety of biological, psychological, and familial processes. Werner and her colleagues followed these individuals from birth through to the age of 40, administering assessments and interviewing participants and their families six different times. They took special note of the 72 individuals who seemed to have the odds stacked against them—growing up in poverty, born with birth defects and complications, living in discordant homes, having parents who were uneducated, suffering from alcoholism or mental illness—but still managing to grow up to become healthy and productive adults, caring, confident, and in satisfying relationships. How did this happen? How did these individuals overcome the odds that the rest of their cohort did not? What did they have? What processes were in place or occurred that changed their trajectory? Others in their cohort developed learning or behavior problems by the time they were 10 years old and had been in trouble with legal authorities, suffered mental health problems, or became pregnant by age 18. Rather than focusing their research on the risk factors, as thousands of studies had done thus far, Werner and her research team took an interest in the protective factors and processes that contributed to the positive outcomes of individuals who could steel themselves against what seemed insurmountable challenges (Werner, 2005; Werner & Smith, 1982).

From her research, Werner found protective factors within the individual, the family, and the community (Werner, 2005). Protective factors within individuals included temperament/disposition, intelligence, problem-solving, and inherent talent. Temperament often manifested itself as early as infancy, with mothers describing their children as cuddly and affectionate. These young children displayed what can already be possibly one of the most important aspects of resilience, the ability to engender positive reactions from others. Other individual protective factors included the ability to quickly learn and pick up information, put things together, organize possessions, and imitate the adults in their lives (Werner, 2005).

Those whose protective factors lay within the family experienced early and close bonds with a significant and stable person who was sensitive to their needs. This significant person may or may not have been the biological parent but rather a grandparent, aunt or uncle, or other surrogate parents or caretakers. Importantly, those most resilient enjoyed a close bond with one caregiver who provided attention and affection to the infant. Infants were rarely separated from their caregiver or were separated only for a short time during the first year of life. Other protective factors included growing up in families with fewer children and children who were at least two years apart in age.

Community protective factors often provided supportive adults, such as teachers, neighbors, or church members (Werner, 2005). These environmental influences tended to capitalize on the physical and social strengths of the individual, enhancing the likelihood that the person would develop their abilities and be successful. Werner and Smith (2001) found that environmental factors also included participation in extracurricular activities, support from friends and important adults, and involvement in YMCA, YWCA, and 4-H. Involvement in church groups also provided youth with support but also meaning, faith, and a sense of control over their lives (Werner & Smith, 2001).

Interestingly, although two-thirds of the initial Kauai cohort were considered high risk for negative outcomes, they were not "doomed to be one of life's losers" (Werner & Smith, 2001, p. 150). By age 40, those with a positive temperament, academic competence, a sense of self-efficacy, and social maturity were more likely to overcome their challenges. Increasing their chances for positive outcomes included emotional support, education, steady employment in jobs they enjoyed, fewer life stressors, service in the armed forces, active participation in a community of faith, and satisfying marriages. A key component present in these survivors was their belief that challenges could be overcome and they had control over their own fate (Werner & Smith, 2001). These resilient individuals overcame their challenges rather than becoming victims of their circumstances.

Project Competence Longitudinal Study on Resilience

Another pioneer in resilience was Norm Garmezy who launched Project Competence Longitudinal Study on resilience in the late 1970s. He and his assistant, Ann Masten, now professor at the University of Minnesota and Director of Project Competence Research on Risk and Resilience (PCR3), along with a number of graduate students at the University of Minnesota, examined resilience within the context of development. Having been a researcher on children at risk for schizophrenia, Garmezy's research focused on risk of psychopathology but also its absence as an indicator of adaptation. After educating and building a solid base of community, mental health, and educational professionals, Garmezy, Masten, student researchers, and well-known international colleagues launched Project Competence, examining resilience in several different cohorts of children with the goal of finding clues as to the protective processes that helped children overcome adversity and become competent adults throughout development (Masten, 2014).

From their work, several key findings emerge, one of which is the "ordinariness" of resilience (Masten, 2014, p. 7). Resilience, often associated with many of our great heroes such as Viktor Frankl, John Glenn, Nelson Mandela, or Abraham Lincoln can also be found in our parents, grandparents, siblings, friends, and colleagues who have also walked through the fires of tragedy, stress, bereavement, and hurt but emerged from it to live lives with purpose and integrity, surviving well and helping others to do the same.

Masten (2014) also notes resilience as a process that develops and changes over time, not a one-time event. It occurs in the face of adversity as we rise to meet challenges, recover, and adapt. Resilience represents the manifestation of several factors and processes, not just one, at the individual and systemic levels that shape development in the face of adversity over time. As people grow and adapt in the face adversity, they grow more competent, and this "competence begets competence" (Masten & Tellegen, 2012, p. 349), so that competence cascades into other areas.

Masten (2014) developed the "short list" (p. 148) of resiliency factors and, similar to Werner, grouped them into three different areas—individual factors (intelligence; problem-solving skills; self-control, emotional regulation, and planfulness; motivation; self-efficacy, faith, hope, and meaning), family factors (effective caregiving and parenting quality, close relationships with other adults, close friendships and romantic partners), and environmental factors (effective communities and neighborhoods, effective schools). Although this list is likely to grow, these findings on resilience tend to be repeated around the globe, in different cultures and circumstances (Masten, 2014).

Initial knowledge about resilience led to studies on interventions to increase resilience, yielding results that indicated the possibility of boosting protective processes, so that assets could be strengthened and protective systems could be put in place to protect those most at risk for negative outcomes. Over time, trends in the study of resilience moved from focusing on the individual and their resiliency traits to viewing resilience as a complex process involving multiple systems at the individual, family, community, and cultural levels, thus widening the scope of what resilience entails throughout development (Masten & Herbers, 2013). These trends also led to focusing on prevention to reduce exposure to risks and keep children and adolescents from being exposed to severe adversity (Masten, 2014).

Positive Psychology

In keeping with the new interest in strengths, Martin Seligman, former president of the American Psychological Association and an expert in the field of cognitive-behavioral psychology, questioned the field of psychology's constant focus on pathology and interventions to address mental disorders without examining the more positive aspects of living, such as happiness, vitality, and mental health. In 2000, he introduced the concept of "positive psychology" in a special edition of the *American Psychologist* (Seligman & Csikszentmihalyi, 2000).

Similar to resiliency, positive psychology focuses on strengths and "how they fulfill an individual" (Peterson & Seligman, 2004, p. 17). Positive psychology focuses not only on how average individuals overcome stress but also on how people thrive and live fulfilling lives. After all, most people do not succumb to difficult events; rather, they adapt, shift, and continue to move forward. These strengths, evident in different contexts and paragons of society, remain stable in a trait-like fashion (Peterson & Seligman, 2004) and, similar to resiliency, are endorsed all over the world (Seligman & Csikszentmihalyi, 2000).

By focusing on mental illness, little is done to move toward prevention. In fact, we have "scant knowledge of what makes life worth living" or "about how normal people flourish under benign conditions" (Seligman & Csikszentmihalyi, 2000, p. 5). Positive psychology desires to shift this focus to examine how to prevent tragic consequences, such as mass shootings, suicide, anxiety, and depression. By focusing on mental illnesses, or the disease model, prevention is hampered. However, by focusing on competency, similar to studies of Werner and Smith, Garmezy, Masten, and others, focus shifts from focusing on weaknesses to building strengths (Seligman & Csikszentmihalyi, 2000).

Positive psychology does not discount stressors, risks, or pathology, but rather shines light on, as Paul Harvey would say, "the rest of the story." "Treatment is not just fixing what is broken; it is nurturing what is best" (Seligman & Csikszentmihalyi, 2000, p. 7). Positive psychologists want to focus not just on illness and health but on all matters in life that make life worth living, that allow the average person to flourish. These competencies and strengths buffer the individual against the impact of life stressors and challenges. By learning more about character virtues and nurturing them in others, positive psychologists believe it may be possible to foster human strengths (Seligman & Csikszentmihalyi, 2000).

Peterson and Seligman (2004) published the first edition of *Character Strengths and Virtues*, the antithesis to the American Psychiatric Association's *Diagnostic and Statistical Manual (DSM-V)* (2014). The DSM-V, providing descriptions and criteria for the diagnosis of mental disorders, gave researchers a common language to diagnose pathology, examine the prevalence of mental disorders, address possible biological, behavioral, and social causes, and describe symptomology (American Psychiatric Association, 2014). On the other hand, Peterson and Seligman, in their text, group 24 strengths into six core virtues. For each of the 24 strengths, they provide a definition, descriptions, example, background, assessment measures, and other relevant information, as well as possible interventions.

Positive psychology continues to encourage research in many of the different areas described in Peterson and Seligman's text. For example, in a cursory search of several databases on EBSCO, over 5,000 articles have been published since the year 2000 on gratitude, over 100,000 on hope, and over 9,000 on vitality. This shift in the focus of research, from stress and risks to focusing on strengths and resiliencies, continues an upward trajectory.

How can we build these resiliencies and strengths? How can we help others be stronger and steel themselves against the storm of negativity and hardships that pound our lives? What is the best approach to building people up, so they don't succumb but overcome challenges and thrive? Positive psychologist Martin Seligman, when talking about raising his daughter, states that it wasn't about correcting her faults but about growing her strength, "amplifying it, nurturing it, helping her to lead her life around it to buffer against her weaknesses and the storms of life" (Seligman & Csikszentmihalyi, 2000, p. 6).

Positive psychologists develop interventions that focus on relieving pain and distress but also on helping people to move beyond their pain. Some of these interventions lend themselves to enhance SF therapy by providing shifts in focus, reframes, and possible suggestions that may be useful between sessions. For example, the therapist asks a client to note times when the problem is not occurring. To carry this further, this activity might be extended to noticing those things that the client likes, enjoys doing, or something good that happens during the week. These types of activities shift the client's focus from problems to strengths and positive areas of life. Similarly, a common positive psychology intervention involves asking individuals to notice when something is good and to savor the event. By doing so, the individual focuses on what is right, thus decreasing the focus on what is wrong (Peterson, 2006). The exercise provides a way to generate exceptions, a common technique in SF therapy (De Jong & Berg, 2013).

The focus on strengths and resiliencies continues to expand. Leaders and counselors in schools focus more on strength building than in times past, often pushing against high-stakes testing to focus on those "at promise" rather than the old label of "at risk" (Galassi & Akos, 2007; Henderson & Milstein, 2003). Although prevention efforts continue to influence system changes in schools and communities, it took 30 years for the resiliency research to shift the focus from those at risk to those who overcome; therefore, it likely will take time and many voices for health providers, lawmakers, and educators to recognize the power of focusing on strengths.

Post-Modern Constructionist Approaches

Before Seligman and colleagues proposed the tenets of positive psychology, new ways to define knowledge emerged. Moving from knowledge based on reason to knowledge based on evidence, an individual's perception of knowledge was thought to be objective, accurate, and reflect what structuralists consider the "underlying structure or essence" (Bidwell, 2007, p. 68). However, postmodernists began to shift the definition of knowledge from that of concepts that are knowable and static to one that defines knowledge as changeable, context specific, relational, and dependent on the negotiation of meaning through language within human interaction.

De Barbaro (2008) classifies postmodern understandings of knowledge into two types: That which pertains to the whole of intellectual climate and how knowledge is viewed and that which focuses on the psychological, philosophical, and artistic areas of understanding. The focus in this text is on the latter view in terms of how postmodern thought affects our work with clients. Through this philosophical lens, we are better able to see how we communicate and use words to nudge individuals into seeing new perspectives on their lives and create new, preferred realities.

Much of the social constructionist postmodern shift in therapy occurred as a result of Milton Erickson's unique style of therapy and those in family therapy who worked at the Mental Research Institute in Palo Alto, California. No longer did these therapists approach clients focusing on causes of behavior or the singular focus of internal dispositions of individuals. Instead, therapists focused on what clients perceived as the problem rather than searching for deeper issues or interpretation. At the beginning stages of this constructivist postmodern shift, change occurred as the therapist acted on systems, most often family systems, in ways that shifted systems' functioning. The therapist described what he saw, changed problematic communication patterns, and remained the expert (Bidwell, 2007).

However, over time, we also see the role of the therapist change. No longer is the therapist the expert (except in asking good questions), the client is. The therapist approaches the client with curiosity and interest in terms of how the client perceives the problem and solutions. The therapist no longer views the client through a certain therapeutic philosophy that, in turn, shifts and perhaps distorts how the client is viewed. Rather, the therapist works *with* the client, ready to be informed by the client regarding how the client views the problem, its effects, and its solutions. How the therapist responds reflects the specific version of discourse the client provides rather than the therapist's belief system about problems and solutions learned in a specific school of therapy (de Barbaro, 2008). De Shazer (1984) describes this cooperation of client and therapist much like a tennis match in which client and therapist work on the same side to defeat the opponent. Of course, this too is a type of lens and is affected by the knowledge, experience, and values of the therapist, but the approach provides a more open and flexible way to help the client.

The constructivist viewpoint might be better understood by considering our own families. For example, just discussing with my younger brother and sister events that occurred in high school, I am amazed at how our versions of common stories are often quite different. Our different perceptions of reality emerge out of our different genetic makeup, different experiences in the family, school, and community, our birth order, age, sex, and other factors.

These different versions of reality play a major role in how we work with children, families, and school staff. Oftentimes, the stories children tell us differ from teachers' versions of the same stories. These views, all valuable, vary widely in terms of the reality being constructed. The teacher sees the child as "being out of his seat and disrupting class." The child views being out of his seat as a way to take a break due to boredom or interest in another child's activities. Both hold valid viewpoints, and no one is wrong, but their realities and versions of truth are different. The postmodern therapist sees these stories through a "not-knowing stance," values each opinion, and views each as having legitimate solutions to the problem. Rather than doing something to the client, the postmodern therapist works with the child and teacher, not to locate the truth, but to gather different perspectives. In seeing problems as different perspectives, the therapist asks questions that elicit new knowledge and uses what the client already knows to solve the problem. Together, therapist and client co-construct solutions to find new ways of doing, knowing, and being. For adults, most of whom are more cognitively advanced and verbally sophisticated in their understanding, this co-construction can be negotiated verbally. But when working with younger clients, who often have different ways of communicating and who are at different developmental levels from that of the therapist, communication must be negotiated through more concrete and playful approaches.

Two therapies relevant to this text arise out of the postmodern, social constructivist approach: Narrative Therapy and Solution-Focused Therapy. Both therapies, highly influenced by language systems and a non-pathologizing belief system, focus more on what goes right than what is wrong (Chang & Nylund, 2013). Both therapies consider the client the expert on his or her problem and use questions as their main interventions. Although SF therapy uses externalizing the problem as a therapeutic technique, narrative therapy sees it as a crucial piece of effective therapy, that is, separating the problem from the client. Both focus on when the problem is not occurring; that is, narrative therapy focuses on exploring and expanding alternative stories, whereas SF therapy focuses on amplifying exceptions to the problem (White & Epston, 1990; De Jong & Berg, 2008).

The theories differ in major areas. The narrative therapist begins by exploring and "deconstructing" the problem and helping the client address how the problem influences the client's life, unlike the SF therapist (de Shazer & Dolan, 2007) who does not believe it necessary to even know what the problem is, much less its influence. However, this does not mean that SF therapists ignore the client's descriptions of the problem, but they notice and focus their responses on times when the problem is not occurring to help the client find ways to continue to make these exception times occur more frequently. Unlike SF therapy, narrative therapy concerns itself with the socio-political context, particularly in terms of gender, class, culture, and economics, and see social advocacy as part of the therapeutic process (Chang & Nylund, 2013).

Narrative Therapy

The narrative therapist focuses on the stories we weave, both problem-saturated and alternative stories that may have only been thinly noted. These alternative stories, much like exceptions in SF therapy, are expanded with thick descriptions to create new stories, so the client re-authors her life more in line with her purposes and values. Since the client often views problem stories as permanent and a part of the person, the therapist helps the client separate the self from the problem, to externalize it, so that "the problem becomes the problem, not the person" (White, 2007, p. 8). Externalizing involves making the problem an entity separate from the person, giving it a name, describing its personal attributes, thoughts, feelings, behaviors, and intentions (White, 2007).

Often, the person ascribes to herself problem attributes, adopting its identity and assuming a reputation with others that includes these problem characteristics. For example, a young girl may struggle with weight issues, being 10 to 15 pounds over the average weight for her size. However, she ascribes what others say about people her size to herself, and thus she decides she is "fat." So, "fat Marie," becomes her personal identity. Since she sees herself in this role, she decides she must not go out for fear others may make fun of her. Becoming more and more withdrawn, her grades slip throughout the year, so that she begins to believe she is not capable of making good grades. By adolescence, she loses the mindset for success and slips into depression, subsequently losing control of her eating habits, thus fulfilling what she decides is her basic identity.

However, the problem is not "fat Marie"; rather, the challenge is her problem story that she incorporates as part of herself. As the therapist works to deconstruct her story and construct a more helpful story, her new story becomes one in which she views herself as healthy and active, thus gaining confidence in herself and her abilities. She gradually begins to make choices that result in lowering her weight while increasing her activity. When the person is not the problem, exceptions to the problem become more evident, and the problem-saturated story is gradually replaced with a positive one.

Solution-Focused Therapy

As noted earlier, ideas underlying SF therapy began with the master therapist, Milton Erickson, who might have been the subject of a text on resilience himself, having overcome what would be considered insurmountable physical illnesses and obstacles. Erickson employed unorthodox ideas and communication techniques to help his clients in therapy. Many of these ideas became established principles of SF therapy, such as not using diagnostic labels, the belief in the client's ability to solve his or her own problems, and the idea that therapy can be brief (Visser, 2013). Another influence, Gregory Bateson, wrote about systems and cybernetics, emphasizing context and communication. Erickson's and Bateson's focus on communication and systems provided the basis for the foundation of the Mental Research Institute, where Insoo Kim Berg studied and met Steve de Shazer, a student of Milton Erickson. Eventually, Berg and de Shazer set up practice at the Brief Family Therapy Center in Milwaukee, Wisconsin. Rather than taking already known theories and techniques, they worked organically to determine what worked with clients, adding and taking away techniques, observing clients behind a one-way mirror, and asking clients about what was helpful. Through this process, based on their background experiences at the Mental Research Institute and the influences of communication theory and systemic family therapy, they developed, practiced, and researched SF therapy (Visser, 2013).

Continuing to work with clients, Berg and de Shazer added to the techniques they found effective and worked with colleagues to conduct empirical research to determine SF therapy's effectiveness (Visser, 2013). Over time, researchers demonstrated its effectiveness with a variety of issues, including substance abuse (de Shazer & Isebaert, 2004; Smock et al., 2008; Miller & Berg, 1995), academic and emotional problems (Daki & Savage, 2010; Thompson & Littrell, 1998), and affective disorders (Knekt, Lindofors, Härkänen et al., 2008; Kramer, Conijn, Oijevaar & Riper, 2014); in a variety of formats, including individual, family, and group therapy (Bond, Woods, Humphrey, Symes & Green, 2013; Carrera et al., 2016; Proudlock & Wellman, 2011; Reimer & Chatwin, 2006); and with populations of different ages and ethnicities (Franklin, Streeter, Kim & Tripodi, 2007; Gingerich & Peterson, 2013; Kim et al., 2015). As of 2017, research on SF therapy included 10 meta-analyses, 143 randomized controlled studies, and 100 comparison studies with 71 favoring SF therapy to be an effective therapeutic approach (MacDonald, 2017).

Solution-focused therapy's effectiveness is based on assumptions the therapist has about the client and the therapeutic process, using unique questions and interventions to help the client uncover her strengths, resources, and solutions to problems and challenges. De Shazer and Dolan (2007, pp. 1–3) lay out the following tenets that guide the practice of SF therapy:

- *If it is not broken, don't fix it.* We tend to focus on what is wrong rather than what is right; however, by focusing on what is right, we instill hope and confidence in the client. Oftentimes, the problem improves or is no longer a problem before the client comes to therapy, so we do not want to go back and rehash the problem if the problem disappears.
- *If it is not working, do something different.* We have heard the saying from an unknown sage that "insanity is doing the same thing over and over again while expecting different results." Often true of clients coming in for therapy, it holds true for therapists as well. If clients do not improve, the SF therapist assumes the blame and does something different. If the client succeeds, the therapist continues to encourage the client to do what works.
- *If it is working, do more of it.* Of course, this is what we should do! We give the client credit for successfully addressing challenges and encourage the client to do more of the same.
- *Small steps can lead to big changes.* Just gaining a sense of success leads the client to develop hope and a sense of self-efficacy, key ingredients in motivation and self-esteem but also key ingredients in reaching goals.

Therefore, the therapist works collaboratively with the client to identify small steps that can be realized in reaching the client's goal.

- *The solution is not necessarily related to the problem.* The focus of SF therapy is on the present and future, not the past. The past cannot be changed, but by looking at what will be different once the problem no longer exists, the therapist and client work backwards, looking at exception times when the problem does not occur and how the client makes this happen.

- *The language for solution development is different from that needed to describe a problem.* In many traditional therapies, conversations begin by talking about the problem and then discussing solutions. In SF therapy, therapy begins by discussing what the client wants to be different and then examining possible times when the solution is already occurring or could occur. Spending time talking about the problem does not lead to solutions; spending time talking about solutions leads to solutions (Berg & de Shazer, 1993).

- *No problems happen all the time; there are exceptions that can be utilized.* "The therapeutic task is to examine those exceptions and get the client to repeat the successful mastery of the problems" (Berg & Dolan, 2001, p. 45). For the client to realize that there may be times when the problem is not occurring or times when the client feels better in the midst of difficulties creates a sense of hope and possibility of change.

- *The future is both created and negotiable.* Based on the constructivist concepts, children and adolescents are not locked into their diagnoses, traumatic experiences, or behavioral mistakes. Rather, through language, the client and therapist work collaboratively to open up possibilities and achieve goals.

Throughout, the therapist demonstrates genuine interest in the client, asks questions out of curiosity using the client's language, and works without judgment and with great respect for the client. Together, client and therapist work to uncover the client's preferred future so that client and therapist will know if they are making progress (Bliss & Bray, 2009).

The therapist's role in SF therapy is that of a collaborator and encourager who walks beside the client, since it is the client that is the expert on her life, problems, and solutions. The therapist treats the client as an equal, recognizing the power differential in the relationship, yet deferring personal expertise regarding the client's problem and solutions. The therapist conveys to the child or adolescent her faith in the client's abilities, strengths, resources, and expertise by using language that assumes change will occur, respecting the client's knowledge and perspective, and by returning responsibility to the client for her progress (Berg & Dolan, 2001; de Shazer & Dolan, 2007; De Jong & Berg, 2013). It is not the role of the therapist to "educate or enlighten clients" (Berg & Dolan, 2001, p. 1), but to view the client through a lens that sheds light on the client's strengths, hopes, resiliencies, and their efforts to achieve their preferred futures.

Conclusions

This very brief review of strength-based approaches examines only a few of the landmark shifts in research from a focus on pathology and risks to a focus on resilience, strengths, and thriving. Understanding the emergence of strength-based research and practice allows the therapist to redefine the client, not as a person with problems and deficits but as a person with amazing strengths who likely overcame many obstacles in the past and possesses strengths to overcome current and future challenges. When the client focuses the lens on client strengths, the client finds empowerment and hope in the therapeutic process. Through the client–therapist relationship, the client incorporates strategies that capitalize on internal and external resources, allowing the client to overcome challenges but also thrive in the face of them.

References

American Psychiatric Association (2014). *Diagnostic and statistical manual of mental disorders* (5th Ed.). Washington, DC: American Psychiatric Press.

Berg, I. K. & de Shazer, S. (1993). Making numbers talk: Language in therapy. In S. Friedman (Ed.), *The new constructive collaboration language in psychotherapy of change*, pp. 5–24. New York, NY: Guilford.

Berg, I. K., & Dolan, Y (2001). *Tales of solutions.* New York, NY: W. W. Norton.

Bidwell, D. R. (2007). Miraculous knowing: Epistemology and solution-focused therapy. In T. S. Nelson & F. N. Thomas (Eds), *Handbook of solution-focused brief therapy*, pp. 65–87. New York, NY: Haworth Press.

Bliss, E. V. & Bray, D. (2009). The smallest solution focused particles: Towards a minimalist definition of when therapy is solution focused. *Journal of Systemic Therapies, 28*(2), 62–74.

Bond, C., Woods, K., Humphrey, N., Symes, W. & Green, L. (2013). Practitioner review: The effectiveness of solution focused brief therapy with children and families: A systematic and critical evaluation of the literature from 1990–2010. *Journal of Child Psychology and Psychiatry, 54*(7), 707–723.

Carrera, M., Cabero, A., Gonzalez, S., Rodriguez, N., Garcia, C., Hernandez, L. & Manjon, J. (2016). Solution-focused group work for common mental health problems: Outcome in routine clinical practice. *Psychology and Psychotherapy: Theory, Research, & Practice, 89*(3), 294–307.

Chang, J. & Nylund, D. (2013). Narrative and solution-focused therapies: A twenty-year retrospective. *Journal of Systemic Therapies, 32*(2), pp. 72–88.

Daki, J. & Savage, R. (2010). Solution-focused brief therapy: Impacts on academic and emotional difficulties. *The Journal of Educational Research, 103*(5), 309–326.

de Barbaro, B. (2008). Why does psychotherapy need postmodernism? *Archives of Psychiatry and Psychotherapy, 10*(3), 43–50.

De Jong, P. & Berg, I. K. (2013). *Interviewing for solutions* (3rd Ed.). Belmont, CA: Brooks/Cole.

de Shazer, S. (1984). The death of resistance. *Family Process, 23*(1), 11–17.

de Shazer, S. & Dolan, Y. (2007). *More than miracles.* Binghamton, NY: Haworth Press.

de Shazer, S. & Isebaert, L. (2004). The Bruges model: A solution-focused approach to problem drinking. *Journal of Family Psychotherapy, 14*(4), 43–52.

Franklin, C., Streeter, C. L., Kim, J. S. & Tripodi, S. (2007). The effectiveness of a solution-focused, public alternative school for dropout prevention and retrieval. *Children & Schools, 29*(3), 133–144.

Galassi, J. P. & Akos, P. (2007). *Strengths-based school counseling.* New York, NY: Routledge.

Gingerich, W. J. & Peterson, L. T. (2013). Effectiveness of solution-focused brief therapy: A systematic qualitative review of controlled outcome studies. *Research on Social Work Practice, (23)*3, 266–283.

Henderson, N. & Milstein, M. M. (2003). *Resiliency in schools.* Thousand Oaks, CA: Corwin Press, Inc.

Kim, J. S., Franklin, C., Zhang, Y., Liu, X., Yuanzhou, Q. & Hong, C. (2015). Solution-focused brief therapy in China. *Journal of Ethnic & Cultural Diversity in Social Work, 24*(3), 187–201.

Knekt, P., Lindfors, O., Härkänen, T., Välikoski, M., Virtala, E., Laaksonen, M. A., Marttunen, M., Kaipainen, M., Renlund, C.; Helsinki Psychotherapy Study Group (2008). Randomized trial on the effectiveness of long- and short-term psychodynamic psychotherapy and solution-focused therapy on psychiatric symptoms during a 3-year follow-up. *Psychological Medicine, 38*(5), 689–703.

Kramer, J., Conijn, B., Oijevaar, P. & Riper, H. (2014). Effectiveness of a web-based solution-focused brief chat treatment for depressed adolescents and young adults: Randomized controlled trial. *Journal of Medical Internet Research, 16*(5), e141, http://doi.org/10.2196/jmir.3261.

MacDonald, A. (2017). *Alisdair MacDonald's Brief Evaluation List.* Retrieved from: https://solutionfocused.net/wp-content/uploads/2018/03/Alasdair-Macdonald_SFBT-Evaluation-List.pdf.

Masten, A. (2014). *Ordinary magic.* New York, NY: Guilford Press.

Masten, A. S. & Herbers, J. E. (2013). Protective factor. In S. S. Lopez (Ed.), *The Encyclopedia of Positive Psychology*, pp. 793–796. Malden, MA: Blackwell.

Masten, A. S. & Tellegen, A. (2012). Resilience in developmental psychology: Contributions of the Project Competence Longitudinal Study. *Development and Psychopathology, 24*(2), 345–361.

Miller, S. D. & Berg, I. K. (1995). *The miracle method.* New York, NY: W. W. Norton.

NBC News (2017). Thanks to football, this Compton student is heading to Oxford. Nightly News with Lester Holt, *NBC News*, May 15. Retrieved from: www.nbcnews.com/nightly-news/video/thanks-to-football-this-compton-student-is-heading-to-oxford-944533571561.

Peterson, C. (2006). *A primer in positive psychology.* New York, NY: Oxford University Press.

Peterson, C. & Seligman, M. E. P. (2004). *Character strengths and virtues.* New York, NY: American Psychological Association.

Proudlock, S. & Wellman, N. (2011). Solution focused groups: The results look promising. *Counselling Psychology Review, 26*(3), 45–54.

Reimer, W. L. & Chatwin, A. (2006). Effectiveness of solution focused therapy for affective and relationship problems in a private practice context. *Journal of Systemic Therapies, 25*(1), 52–67.

Seligman, M. E. P. & Csikszentmihalyi, M. (2000). Positive psychology: An introduction. *American Psychologist, 55*, 5–14.

Smock, S. A., Trepper, T. S., Wetchler, J. L., McCollum, E. E., Ray, R. & Pierce, K. (2008). Solution-focused group therapy for level 1 substance abusers. *Journal of Marital and Family Therapy, 34*(1), 107–120.

Thompson, R. & Littrell, J. (1998). Brief counseling for students with learning disabilities. *Professional School Counseling, 2*(1), 60–67.

Visser, C. F. (2013). The origin of the solution-focused approach. *International Journal of Solution-Focused Practice, 1*(1), 10–17.

Werner, E. (2005). Resilience and recovery: Findings from the Kauai longitudinal study. *Research Policy, and Practice in Children's Mental Health, 19,* 11–14.

Werner, E. E. & Smith, R. S. (1982). *Vulnerable but invincible: A longitudinal study of resilient children and youth.* New York, NY: McGraw-Hill.

Werner, E. E. & Smith, R. S. (2001). *Journeys from childhood to midlife.* Ithaca, NY: Cornell University Press.

White, M. (2007). *Maps of narrative practice.* New York, NY: W. W. Norton.

White, M. & Epston, D. (1990). *Narrative means to therapeutic ends.* New York, NY: W. W. Norton.

CHAPTER 3

Creative and Playful Approaches

Elizabeth R. Taylor and Amanda Allison

There he sat on the other side of the board waiting for me to play my turn. He had quickly played his turn as soon as I let my hand off my black checker. He chose red checkers, maybe to match his flaming red hair? He was winning, and he knew he was winning and couldn't wait to finish the game, so he could say he won! That was how we played checkers. He moved his checkers, and then I moved mine in a way that he could capture them. I would let him know how amazed I was at his skills and his ability to think ahead about what move to make. We had been meeting twice a week at the private school he attended. By his history, you would think he would be highly successful, since most teachers spoke about his intelligence and kindness to others, and his parents bragged about his love for animals. But, this little boy struggled. Challenged by problems with self-regulation, he developed a reputation, alongside his reputation for kindness, for being in trouble, always out of his seat and in everyone else's business, talking incessantly. As soon as a problem broke out on the playground, teachers quickly identified him as the problem due to his red hair and fair skin that stood in contrast to his playmates. Due to his high activity level, he developed few friendships with peers and a poor reputation with teachers. However, over the past month, his behavior and grades improved, as he gradually calmed. We talked about many different subjects, particularly animals. We talked about his struggles with friends and academics but also his strengths in math and science.

Now, here we were playing checkers as we had done so many, many times while we talked about who and what were important to him. I moved my black checker a little closer to his red checker and waited for him to jump my checker and claim his win. However, this time, without looking at me, he stated, "This time I am going to let you win." Dumbfounded, I wasn't sure what to do, as this sudden change in our game left me speechless. He moved his red checker closer to mine, so I could jump it and take his checker. Realizing the importance of this step in our relationship, I jumped his checker and, as I had done after every game, stated, "Good game!" He grinned and seemed quite pleased with himself. Over the course of our therapy, he gradually gained a sense of control and well-being. Feeling more competent, he could risk letting me win.

Creative and playful approaches take many forms. Games, expressive arts, and other forms of play allow the therapist to communicate with clients using media and materials that appeal to their interests, strengths, and talents. The use of these approaches provides the SF therapist with a variety of ways to capitalize on the strengths clients bring to therapy, while tapping into different areas of the brain responsible for attachment, memory, and self-regulation.

Play

Play is not work; it holds a natural, intrinsic value (Landreth, 2002). "Unlike adults, whose natural medium of communication is verbalization, the natural medium of communication for children is play and activity" (Landreth, 2002, p. 9). Researchers continue to demonstrate that play performs an important role in the development of the brain—rehearsing behaviors and creating neural connections, learning to socialize and problem-solve, and developing creativity. Not only is play a requirement for children, it plays an important role in coping and development throughout life (Brown, 2009). Not surprisingly, Rhea (2014), as a result of reinstating recess in elementary schools throughout the school day, finds that school staff deal with fewer discipline problems, as children fidget less, engage in fewer off-task behaviors, increase their learning, and raise their test scores (DeNisco, 2016; Hernandez, 2017; Ndoni, 2016).

Unfortunately, academic testing sacrifices play and recess on the proverbial altar of achievement without an understanding of developmental needs, attention span, and appropriate learning practices. At home, parents often restrict their children's play due to fears of abduction and neighborhood violence. Yet, through play children and adolescents find ways to express themselves, develop social skills, learn to play cooperatively, develop creativity, work through difficult challenges, and find solutions. Youth let off steam, express the inexpressible, and develop coping skills through active play; however, many do not have the opportunity to engage in play that is proven to be so important in releasing stress and anxiety.

Play performs an important preventative function in the lives of individuals but also as an intervention to assist youth in coping with personal challenges. The Association for Play Therapy (APT), established in 1982 to promote the value and practice of play and play therapy, defines play therapy as "the systematic use of a theoretical model to establish an interpersonal process wherein trained play therapists use the therapeutic powers of play to help clients prevent or resolve psychosocial difficulties and achieve optimal growth and development" (Association for Play Therapy, 2017). Play therapy offers a developmentally appropriate approach for helping children and adolescents communicate their feelings, thoughts, and experiences, practice new behaviors, take on different perspectives, and rehearse new roles. Ideally, play therapy includes play in the context of a well-organized play room with carefully selected toys and expressive materials (Landreth, 2002), but the therapist may also provide play therapy in homes, schools, medical settings, and community centers (Burns-Nader & Hernandez-Reif, 2016; Drewes & Schaefer, 2010; Ginsberg, 1976; Hendon & Bohon, 2008; Webb, 2011). Play therapy often occurs in disaster settings and crisis centers as therapists work with children and adolescents to make sense of a tragedy and assimilate traumatic experiences (Jordan, Perryman & Anderson, 2013; Webb, 1999).

Variations exist in how play therapy is conducted, including how much control the therapist exerts over the session, toys, and materials used, how the therapist interacts with the client, use of interpretation, and direct application of techniques, differing according to the theoretical orientation. Some (Schaeffer, 1993; Kaduson, Canglelosi, & Schaefer, 1997) suggest that an eclectic approach may be more appropriate, wherein the therapist, knowledgeable in several different areas of play therapy, selects the most appropriate approach to use with clients according to clients' needs.

Play therapy dates back to Sigmund Freud (1909/1955), Hug-Hellmuth (1921), and Anna Freud (1928) working in the psychoanalytic tradition, but it wasn't until 1932, when Melanie Klein first used play as the primary medium and substitute for verbal expression in therapy with children, that play therapy became a viable approach in working with children. Since Psychoanalytic Play Therapy, other play therapy approaches have emerged, most notably Client-Centered Play Therapy (Axline, 1947; Landreth, 1978, 1991), Adlerian Play Therapy (Kottman, 1995), Family Play Therapy (Gil, 1994), Theraplay (Jernberg, 1979), Gestalt Play Therapy (Oaklander, 1988), as well as a host of others, all emphasizing a strong relationship between child and therapist.

Nims (2007) discusses the application of SF techniques to play therapy. Leggett (2009) also introduces SF play therapy (SFPT) using literature and visual arts, as well as providing a general overview of SFPT. King (2017) describes more fully the integration of SF therapy with play therapy when working with children and families, incorporating recent neurological findings and techniques for addressing trauma into her work. SFPT remains goal-focused, and the process of reaching those goals continues to be playful, creative, and driven by the client.

Play therapy approaches incorporate many different creative and playful techniques, including sandtray, puppets, games, art, music, writing, and phototherapy. Since each of these techniques is used throughout the text to enhance the therapeutic process with children and adolescents, they are discussed in further depth in this chapter. A general overview of each technique is provided to give the reader some background when applying it to SF therapy.

Sandtray

Recent findings on the use of sandtray in therapy indicate that out of 100 toys in the playroom, children most prefer the sandtray (Ray et al., 2013). Not only is sandtray the most preferred, but it may be the most important. Lowenfeld (1935/2008) writes that the most important toys in the playroom are those that are part of the "world cabinet," that is, the sandtray and miniatures. What makes sandtray such a vital part of play therapy?

It connects us with our beginnings. "As we connect with the sand, we cannot help but feel the connection to the Spirit within, and the Creation without" (Homeyer & Sweeney, 2011, p. 13). Sand, common to most children and adolescents, provides a safe way to connect client and therapist. Sometimes, the child or adolescent spends the first few minutes just pushing the sand through his hands without speaking, allowing the client to calm himself, to get used to the sandtray and the therapeutic space, and to find ways to connect with the therapist (Taylor, 2009). Further, sandtray offers the client a way to express himself nonverbally without self-judgment and thus facilitates a positive relationship with the therapist but also a positive sense of the therapy process (Gil, 2006).

Sandtray is particularly applicable to SF therapy since it follows a constructivist approach, in that the client is the expert and the client creates, from his perspective, the world as he sees it using miniatures that he selects. The client communicates to the therapist through the miniatures and sand what life looks like through the client's eyes, its challenges, and possible solutions. In the style of constructivism, the client externalizes the problem in the sandtray and thus finds new perspectives on the problem, solutions, and resources. The therapist acts as witness to the process and over the course of therapy asks questions and makes comments on the sandtray the client creates, focusing on strengths, solutions, and personal and interpersonal resources (Taylor, 2009, 2015).

The sandtray, usually a plastic or wood container (30 inches by 20 inches by 3 inches deep), provides a container for the client to project his or her world. Miniatures are carefully selected with attention to the family and culture of the client. In SF sandtray, miniatures also include those items that allow for finding strengths and addressing future-focused questions. Items to consider for inclusion when using SFPT include a fairy godmother, a wishing well, a treasure chest, an Aladdin's lamp, colored stones or jewels, sports goals, a lighthouse, and other items representing goals, strengths, and resources (Taylor, 2009, 2015).

Sandtray offers a constructivist approach in which the client creates her world and the therapist responds to this construction verbally and through the sandtray. Not only does the client create her world where challenges exist but also where exceptions to problems and personal and social resources also exist, waiting to be discovered. The sense of control the client possesses in creating her world provides numerous options for creating new stories with new possibilities.

Puppets

Puppets provide a natural and developmentally appropriate approach to empower the young child. The child communicates through puppets, thus externalizing the problem and opening opportunities to find exceptions. Therapists often find puppets useful individually, in family therapy, and in groups (Guterman & Martin, 2016). "The only limits to the potential applications of puppets in elementary school counseling would be the limits of the counselor's and child's imaginations" (Carter & Mason, 1998, p. 2).

Puppets should be carefully selected. Hartwig (2014, p. 208) suggests using the "three Fs" in choosing puppets—those that fall into the category of friendly, such as dogs, cheerleaders, and butterflies; foolish, such as monsters, chickens, puppets with googly eyes; and frightening, such as snakes, wolves, witches, and sharks. Puppets, such as Santa Claus, that represent universal symbols should not be included in the selection, since children would likely not create their own meaning for this type of puppet. A variety of ethnicities should also be included in the puppet selection. To help children identify with the puppets may require creating or adding materials that reflect the characteristics of the child, such as crutches, glasses, or a wheelchair. For those with visual impairments, it is helpful to make the puppets using a variety of textures so they can be easily identified through touch (Carter & Mason, 1998).

Irwin (2002) recommends as many as 15 to 20 puppets that represent a range of feelings and actions. Many objects can be used as puppets; one only needs to google "making puppets" to find multiple ways to make puppets using paper bags, socks, tongue depressors, and various other materials. Puppets already made are also readily available for purchase. Puppets should fit the hands of children and therapists, be easily manipulated, and soft. The therapist should also consider how to keep puppets clean, whether that means taking them to the dry cleaners or washing them in soapy water or the washing machine (Carter & Mason, 1998).

Sometimes, a stage helps in providing a barrier and needed distance between the child and the therapist, each using a puppet. The therapist may elect to buy a stage or create her own using appliance boxes or even a small table turned on its side (Carter & Mason, 1998).

The child may communicate through the puppet in such a way that it is easier for her to express herself and discuss her strengths and concerns. Communication may involve an unstructured scenario or the therapist and client can create their own puppet show in a mutual storytelling type of approach beginning with "once upon a time," and then alternating story lines. Regardless of how the therapist uses the conversation between puppets, the therapist puppet responses should be neutral and reflective rather than adding to the story (Carter & Mason, 1998).

Puppets provide an alternative approach to communication, one that children find friendly and simple. Having appropriate puppets available allows children to give voice to their concerns and an opportunity to role play new ways of behaving, practicing possibilities without the risk of shame or failure.

Games

Games provide an effective approach for engaging children and adolescents in individual and group therapy, practicing new skills, assessing client strengths, and teaching a variety of important skills necessary for success in the social and academic domains, such as self-control, creating and following rules, dealing with frustration and anxiety, and behaviors associated with winning and losing in competition (Friedberg, 1996; Martinez & Lasser, 2013; Oren, 2008). By playing games with clients, the therapist gains insight into the cognitive and affective strengths of clients, as well as possible challenges. "The choice of game, the way it is played and the interaction with the therapist, reveal the emotional state, difficulties and interactions of children in their social and family frameworks" (Bellinson, 2002; Oren, 2008, p. 365).

Playing games accesses different levels of the brain. For example, the cortex and cortical regions of the brain are activated as clients connect through the game with the therapist or one another. As clients work through the rules and structure of the game, the limbic system, responsible for motivation and attention, becomes activated within a climate of fun. As clients experience success and frustration, they learn to balance their thoughts and feelings, one of the roles of the cerebellum. Games also help clients interact, process, and integrate different areas of the brain by playing within guidelines, negotiating relationships, reality-testing, and striving for a healthy existence (Stone, 2016).

Many premade games exist that address any number of social-emotional topics for children and adolescents, but it may be more expedient to design a game that specifically targets strengths and resiliencies in developmentally appropriate ways for a specific client or clients. One approach involves taking games familiar to youth and adapting them to the therapeutic situation. For example, the game of "Operation" offers a way for children to practice self-regulation skills within the game mode, and, as noted in the case study of this chapter, playing a game of Checkers can foster the client–therapist relationship.

The therapist might also elect to have clients create their own game. By doing so, specific developmental needs are addressed with the client's targeted goals or hoped-for outcomes. Martinez and Lasser (2013) outline a specific approach to helping middle-school adolescents design their own game as individuals or as a group, employing creative and cognitive processes to plan and design the game, and then consider scenarios in which certain skills may be needed. They find that the creation and use of the game requires therapeutic flexibility but also some structure in creating the game. However, the ability of clients to create a game that sets up personal challenges and provides their own solutions offers the SF therapist an appropriate and hopeful avenue for empowering clients to find solutions and reach their goals. When playing games in groups, using games that require teamwork helps clients develop altruistic and supportive relationships with other team members, as long as the therapist encourages supportive behaviors and facilitates the positive aspects of being a part of a team.

Art

Many have stated that art is necessary to living. Pablo Picasso wrote, "Art washes from the soul the dust of everyday life." An anonymous writer stated,

"EARTH" without "ART" is just "EH." The famous clergyman and abolition-ist Henry Ward Beecher stated, "Every artist dips his brush in his own soul and paints his own nature into his pictures." These sayings made their way into everyday vernacular because we recognized, as a society, the immediacy of the arts in helping manage life stresses and creating a productive, competitive workforce in the 21st century.

The arts nourish human beings at their deepest levels. Anthropologist Ellen Dissanayake, in her book *Homo Aestheticus* (1992), makes the claim that making art is as necessary to survival as food, clothing, shelter, and even procreation. Art as a therapeutic process enables us to be whole and exhale the stresses of life. "Just as science has the power to transform raw materials into medicine or technology into curative therapy, so art—in all its varied incarnations—has the power to transform" (Kropf, 2009, p. 778).

"Therapeutic art" can be defined as a process of using art to enhance the quality of life in three ways. First, the therapist develops a relationship and con-nects with the person with whom art is being made by verbally (or physically in some cases) tracking the person's actions. Second, the therapist creates a prompt for art making that lends itself to reflection. For example, the therapist asks the client to trace a car or house key as many times as the client wants and then illustrate the "keys' the client needs in life to be successful. A third way the therapist uses art to enhance the client's quality of life involves choosing materials and processes that reach intended goals and support the art maker in being successful. The therapist differentiates instruction, with consideration of the client's developmental level and learning differences, by demonstrating multiple ways to achieve success. In order to further assist the client in being successful, the therapist allows the client to experiment beforehand so that she is familiar with the materials and process and feels safe in art-making activities.

Children progress through developmental stages in art, just as they do in other areas of their lives. They begin scribbling, then making shapes, drawing symbols and then real objects (Day & Hurwitz, 2012). This artistic devel-opment occurs in concert with children's physical, emotional, social, and cognitive development, so that children's art work often indicates the present levels of functioning in each of these areas and provides an understanding of the child's overall development.

Art making, especially when viewed as a special experience, activates the emotion and memory center of the brain, the amygdala; therefore, when a pos-itive counseling experience provides a special experience for clients, it is likely to be remembered. In therapeutic art, we want to condition clients to associ-ate positive thoughts, beliefs, and intentions with the artworks they create. To do this, we activate the amygdala as we provide therapeutic experiences that include multisensory approaches, novelty, and embodied learning. When the child engages multiple senses (sight, smell, taste, touch, movement), when they do something new (use a new art material, take a new approach to introducing something, learn in a new environment), and when they act out or role play an event or person or state of being, then the chances increase that the child remembers the event with the positive thoughts, actions, beliefs and intentions associated with it. The art work acts as a method of visualization, a reminder of the prize the client seeks, the target for which the client aims, and the goals the client accomplishes. As such, making art provides a powerful and a significant tool in the healing endeavor. Researchers (Bolwerk, Mack-Andrick, Lang, Dorfler & Maihofner, 2014) suggest that engaging clients in art making activates neural activity and increases neural connections that help clients cognitively regulate emotions, reduce negative emotions, increase self-awareness and focus, enhance memory, and increase psychological resilience.

Coloring and Drawing

A child uses coloring and drawing to fulfill an array of developmental needs. The piece of paper that the child uses to draw or color can be conceived of as a physical representation of the child's world. It is a contained space, therefore filling it in produces a sense of control, completion, and closure. Coloring provides a way for a child to self soothe, much like rocking a baby. Through coloring and drawing, the child proves her existence. She creates a mark that was not there before (Malchiodi, 1998). To the dismay of her parents, a toddler experiences joy in her first mark on a wall. This connection between art making and personal agency grows stronger with age. The adult mentor encourages this agency by paying attention to the drawing the child creates and making observational comments, such as "I see you are using a lot of strong blue lines," thus making the child feel valued because the adult pays attention to her creation.

The child feels a genuine pleasure in the act of moving a crayon smoothly over and filling in a piece of paper. Researchers (Curry & Kasser, 2005) find that coloring in a geometric pattern evokes a meditative state and reduces anxiety in college students. Not surprisingly, coloring books for children and adults sell to those who use coloring to de-stress, experience calm, and induce the meditative experience.

Coloring and drawing may also be used as a means of distraction, as the individual experiences a state of flow, where the mind's throttle is fully open and activities feel seamless (Forkosh & Drake, 2017). When a child is given a task to draw something, it poses a cognitive challenge. With appropriate supports, the child meets the challenge and engages in the activity, taking his mind off other concerns.

Drawing and coloring activate different areas of the brain (Forkosh & Drake, 2017). When coloring and shading, the reward and self-regulating centers of the brain located in the prefrontal cortex seem to awaken (Kaimal et al., 2017). Kaimal, Ray and Muniz (2016) substantiate the claim that art making can be relaxing by measuring pre- and post-cortisol levels of individuals after a 45-minute session of art making. Participants state that they find art making relaxing and helpful, and their lowered cortisol levels substantiate their statements.

Clay/Play Dough

Clay offers a medium that evokes the kinesthetic, visual, and olfactory senses, activating various parts of the brain. Rather than focusing on images and objects, the use of clay addresses haptic perception—that is, the sense of touch—activating neural pathways responsible for the tactile and kinesthetic senses (Elbrecht & Antcliff, 2014). Clay often serves as a highly satisfying medium for those who have severe handicapping conditions, such as mental retardation, psychosis, visual and hearing deficits, or autism (Henley, 1991), but also with other issues such as anxiety, negative mood, and trauma (Elbrecht & Antcliff, 2014; Kimport & Robbins, 2012; McGrath, 2017). For those who work with clients who have experienced trauma, clay provides a sensorimotor experience that accesses those areas of the brain that trauma often affects (Elbrecht & Antcliff, 2014) and provides a bridge to discussing the trauma itself at more cognitive levels, allowing the client to move forward in addressing goals and a hoped-for future.

Working with clay or play dough offers several advantages. First, clay provides a non-verbal, three-dimensional medium through which children and adolescents control the process and outcome. Play dough or clay can be molded and controlled within limits, so that the child controls the process of forming the play dough and the eventual shape it takes. As the client creates and molds the clay, the brain receives feedback through the tactile sense and motor and muscle movement (Elbrecht & Antcliff, 2014). Kruk, Aravich, Deaver, and deBeus (2014) surmise that the use of clay invokes a meditative state, explaining the reduction of anxiety and decrease in negative mood in study participants. Like other forms of expression, working with clay or play dough provides a safe outlet for anger and aggressive feelings, regardless of age.

Music Therapy

Victor Hugo states, "Music expresses that which cannot be said and on which it is impossible to be silent." Indeed, music appeals to all ages and is imbedded in most cultures and religions. Even the most severely handicapped children tend to be affected by the sound of music.

For example, while working at a state institution for the cognitively and physically impaired, I was assigned to work with a blind 18-year-old girl who could walk but, due to her frequent and violent outbursts, was restrained to her chair. Unable to tolerate clothing, she sat naked amidst other bedfast patients. If a staff member approached her she would reach behind and grab part of her excrement and throw it. This made it almost impossible to care for her and staff were often repelled by her smell. However, over time, I found that she responded to the sound of a simple music box. When approaching her, I turned on the music box and she stopped screaming and calmed to the music. After several weeks, I could approach her while the music played and stroke her arm. Eventually, staff found the magic of playing music for her, and she allowed them to attend to her basic needs while she tuned into music.

Therapeutically, music provides healing at the deepest levels of brain development, within the brainstem and cerebellum. Infants, even in the womb, respond to music and listen to the heartbeat of their mothers. Music, in a variety of forms, provides healing, as it "is all-encompassing in its engagement of the whole person, the embodied self" (McGrath, 2017).

Researchers and clinicians support the use of music to calm those with anxiety, decrease agitation and aggression, and increase positive mood (Magee, 2011). School counselors find that using music reduces children's anxiety, it motivates, and it increases self-esteem (Bowman, 1987; McFerran, Crooke & Bolger, 2017). Music provides a way to teach social skills, such as eye contact, listening, and taking turns (Magee, 2011), and helps children to develop confidence and build relationships (Hadley & Steele, 2014).

Therapists use music with children, adolescents, and adults suffering from traumatic brain injuries to help them improve self-regulation (Magee, 2011), with children and adolescents affected by natural disasters to help with coping associated trauma (Davis, 2010), in bereavement groups (Krout, 2015), and for young women at risk of depression (McFerran, Crooke & Bolger, 2017). Researchers find that music benefits children and adolescents undergoing medical procedures (Standley & Whipple, 2003), treating pain and anxiety (Klassen, Liang, Tjosvold, Klassen, & Hartling, 2008), and lowering blood pressure (Bradt & Dileo, 2009). Using different music approaches, such as body percussion, songwriting, and dancing, fosters school and peer engagement (McFerran, Crooke & Bolger, 2017).

Therapists use music in different ways—to calm clients, help clients express themselves, and teach clients to create their own music and words. "Children who have difficulty expressing themselves verbally may be able to do so through singing, playing an instrument, or writing a song" (Newcomb, 1994, p. 150). Therapists do not need to be skilled musicians; they only need to bring a few skills and their energy to the process. Researchers and clinicians (McFerran, Crooke & Bolger, 2017; Newcomb, 1994) emphasize that the therapist should tailor the music to the child's or adolescent's developmental level and interests and make it inclusive so all can participate without fear of judgment. The therapist selects music with consideration for client preferences in terms of the type of music and how it is played (live or recorded, rhythm, and instrumentation) (Magee, 2011).

Rhythm plays a significant role when using music in therapy, since rhythm involves all aspects of life, such as the heart beating, breathing, walking, and even communication between two people. The mother rocks the child and attunes to the child's communication patterns in a back-and-forth rhythm that builds neural connections, allowing the child to regulate the self and develop relationships to and with the world. Rhythm experiences, such as drumming, swaying and dancing to music, and using different percussion instruments (e.g., rhythm sticks, triangle, castanets, tambourine, and maracas) in time to music provide ways to practice rhythm. By clapping hands, tapping feet, and body drumming, youth practice rhythm that helps develop self-regulation skills (Ho, Tsao, Block & Zeltzer, 2011).

Music tends to connect people when listening, creating, and playing music together. Sassen (2012) illustrates such a connection through her program "Drums and Poems," which focuses on building positive relationships and enhancing the culture of children and adolescents as they create rhythms and write poems, and then blend these two expressive art forms together. The focus of the program does not lie with the product of the writing and playing but with the relational processes involved. Through this expressive modality, immigrant and low-income children find connections and experience joy due to feelings of inclusion and being valued by peers. Rather than being the victim of someone with power over them, they experience "power-with" (Sassen, 2012, p. 242).

Writing

Writing offers a way for the therapist to connect with the client, so that the client can express what may be difficult to express verbally. Through writing, the client assimilates and validates difficult circumstances and considers new possibilities and solutions. As viewed through a constructivist lens, the client and therapist collaboratively construct new ways of being and doing by externalizing thoughts and feelings onto paper or a computer screen. Various forms of writing used therapeutically include letter writing, journaling, creative writing, structured writing, and poetry (Brand, 1987; White & Epston, 1990).

White and Epston (1990), originators of narrative therapy, present letter writing or "storied therapy" as a therapeutic medium. The therapist writes a letter to the client, for the client, or to the client's close affiliations (parents, friends, teachers). Through this form of narrative therapy, the therapist aims to assist clients in externalizing and redefining their relationship with the problem, to document solutions, and to celebrate victories over problems. Letters specifically address any number of areas, such as summaries of the sessions, reframes of the problem, client strengths, changes the client makes or hopes to make, goals, and suggestions for noticing positive changes.

Davis and Voirin (2016) describe the use of reciprocal writing through the perspectives of narrative and SF therapy as an approach for creating dialogue, asking questions, emphasizing strengths and deemphasizing negative aspects of the problem, creating goals and possible solutions, externalizing the problem, and reauthoring personal stories. The benefits of the reciprocal writing approach include helping clients focus on solutions rather than problems, providing clients with a written record to keep outside of the therapy session to review, a visual of their status and progress made, and an approach for those reluctant to verbalize due to shyness, shame, or speaking difficulties. Reciprocal writing also offers a means for strong emotion to be reduced and "make the counseling experience more realistic, personal, and practical to the individual's life" (Davis & Voirin, 2016, p. 74).

Writing may also be useful in group therapy. For example, the therapist provides time before group starts for clients to write anything that comes to their minds without worrying about punctuation or spelling. Sentence starters can be helpful in focusing clients on a specific topic, for example, "When I need help, I know I can . . .," or "I am strong enough to . . .," or "My favorite place to go is . . . ."

The client might also write letters to externalize problems and focus on future solutions. For example, those who feel victimized or angry may find letter writing to be an approach that externalizes the problem and allows consideration of different solutions. Asking clients to write a letter *from* their future self provides a way for clients to come up with their own solutions as they consider the possible strengths and solutions they use to reach their goals. Clients may also write a letter *to* their future self, projecting into the future and giving advice for overcoming obstacles and achieving goals.

Combining writing with other expressive and creative approaches allows clients to use multiple modalities, as they illustrate what they write using collage, drawing, or painting. Clients put words to pictures or add pictures to words to provide a more in-depth, individualized expression of challenges, strengths, and solutions. Another form of creative writing, poetry, can be combined with music and various image-making approaches, such as drawing, painting, and photography. For example, the therapist asks the client to write new words to a familiar musical tune, providing an easy way to experiment with putting thoughts and ideas into poems and then to music.

Phototherapy

Phototherapy provides a therapeutic approach that serves to increase therapeutic efficacy and cement changes by employing photographic images to encourage verbal or nonverbal expression and explore various levels of psychological content individually and in groups (Wadeson, 2000; Williams, 1987). Photographs are used in therapy to raise and maintain self-esteem and the self-concept, enhance a sense of self, increase an individual's sense of mastery and competence, foster self-expression, increase socialization skills, and explore family-of-origin issues (Blinn, 1987; Fryrear, Nuell & White, 1977; Hubbard, Romero & Thomas, 1987; Juhnke, 1995; Miller, 1962; Mitchell & Weber, 1998; Spire, 1973; Wadeson, 2000). Researchers indicate that photographs in therapy can be used effectively with children, adolescents, and adults; through different therapeutic modalities, including individuals, couples, groups, and families; and with a variety of clients with varying concerns, including inpatients and outpatients, those with learning disabilities, and military veterans (Anderson & Malloy, 1976; Jackson & Jackson, 1999; Miller, 1962). Photographs may also be employed as a catalyst to promote verbal and written expression, as well as a way to document progress (Wadeson, 2000; Williams, 1987). Photography appeals to all ages and tends to break down barriers for those with disabilities or severe psychiatric disorders. Fisk (1994) notes the value of photography quoting Lewis Hine: "If I could tell a story in words, I wouldn't need to lug a camera" (p. 265).

The photographer creates an environment by selecting certain situations and ignoring others. These situations provide information about the self and the world (Ziller, 1990), explaining why the significance of a photograph is peculiar to each individual, reflecting unique perspectives of the world and glimpses into the client's personality (Weiser, 1993). For example, persons who have a tendency toward shyness tend to take pictures of non-persons, preferring aesthetics (Ziller & Rorer, 1985).

Bermer (1993) describes a psychoanalytic use of photographs in therapy. Similar to De Jong and Berg (2013), the psychoanalytic therapist takes the stance of "not knowing" when using photographs in therapy. However, unlike SF therapists, Bermer focuses on "incongruities" (p. 80) and "contradictions" (p. 80), the "family problem" (p. 80), and individual feelings of inadequacies, whereas SF therapists focus on clients' personal strengths and resources.

Other similarities exist between SF therapy and the use of photography in therapy. For example, the therapist respects the individual for his uniqueness and perceptions and emphasizes the client's personal control (De Jong & Berg, 2013; Weiser, 1993). Martin and Spence (1988) describe a co-therapy approach in which individuals visually reframe past attitudes and activities, not focusing so much on accuracy of memories, but on changing perceptions and creating new meanings. They utilize an ongoing process of self-photographs and words to facilitate changing self-images and perceptions. Taking photographs empowers clients with the freedom to create the self and look at possibilities (Weiser, 1993). Winburn, King, and Burton (2017) also describe the use of self-photographs, "selfies," as a way for children to choose how they want to represent themselves in a picture. Self-photographs allow clients to create personal narratives with a new sense of control, facilitate self-expression, and develop a better understanding of others' viewpoints.

Wolf (2014) states that using phototherapy enables "clients to create powerful visual metaphors that are then used to achieve deeper self-understanding and personal insight during the therapy process" (p. 183). He believes that children and particularly adolescents are more likely to engage in the use of photography than other forms of art due to perfectionism and fears of failure. Although he speaks from a psychoanalytic perspective, Wolf concedes that phototherapy interventions depend on the therapist's clinical training. To that end, he provides a plethora of ideas in the use of photography in therapy but also ways to manipulate photos digitally.

As research indicates, the use of photographs continues to provide a unique, non-verbal approach for therapists, one that tends to be congruent with SF therapy. By using photographs, either in taking them or viewing them, the therapist employs a unique, meaningful, and nonverbal and verbal approach in communicating with clients through a developmentally appropriate modality.

The many creative and tangible approaches presented provide the therapist with different ways to communicate with clients and capitalize on their strengths. Many of these approaches, common to other therapeutic disciplines, allow the therapist to expand on SF therapy techniques to incorporate multisensory approaches and increase therapeutic effectiveness.

References

Anderson, C. M. & Malloy, E. S. (1976). Family photographs: In treatment and training. *Family Process, 15*(2), 259–264.

Association for Play Therapy (APT) (2017). *About APT.* Retrieved from: www.a4pt. org/page/AboutAPT.

Axline, V. (1947). *Play therapy: The inner dynamics of childhood.* Boston, MA: Houghton-Mifflin.

Bellinson, J. (2002). *Children's use of board games in psychotherapy.* Northvale, NJ: Jason Aronson, Inc.

Bermer, L. (1993). *Beyond the smile.* London: Routledge.

Blinn, L. M. (1987). Phototherapeutic intervention to improve self-concept and prevent repeat pregnancies among adolescents. *Family Relations, 36*, 252–257.

Bolwerk, A., Mack-Andrick, J., Lang, F. R., Dorfler, A. & Maihofner, C. (2014). How art changes your brain: Differential effects of visual art production and cognitive art evaluation on functional brain connectivity. *PLOS ONE, 9*(7), 1–8.

Bowman, R. P. (1987). Approaches for counseling children through music. *Elementary School Guidance & Counseling, 21*(2), 281–288.

Bradt, J. & Dileo, C. (2009). Music for stress and anxiety reduction in coronary heart disease patients. *The Cochrane Library,* Dec 28; (12): CD006577.

Brand, A. G. (1987). Writing as counseling. *Elementary School Guidance & Counseling, 21*(4), 266–275.

Brown, S. (2009). *Play.* New York, NY: Penguin Press.

Burns-Nader, S. & Hernandez-Reif, M. (2016). Facilitating play for hospitalized children through child life services. *Children's Health Care, 45*(1), 1–21.

Carter, R. B. & Mason, P. S. (1998). The selection and use of puppets in counseling. *Professional School Counseling, 1*(5), 50–53.

Curry, N. A. & Kasser, T. (2005). Can coloring mandalas reduce anxiety? *Art Therapy: Journal of American Art Association, 22*(2), 81–85.

Davis, K. M. (2010). Music and expressive arts with children experiencing trauma. *Journal of Creativity in Mental Health, 5*(2), 125–133.

Davis, N. L. & Voirin, J. (2016). Reciprocal writing as a creative technique. *Journal of Creativity in Mental Health, 11*(1), 66–77.

Day, M. & Hurwitz, A. (2012). *Children and their art.* Boston, MA: Wadsworth.

De Jong, P. & Berg, I. K. (2013). *Interviewing for solutions* (4th Ed.). Belmont, CA: Brooks/Cole.

DeNisco, A. (2016). Texas schools test brain benefits of recess. *District Administration, 52*(3), 24.

Dissanayake, E. (1992). *Homo aestheticus: Where art comes from and why.* New York, NY: Free Press.

Drewes, A. & Schaefer, C. E. (2010). School-based play therapy (2nd Ed.). Hoboken, NJ: John Wiley & Sons.

Elbrecht, C. & Antcliff, L. R. (2014). Being touched through touch. Trauma treatment through haptic perception at the Clay Field: A sensorimotor art therapy. *International Journal of Art Therapy, 19*(1), 19–30.

Fisk, D. L. (1994). A second look: Photography as an experiential and therapeutic tool. *Experiential education: A critical resource for the 21st century.* Proceedings from the Manual of the Annual Interactional Conference of the Association for Experiential Education, Austin, TX. Abstract retrieved from: https://files.eric.ed.gov/fulltext/ED377016.pdf.

Forkosh, J. & Drake, J. E. (2017). Coloring versus drawing: Effects of cognitive demand on mood repair, flow, and enjoyment. *Art Therapy, 34*(2), 75–82.

Freud, A. (1928). *Introduction to the technique of child analysis* (L. P. Clark, trans.). New York, NY: Nervous and Mental Disease.

Freud, S. (1955). *Analysis of a phobia in a five year old boy* (original work published in 1909). London: Hogarth Press.

Friedberg, R. D. (1996). Cognitive-behavioral games and workbooks: Tips for school counselors. *Elementary School Guidance and Counseling, 31*(1), 11–20.

Fryrear, J. L., Nuell, L. R. & White, P. (1977). Enhancement of male juvenile delinquents' self-concepts through photographed social interactions. *Journal of Clinical Psychology, 33*, 833–838.

Gil, E. (1994). *Play in family therapy.* New York, NY: Guilford Press.

Gil, E. (2006). *Helping abused and traumatized children.* New York, NY: Guilford Press.

Ginsberg, B. G. (1976). Parents as therapeutic agents: The usefulness of filial therapy in a community mental health center. *Journal of Community Psychology, 4*(1), 47–54.

Guterman, J. T. & Martin, C. (2016). Using puppets with aggressive children to externalize the problem in narrative therapy. In A. A. Drewes & C. E. Schaefer (Eds), *Play therapy in middle childhood*, pp. 135–150. Washington, DC: American Psychological Association.

Hadley, S. & Steele, N. (2014). Music therapy. In E. J. Green & A. Drewes (Eds), *Integrating expressive arts and play therapy with children and adolescents*, pp. 149–179. Hoboken, NJ: John Wiley & Sons, Inc.

Hartwig, E. (2014). Puppets in the playroom: Utilizing puppets and child-centered facilitative skills as a metaphor for healing. *International Journal of Play Therapy, 23*(4), 204–216.

Hendon, C. & Bohon, L. M. (2008). Hospitalized children's mood differences during play and music therapy. *Health and Development, 34*(2), 141–144.

Henley, D. R. (1991). Facilitating the development of object relations through the use of clay in art therapy. *American Journal of Art Therapy, 29*(3), 69–76.

Hernandez, M. (2017). Recess 4 times a day? Little Elm ISD says it helps in the classroom. *WFAA Television Station.* Retrieved from: www.wfaa.com/article/news/education/recess-4-times-a-day-little-elm-isd-says-it-helps-in-the-classroom/497319924.

Homeyer, L. E. & Sweeney, D. S. (2011). *Sandtray therapy* (2nd Ed.). New York, NY: Taylor & Francis.

Ho, P., Tsao, J. C., Block, L. & Zeltzer, L. K. (2011). The impact of group drumming on social-emotional behavior in low income children. *Evidence Based Complementary and Alternative Medicine, 250708*, 10.1093/ecam/neq072, pp. 1–16.

Hubbard, J. T., Romero, D. H. & Thomas, S. B. (1987). A guide to photography in educational and counseling sessions. *Perspectives in Psychiatric Care, 24* (1), 20–24.

Hug-Hellmuth, H. (1921). On the technique of child-analysis. *International Journal of Psychoanalysis, 2*, 287–305.

Irwin, E. C. (2002). Using puppets for assessment. In C. E. Schaeffer & L. Carey (Eds), *Family play therapy techniques* (2nd Ed.), pp. 101–113. Northvale, NJ: Jason Aronson, Inc.

Jackson, E. & Jackson, N. (1999). *Learning disability in focus: The use of photography in the care of people with a learning disability.* Philadelphia, PA: Jessica Kingsley Publishers.

Jernberg, A. (1979). *Theraplay: A new treatment using structured play for problem children and their families.* San Francisco, CA: Jossey-Bass.

Jordan, B., Perryman, K. & Anderson, L. (2013). A case for child-centered play therapy with natural disaster and catastrophic event survivors. *International Journal of Play Therapy*, 22(4), 219–230.

Juhnke, G. A. (1995). Mental health counseling assessment: Broadening one's under-standing of the client and the clients presenting concerns. (Report EDO-CG-95-3). Greensboro, NC: ERIC Clearinghouse on Counseling and Student Services. Retrieved from: www.counseling.org/resources/library/eric%20digests/95-03.pdf.

Kaduson, H., Canglelosi, D. & Schaefer, C. (1997). *The playing cure: Individualized play therapy for specific childhood problems*. Northvale, NJ: Jason Aronson.

Kaimal, G., Ray, K. & Muniz, J. (2016). Reduction of cortisol levels and participants' responses following art making. *Art Therapy*, 33(2), 74–80.

Kaimal, G., Ayaz, H., Herres, J., Dieterich-Hartwell, R., Makwana, B., Kaiser, D. H. & Nasser, J. A. (2017). Functional near-infrared spectroscopy assessment of reward perception based on visual self-expression: Coloring, doodling, and free drawing. *The Arts in Psychotherapy*, 55, 85–92.

Kimport, E. R. & Robbins, S. (2012). Efficacy of creative clay work for reducing negative mood: A randomized controlled trial. *Art Therapy*, 29(2), 74–79.

King, P. K. (2017). *Tools for effective therapy with children and families: A solution-focused approach*. New York, NY: Routledge.

Klassen, T. P., Liang, Y., Tjosvold, L., Klassen, J. A. & Hartling, L. (2008). Music for pain and anxiety in children undergoing medical procedures: A systematic review of randomized controlled trials. *Ambulatory Pediatrics*, 8(2), 117–128.

Klein, M. (1932). *The psychoanalysis of children*. London: Hogarth Press.

Kottman, T. (1995). *Partners in play: An Adlerian approach to play therapy*. Alexandria, VA: American Counseling Association.

Kropf, A. (2009). The transforming power of art. *American Journal of Public Health*, 99(5), 778.

Krout, R. E. (2015). Music therapy for grief and loss. In B. L. Wheeler (Ed.), *Music therapy handbook*, pp. 401–411. New York, NY: Guilford Press.

Kruk, K. A., Aravich, P. F., Deaver, S. P. & deBeus, R. (2014). Comparison of brain activity during drawing and clay sculpting: A preliminary qEEG study. *Art Therapy*, 31(2), 52–60.

Landreth, G. (1978). Children communicate through play. *Texas Personnel and Guidance Association Journal*, 1, 41–42.

Landreth, G. L. (1991). *Play therapy: The art of the relationship*. Muncie, IN: Accelerated Development.

Landreth, G. L. (2002). *Play therapy: The art of the relationship* (2nd Ed.). New York, NY: Routledge.

Landreth, G., Bratton, S., Kellman, T. & Blackard, S. R. (2008). *Child parent relationship therapy*. New York, NY: Routledge.

Leggett, E. S. (2009). A creative application of solution-focused counseling: An integra-tion with children's literature and visual arts. *Journal of Creativity in Mental Health*, 4(2), 192–200.

Lowenfeld, M. (1935, 2008). *Play in childhood*. Portland, OR: Sussex Press.

Magee, W. (2011). Music therapy with children, adolescents, and adults with severe neurobehavioral disorders due to brain injury. *Music Therapy Perspectives*, 29(1), 5–13.

Malchiodi, C. A. (1998). *Understanding children's drawings*. New York, NY: Guilford.

Martin, R. & Spence, J. (1988). Photo therapy: New portraits for old, 1984 onwards. In J. Spence (Ed.), *Putting myself in the picture*, pp. 172–193. London: Camden Press.

Martinez, A. & Lasser, J. (2013). Thinking outside the box while playing the game: A creative school-based approach to working with children and adolescents. *Journal of Creativity in Mental Health*, 8(1), 81–91.

McFerran, K. S., Crooke, A. H. D. & Bolger, L. (2017). Promoting engagement in school through tailored music programs. *International Journal of Education and the Arts*, 18(3), 28.

McGrath, E. (2017). *The role of music and rhythm in the development, integration, and repair of self*. In E. Prendiville, & J. Howard (Eds), *Creative Psychotherapy*, pp. 83–100. New York, NY: Routledge.

Miller, M. F. (1962). Responses of psychiatric patients to their photographed images. *Diseases of the Nervous System*, 23, 296–298.

Mitchell, C. & Weber, S. (1998). Picture this! The class line-ups, vernacular portraits and lasting impressions of school. In J. Prosser (Ed.), *Image-based research: A sourcebook for qualitative researchers*, pp. 197–213. Bristol, PA: Falmer Press.

Ndoni, K. (2016). Recess rocks. *Scholastic Administrator*, 15(2), 12.

Newcomb, N. S. (1994). Music: A powerful resource for the elementary school counselor. *Elementary School Guidance & Counseling*, 29, 150–155.

Nims, D. R. (2007). Integrating play therapy into solution-focused brief therapy. *International Journal of Play Therapy*, 16(1), 54–68.

Oaklander, V. (1988). *Windows to our children*. Highland, NY: Center for Gestalt Development.

Oren, A. (2008). The use of board games in child psychotherapy. *Journal of Child Psychotherapy*, 34(3), 364–383.

Ray, D. C., Lee, K. R., Meany-Walen, K. K., Carlson, S. E., Carnes-Holt, K. L. & Ware, J. N. (2013). Use of toys in child-centered play therapy. *International Journal of Play Therapy*, 22(3), 43–57.

Rhea, D. (2014). Give students time to play. *Education Week*, 33(22), 21.

Sassen, G. (2012). Drums and poems: An intervention promoting empathic connection and literacy in children. *Journal of Creativity in Mental Health*, 7(7), 233–248.

Schaeffer, C. (Ed.) (1993). *The therapeutic powers of play*. Northvale, NJ: Jason Aronson.

Spire, R. H. (1973). Photographic self-image confrontation. *American Journal of Nursing*, 73, 1207–1210.

Standley, J. M. & Whipple, J. (2003). Music therapy in pediatric patients: A meta-analysis. In S. Robb (Ed.), *Music therapy in pediatric health-care: Research and evidence-based practice*, pp. 19–30. Silver Springs, MD: American Music Therapy Association.

Stone, J. (2016). Board games in play therapy. In K. J. O'Connor, C. E. Schaefer & L. D. Braverman (Eds), *Handbook of play therapy*, pp. 309–326. Hoboken, NJ: John Wiley & Sons.

Taylor, E. R. (2009). Sandtray and solution-focused therapy. *International Journal of Play Therapy*, 18(1), 56–68.

Taylor, E. R. (2015). Solution-focused sandtray for children. In H. G. Kaduson & C. E. Schaeffer (Eds), *Short-term play therapy for children* (3rd Ed.), pp. 150–174. New York, NY: Guilford Press.

Wadeson, H. (2000). *Art therapy practice*. Hoboken, NJ: John Wiley & Sons.

Webb, N. B. (1999). *Play therapy with children in crisis* (2nd Ed.). New York, NY: Guilford Press.

Webb, N. B. (2011). Play therapy for bereaved children: Adapting strategies to community, home, & school settings. *School Psychology International*, 32(2), 132–143.

Weiser, J. (1993). *PhotoTherapy techniques*. San Francisco, CA: Jossey-Bass.

White, M. & Epston, D. (1990). *Narrative means to therapeutic ends*. New York, NY: W. W. Norton.

Williams, B. (1987). Reaching adolescents through portraiture photography. *Child and Youth Quarterly, 16*(4), 241–248.

Winburn, A., King, A. & Burton, E. (2017). Me, my selfie, and I. *Mining Report, 12*(1), 6–9.

Wolf, R. I. (2014). The therapeutic uses of photography in play therapy. In E. J. Green & A. A. Drewes, *Integrating expressive arts and play therapy with children and adolescents*, pp. 181–203. Hoboken, NJ: John Wiley & Sons.

Ziller, R. C. (1990). *Photographing the self*. Newbury Park, CA: Sage Publications.

Ziller, R. C. & Rorer, B. A. (1985). Shyness-environment interaction: A view from the shy side through auto-photography. *Journal of Personality, 53*(4), 626–639.

CHAPTER 4

Client Considerations

Elizabeth R. Taylor

He was a large boy, seemed too big for an 11-year-old, but he had been referred for testing due to problems with reading and he was failing many of his other subjects. We went through the vocabulary section of the intelligence test, and he had some difficulty but not as much as I expected considering his poor grades. However, when I laid out the blocks for block design and gave him the instructions, in seconds he completed the puzzle, matching the design with the picture on the card. I gave him the next designs that progressively became more and more difficult. Each time he completed them quickly, taking his large hands and moving the blocks quickly into place. I was amazed! His problems in reading had certainly masked his strengths in problem-solving. I looked at him and smiled, and slowly this somber child smiled back, as we both realized his strength.

Children attending therapy often come with emotional, physical, and cognitive challenges, including learning disabilities, developmental delays, health challenges, and physical handicaps. These unique characteristics often cast a shadow over the individuals' many strengths and coping skills. Solution-focused therapy provides an approach where individuals can redefine themselves in terms of their strengths, resiliencies, and capacities to learn, cope, and thrive rather than in terms of their disabilities or handicaps.

The federal government, through the Individuals with Disabilities Act (2004), outlines 14 different disabilities that may affect youth's learning and academic opportunities: Autism, Deaf-Blindness, Deafness, Developmental Delay, Emotional Disturbance, Hearing Impairment, Intellectual Disability, Multiple Disabilities, Orthopedic Impairment, Other Health Impairments (includes Attention Deficit Disorder), Specific Learning Disability, Speech or Language Impairment, Traumatic Brain Injury, and Visual Impairment Including Blindness. In schools, children diagnosed with these disabilities qualify to receive special education services depending on the need and severity of the disability (sites.ed.gov/idea). Currently, 6.5 million youth qualify for services (sites.ed.gov/idea/about-idea), so therapists will likely treat a child with a disability and his or her family.

Although different disabilities manifest themselves in specific and unique ways in children and adolescents, they carry common socioemotional concerns that often include problems in making friends, bullying, low self-esteem, isolation and loneliness, physical and/or sexual abuse, and family dysfunction. For example, those with specific learning disabilities, the largest group of diagnosed disabilities, are more at risk than the normal population for social-emotional problems due to their inability to read social cues, to initiate interactions, or resolve conflicts with peers (Brinton, Fujiki, Spencer & Robinson, 1997; Brinton, Fujiki & McKee, 1998; Liiva & Cleave 2005; Stevens & Bliss, 1995; Timler, 2008). Those with Attention Deficit Disorder often have lower reading scores, more problems with social acceptance, and higher dropout rates (Rabiner, Godwin & Dodge, 2016).

Since disabilities are constructed and defined by the social norms of the society in which the person lives, not everyone agrees with the definitions of disabilities or their causes, and disabilities tend to vary by culture and social expectations. The perspective of western cultures tends to be based on a deficit model, the medical model of disability. "In this model, it is not the disability itself that defines the nature of the difficulty, but rather the way society describes and reacts to the issue" (Smith, 2007 in Carmichael, 2016, p. 401). In other words, society constructs the language that defines the disability. For example, we used to diagnose children with Asperger's, but we now use the term autism to cover a wide spectrum of specific behavioral characteristics. A second example is that of Attention Deficit Disorder, which tends to be diagnosed frequently in our society; however, this upsurge in those who carry the diagnosis occurs as society shifts from an agricultural to a more technological society, requiring longer days in school and dismissing recess as unimportant to learning. Therefore, it is important to consider a disability within the context of social expectations and focus on client strengths, particularly within the therapy context. The disability describes only one aspect of the individual's life in the face of society's expectations and should not define the person.

Olkin (2001) states that the main disability depends on who views it. Those looking from the outside view the disability as the impairment, but those with the disability view social factors as the main impairment. "Disability is a highly visible 'otherness.' It offers an identity of sorts, but also a kind of invisibility as a person" (Learmonth & Gibson, 2010 p. 60). Those with disabilities also have strengths that enable to them cope and thrive in the face of their challenges. The therapist working with clients who have disabilities needs to be aware, not only of handicapping conditions and their limitations, but of clients' unique learning strategies and strengths.

Use of SF Therapy with Youth with Disabilities

Solution-focused therapy offers many advantages for working with children who have been diagnosed with a disability. For example, SF therapy focuses on the perspective of the client rather than on what others think the client needs.

Solution-focused therapy's focus on strengths counters the negative focus that others often have on weaknesses and disabilities. Focusing on strengths increases the child's feelings of self-efficacy and hope in the face of personal challenges. A strengths focus also increases the child's attention to resources that may be employed to compensate for challenges. Two children with disabilities, after participating in a SF therapy group with other children who have learning disabilities, stated, "I got to talk to someone who didn't tell me what to do or just give me advice," and "I changed so much in one day that my friends noticed I was happier" (Thompson & Littrell, 1998).

Many of the techniques employed in SF therapy provide concrete and easily adaptable techniques that can be modified to meet the child's needs. For example, the use of externalizing the problem, often used in SF therapy, allows the client to see the disability outside of himself, making it more manageable. Solution-focused therapy uses scaling and relationship questions that provide concrete ways for clients to create goals and assess their progress. The therapist's frequent use of compliments with a focus on the client's role in creating success reinforces agency and calls attention to positive behaviors leading to change. In addition to focusing on strengths, the therapist works with the client to break the goal down into manageable tasks, so the client more likely experiences success. The SF therapist's collaborative approach with a focus on strengths increases the client's sense of control and agency, shrinking the problem to a manageable size, and redefining the client in terms of what he can do, not what he can't.

Before working with clients who have been diagnosed with a disability or major health problem, it is helpful to gain experience by volunteering in schools, hospitals, or agencies with children and adolescents with disabilities, health challenges, and physical limitations. Through such experiences, the therapist becomes more comfortable in the often hands-on needs that working with those who have disabilities often entails. The therapist also learns what parents and caregivers must manage each day and the emotional, physical, and social toll that it often takes on them and their families.

Those who work with clients with disabilities require an understanding not only of the disability but also of client and family resources, including:

- financial resources, such as Medicare or social security;
- medical resources, for example in rural communities, often require families to travel long distances to meet with specialists or to be fitted for medical equipment;
- extended family resources, including aunts and uncles, grandparents, and other extended family who can provide emotional support, address physical needs, help with travel, and give respite care;
- spiritual support in terms of connection to God or a transcendent power and a community of like-minded believers;
- friendships with those who accept the child's disability and provide emotional support but also recreational engagement.

Considerations for Working with Children or Adolescents with Disabilities

Therapist's Office

Before working with those who have disabilities or handicaps, the therapist ensures the office provides an accessible environment. Knowing client needs ahead of time provides the therapist with knowledge about how to accommodate the therapy space. The following provide considerations regarding how the space and furnishings might need adjustment:

- Doorways allow space for a wheelchair and have flat thresholds that do not impede walking or wheelchair mobility.
- Book and toy shelves are at eye-level.
- Shelves and fixtures (sandbox, doll house, etc.) are stabilized.
- The therapy room remains uncluttered, so that clients can easily find and access what is needed, and distraction is minimized. Those with visual impairments, physical disabilities, and attention challenges often function better when the space and materials are organized.
- Toys and materials remain in the same place each session.
- The therapy room's location provides a quiet environment, so clients are not disturbed or distracted.
- The client can see the therapist's face and gestures in case of a hearing impairment or communication disorders.
- The therapy room accommodates visual or technical devices that might be needed.

Physical Handicaps

To allow for those with specific physical handicaps, the therapist considers specific accommodations according clients' needs.

- Those who have fine motor concerns often require adjustments in what they use to write and color, preferring larger pencils and crayons. Other toys and art tools may also need to be adapted to address physical needs. For example, Carmichael (2016) suggests using foam rollers placed around paint brushes to make the brushes easier to hold or using bean bags as substitutes for balls to make them easier to handle and catch. "Generally, the less mature the physical development of the child, the larger the toys and other supplies need to be" (Carmichael, 2016, p. 409). Those who have difficulty with writing and drawing may work better with clay or printing with objects, such as a cork (Silver, 1989).
- For clients with low vision or blindness, the therapist uses materials with different textures, colors, sizes, shapes, and sounds. Good lighting and high contrast are particularly helpful to those with low vision. Sculpture

and working with clay provide art forms particularly appealing to those with visual impairments. For example, Georgia O'Keefe turned to sculpting in her later years as her sight began to fail.

- If the client has a hearing impairment, the therapist remains within range of the child's hearing. If the child has hearing devices, the therapist talks in a normal tone of voice unless the child does not seem to hear. Those with hearing loss do not always know what they are missing, so it is important to continually watch their responsiveness to questions and comments. For those who have no hearing and require sign language, the therapist visits with the client and parents about making a referral to a therapist who uses sign language or how to include a person to interpret using sign language in the therapy room for the therapist.
- Considerations for those with physical disabilities and challenges include: Making sure chairs fit the client appropriately, opening up space or finding a room that can accommodate a wheelchair, and providing soft cushions or pillows for those who cannot sit for long periods of time.

The Therapy Process

When working with those who have disabilities, the therapist takes into consideration how children work and learn. Many of the ideas presented below also apply to those who do not have a disability; however, these suggestions consider how children with disabilities function best. The therapist should remain flexible and consider each individual client's needs.

- Lay out the schedule in writing or pictures, so the client knows what to expect.
- Maintain eye contact (as appropriate).
- State questions and instructions clearly and concretely.
- Be sure that the client can be successful in completing tasks.
- Review past sessions to remind those with learning differences of what occurred previously.
- Repeat questions or comments in case the client has difficulty with processing information, hearing, communication, or attention.
- Anticipate issues with transition by providing a verbal or nonverbal signal within five minutes of transition or ending the session.
- Take breaks for those whose stamina is limited due to health impairments or physical disabilities, or who have attention problems.
- Make sessions shorter for those with issues of stamina or attention. However, for some clients, longer sessions work better, as it provides time to take short breaks, so the client does not get too tired. For those with attention problems, longer sessions provide an opportunity for clients to settle into the session.
- In order to better accommodate clients' special needs, therapy sessions may need to take place in the home, hospital, rehab centers, or other locations.

- Be prepared for cancellations or arriving late. Those clients who are medically fragile may experience health crises and concerns, and clients with physical disabilities or who must bring adaptive equipment may not always be able to arrive on time.

Working with Parents and Siblings

When working with children and adolescents who have disabilities, parents and siblings should be included as part of the therapy process. The client may wish to see the therapist alone, but family therapy should be considered. For example, researchers find filial play therapy to be effective with children diagnosed with different types of disabilities, including learning disabilities, cerebral palsy, and deaf and hard of hearing (Carmichael, 2016). Turns, Eddy, and Jordan (2016) find SF therapy effective when working with siblings of children with autism. Others (Lloyd & Dallos, 2008) find SF therapy helpful for families who have a child with severe intellectual disabilities.

The therapist working with those who have disabilities may want to investigate special education services in the school and community. Sometimes, parents do not know about services or do not know how to advocate for their child. The therapist may be an integral part of the special education team thus giving the therapist a better understanding of the client's challenges and techniques that may be helpful.

Parents may call upon the therapist to interpret psychological reports and explain assessment scores. A general knowledge of assessment information and how children qualify for special education services can be helpful when addressing whether or not specific services can be provided. Similarly, by building collaborative relationships with the school psychologist and diagnostician, the therapist has better access to information about what specific services are being provided and by whom, as well as providing resources when the therapist has questions.

Many children with disabilities do not receive counseling services and need advocates to request therapy when their needs impede their ability to fully embrace opportunities and learn effectively. SF therapy services offer an amazing opportunity for the mental health professional to empower those who struggle with cognitive, physical, emotional, and interpersonal limitations. A SF therapist who focuses on clients' internal and external resources fills a void in empowering youth with challenges.

References

Brinton, B., Fujiki, M. & McKee, L. (1998). Negotiation skills of children with specific language impairment. *Journal of Speech, Language, and Hearing Research, 41*(4), 927–940.

Brinton, B., Fujiki, M., Spencer, J. C. & Robinson, L. A. (1997). The ability of children with specific language impairment to access and participate in an ongoing interaction. *Journal of Speech, Language, & Hearing Research, 40*(5), 1011–1025.

Carmichael, K. D. (2016). Play therapy with children with disabilities. In K. J. O'Connor, C. E. Schaeffer & L. D. Braverman (Eds), *Handbook of play therapy*, pp. 397–415. Hoboken, NJ: John Wiley & Sons.

Learmonth, M. & Gibson, K. (2010). Art psychotherapy, disability issues, mental health, trauma, and resilience: 'Things and people.' *International Journal of Art Therapy*, 15(2), 53–64.

Liiva, C.A. & Cleave, P. L. (2005). Roles of initiation and responsiveness in access and participation for children with specific language impairment. *Journal of Speech, Language, & Hearing Research*, 48(4), 868–883.

Lloyd, H. & Dallos, R. (2008). First session solution-focused brief therapy with families who have a child with severe intellectual disabilities: Mothers' experiences and views. *Journal of Family Therapy*, 30(1), 5–28.

Olkin, M. (2001). *What psychotherapists should know about disability*. New York, NY: Guilford.

Rabiner, D. L., Godwin, J. & Dodge, K. A. (2016). Predicting academic achievement and attainment: The contribution of early academic skills, attention difficulties, and social competence. *School Psychology Review*, 45(2), 250–267.

Roeden, J. M., Maaskant, M. A., Bannink, F. P. & Curfs, L. M. G. (2011). Solution-focused brief therapy with people with mild intellectual disabilities: A case series. *Journal of Policy and Practice in Intellectual Disabilities*, 8(4), 247–255.

Shaw, A. (2017). 7 things every child with dyslexia wishes you knew. *Exceptional Parent Magazine*, March.

Silver, R. A. (1989). *Developing cognitive and creative skills through art: Programs for children with communication disorders or learning disabilities* (3rd Ed.). New York, NY: Ablin Press.

Smith, D. (2007). *Introduction to special education: Making a difference*. Columbus, OH: Allyn & Bacon.

Stevens, L.J. & Bliss, L.S. (1995). Conflict resolution abilities of children with specific language impairment and children with normal language. *Journal of Speech & Hearing Research*, 38, 599–611.

Thompson, R. & Littrell, J. (1998). Brief counseling for students with learning disabilities. *Professional School Counseling*, 2(1), 60–67.

Timler, G. R. (2008). Social knowledge in children with language impairments: Examination of strategies, predicted consequences, and goals in peer conflict situations. *Clinical Linguistics & Phonetics*, 22, 741–763.

Turns, B., Eddy, B. P. & Jordan, S. S. (2016). Working with siblings of children with autism: A solution-focused approach. *Australian and New Zealand Journal of Family Therapy*, 37(4), 558–571.

CHAPTER 5

Solution-Focused Therapy and Integration with Creative and Tangible Approaches

Elizabeth R. Taylor

I went to visit a young student who was working on her first practicum in an elementary school. She was counseling a 4th grade boy in a low-income elementary school. The boy was somewhat large for his age but very soft-spoken. She began by asking him "What's better?" Silence. He didn't move. I was sitting across the room and trying not to look up so as not to disrupt the session. She asked "What did you do this weekend?" She was still trying to be upbeat and encouraging. More silence. I felt terrible for her. Here I was trying to observe her counseling skills and her client does not utter a word. He just looked at her then looked away, played with the hair on his arm, then untied and tied his shoes.

Everything was quiet for several minutes, and then she continued to try to ask him questions. After a few more questions, another long silence ensued. I looked up and saw them sitting almost knee to knee, and she was writing down questions on a notepad on her lap. She turned it to him, and he wrote back to her. They continued this for quite a while until, eventually, he became comfortable enough to speak, very quietly, but speak nonetheless. How wonderful that my student was clever and flexible enough to allow him an alternative to verbal communication.

Introduction

Solution-focused therapy offers a unique approach for working with children and adolescents, and, since clients are considered the experts on their own lives, SF therapy gives them control. Not surprisingly, the reasons for clients' referral to therapy often involves their need for control in an often painful, uncertain, and uncontrollable world. Their behaviors—not talking or telling lies, sitting quietly and not participating or constantly being out of their seat and running around the room, meekly allowing others to bully and harass them or acting as the aggressor against peers and adults, being a loner and acting in socially inappropriate ways—often the result of difficult circumstances, overwhelm their abilities to cope in healthy ways. However, in SF therapy, the therapist recognizes clients' strengths and gives clients credit for knowing what they need, listening intently to their perspectives about what might be helpful.

Solution-focused therapy's effectiveness, based on the assumptions of the therapist about the client and the therapy process, uses unique questions and interventions to help the client uncover personal strengths, resources, and solutions to problems and challenges. The SF therapist considers the following to be true of the client and the therapy process:

- the client possesses the resources necessary to solve his or her problem (De Jong & Berg, 2013);
- the therapist and client work as collaborators, with the client being the expert on his or her problem (Bliss & Bray, 2009; De Jong & Berg, 2013);
- therapy is goal-directed (de Shazer & Dolan, 2007);
- spending time talking about the problem does not lead to solutions; spending time talking about solutions leads to solutions (Berg & de Shazer, 1993);
- problems and their solutions are interactional and contextual (Lethem, 2002; Ray & Brasher, 2010).
- the therapist acts as a catalyst in creating a relationship and context in which clients come to know their strengths and resources (Thomas & Nelson, 2007).

Throughout the therapy process, the therapist highlights client strengths and resiliencies through intense interest, expressions of amazement, and compliments. Continuing with a focus on solutions, the therapist questions how the client may have coped or solved the problem in the past, and asks about exceptions to the problem and the details of how exceptions to the problem are different, including how the exceptions to the problem affect the client and important others. The therapist listens for what works from the client's perspective, not a preconceived philosophy (Bliss & Bray, 2009).

In SF therapy, all conversation between client and therapist involves intervention. The questions a therapist asks, how the therapist responds, and even the therapist's body language tilt therapy in one direction or another. Like the trails on a mountainside, the therapist determines which path to take by shifting the conversation one way or another through focused attention, body language, and carefully crafted questions. The therapist, in many therapeutic traditions, may choose to ask questions about a problem, so that the conversation moves down a trail that discusses the problem. On the other hand, the SF therapist may tune in and intently listen to information about the client's strengths and abilities to handle the problem, resulting in a shift in the conversation down a trail of possibilities. The therapist asks questions that differentiate the paths the conversation takes, for example if the therapist asks "why" questions, the path may become rocky and challenging due to the client's inability or reluctance to explain her motives. On the other hand, if the therapist chooses "how" questions, the client tends to feel empowered and takes credit for personal successes. The therapist's questions "generate entirely different responses that the counselor can pursue" (Berg & Dolan, 2001, p. 80). For this reason, the therapist must remain sensitive to the client's ability and preferences in communication, giving opportunities to use multiple modalities whether through verbal exchanges, playful activities, art, music, or other forms of communication.

In the constructivist model, the interaction and communication between therapist and client build on one another as solutions are co-constructed through ongoing interaction. The outline that follows provides a general overview of the process of SF therapy; however, how therapy proceeds depends on different characteristics of the client and therapist, their relationship, reciprocal communication responses, the overall process of therapy, as well as events that occur outside the session that cannot be controlled or predicted.

Beginnings

The first stage begins with meeting the client, building a relationship, and learning about who and what are important to the client. Regardless of what theory the therapist chooses to use or what technique the therapist employs, the relationship provides the impetus for change, and, except under the most unusual circumstances, positive change cannot occur without a positive relationship. Building the relationship involves learning about the client, the client's family and friends, and significant others. The therapist asks questions and uses creative approaches to find out what the client enjoys doing, where he likes to go, what music is appealing, places where he feels safe, and other information that may prove helpful in building the relationship and understanding client resources and challenges. The therapist explores this information out of a genuine interest in the client and client responses. Listening entails more than focusing on client words; it includes a focused interest in the client's preferred mode of communication, whether through words or concrete and creative modalities, such as sandtray, drawing, writing, photography, or other modes of expression.

Digging for Treasure

As the therapist gains an understanding of the client, the SF therapist focuses on digging for treasure, uncovering strengths, resiliencies, positive personality traits, and talents. Unlike therapies that focus on and assess the client for problems and problematic interactions, the SF therapist listens for strengths the client employs to solve problems, how the client finds solutions, and what is different when problems do not occur. The therapist, a vigilant treasure seeker, focuses on strengths the client exhibits in the face of difficulties, how the client meets challenges successfully, and what resiliencies and resources he employs to cope and overcome problems.

Digging for treasure also involves finding exceptions, those times when the problem might have occurred but didn't. The therapist asks questions such as

"What is different when your teacher isn't on your back?" or "What are you doing differently when the problem is not so bad?" Asking about exceptions shifts the problem-focused conversation to a focus on strengths, providing hope that change can occur and solutions exist to help the client overcome or, at least, cope with the problem.

Relationship Questions

As therapists notice client strengths, they also notice the interpersonal resources the client possesses that can be helpful in finding solutions. By asking relationship questions—questions that vicariously include attitudes, behaviors, and dispositions of important others in the client's personal circle of family and friends—the client and therapist uncover personal resources and reciprocal influences that affect client goals. Asking relationship questions includes asking how others see the client's behaviors and the reciprocal influences the client has on others. Through relationship questions, the therapist assists the client in a way that does not imply blame in order to look at how possible solutions may be effective or ineffective and how others might view such solutions. Relationship questions might also be asked when setting goals, so that the client notices that he or she has a reciprocal effect on others, providing a voice for those who may not be in the room but play important roles in providing support for the client (De Jong & Berg, 2013). For example, the therapist might ask the client "What would your mother notice you doing differently when you reach your goals?" or "What would your mother say when you reach your goal?"

Compliments

The therapist employs different types of compliments throughout SF therapy. Direct compliments involve commenting on strengths and resiliencies the client indicates throughout the conversation, such as "I am impressed that you got your homework done." Indirect compliments involve asking clients details about how they cope with a problem or how they find solutions, for example, the client states that she avoided getting into trouble on the playground. The therapist provides an indirect compliment, "Wow! How did you do that?" and then asks for details about how the client played without getting into trouble. Gathering these details through indirect compliments increases the client's sense of control and self-efficacy, empowering the client.

The flow of the interview is important. Being 'solution-forced' (Nylund & Corsiglia, 1994, p. 5), that is, jumping in with compliments prematurely or demanding answers to SF questions, can undermine the therapy process and is often the result of the therapist not listening intently to the client's words and perspective. Nylund and Corsiglia (1994) see these mistakes as a novice error, often linked to excessive enthusiasm and heavy caseloads. They emphasize the importance of pace and timing in solution-focused interviews.

The Miracle Question and Other Future-Focused Questions

The therapist works with the client to set goals based on what the client wants to be different, and together client and therapist co-construct solutions. For example, a common first goal question entails asking the client, "What are your best hopes for our meeting today?" Another possible question, the presupposition question, asks the client about what positive changes the client noticed since deciding to come in or making the appointment for therapy, allowing the client to consider changes that are already occurring.

The SF therapist works in collaboration with the client to set goals and examine and amplify successes. One key question employed by SF therapists is that of the "miracle question." When asking the miracle question (MQ), the therapist prepares the client for a shift in conversation by stating something like, "Now, I want to ask you a strange question" (De Jong & Berg, 2013, p. 91). Then, with expression, the therapist asks,

> Suppose that while you are sleeping tonight a miracle happens. The miracle is that the problem that brought you here today is solved. But because you are asleep, you don't know that the miracle has happened. When you wake up, what would be the first sign to you that things are different, that a miracle has happened?
>
> (De Jong & Berg, 2013, p. 93)

Once clients describe the miracle, the therapist asks questions to break the goal down into smaller steps. For example, the therapist asks about times when even a little bit of the miracle occurred and gathers details about these successes, what happened, how others were affected, and the specifics of what the client did that caused this success to occur. In this way, the client uncovers what is already working or might work, so that he or she can do more of it (De Jong & Berg, 2013).

Sometimes, the therapist asks other future-focused questions instead of the MQ to help clients develop their goals. For example, the therapist might ask, "Suppose next week, your mom notices that things are better, and the problem isn't bothering you, what will you say is different?" or "Imagine that it is five years in the future, and you have overcome this problem. What would you be doing?" Therapists use many different approaches and questions to set goals. They also may reword questions or use tangible and concrete language and materials to make them developmentally appropriate, such as a magic wand, drawing, a wishing well, a letter from the future self to the current self, and others that will be presented later in this text.

Scaling Questions

To help clients break down the MQ into smaller goals, the therapist often follows up the MQ with a scaling question (SQ). The therapist asks the client to assess where the client thinks she is in terms of the miracle she described.

For example, the therapist might ask the client, "On a scale of 1 to 10, where do you think you are in terms of [miracle description], with 0 being that none of this miracle is happening and 10 being that the miracle is happening all the time?" If the client answers that he or she is a 4, then the therapist might ask a small goal question such as "Suppose you were a 5, what would you be doing differently?"

Generally, the therapist asks SQs each session to better understand progress, how the client maintains this status (if the number on the scale is the same), or how the client is coping (if the number on the scale goes down) (de Shazer & Dolan, 2007). Scaling questions provide the therapist with tools to not only help break the miracle down into smaller steps but also to assess progress, possibilities of reaching goals, motivation, and other dispositions.

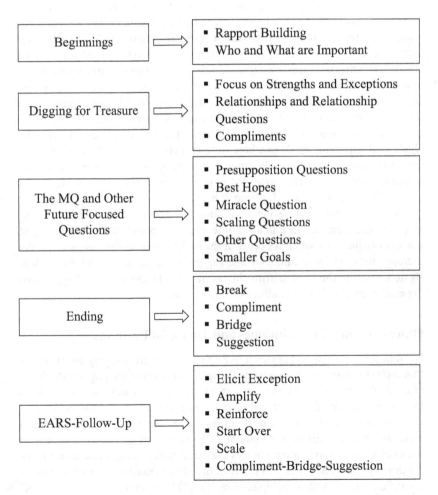

Figure 5.1 Process of Solution-Focused Therapy.

Ending the Session

The process of ending the session begins with the therapist taking a break to consider a message to give to the client. The therapist may take a few minutes in session or step out of the session to consider the challenges the client discusses, compliments to give the client that recognize the solutions and strengths the client brings to therapy, and to suggest one or two possible actions to do before the next meeting. The therapist then delivers the message to the client for consideration. This ending process—compliment-bridge-suggestion—recognizes the client's strengths and challenges and provides suggestions based on what the client discussed (De Jong & Berg, 2013).

EARS-Follow-Up Sessions

Solution-focused therapy is generally short-term, rarely more than eight sessions, and sometimes only one session is needed (Iveson, 2002). Follow-up sessions continue through a process using the acronym EARS. The first step involves eliciting (E) the exceptions, beginning with the first question "What's better?" The therapist then amplifies (A) these exceptions by paying attention to any hints of success or differences from the problem that may be occurring and asking detailed questions about how this occurred, who was present, and the client's role. Direct and indirect compliments to reinforce (R) the client continue throughout the session. For example, the therapist might also ask the client, with amazement, "Wow, how were you able to do that?" Sessions continue to follow the process of eliciting exceptions, amplifying them, reinforcing solutions, and then starting over (S) with the same process beginning again with, "What else is better?" (De Jong & Berg, 2013).

The therapist asks scaling questions during each of the follow-up sessions to assess progress and set new goals. Sometimes this occurs at the beginning of the session, but most often it occurs at the end. Similar to the first session, the therapist uses the compliment-bridge-suggestion sequence to end the session. By doing so, the therapist affirms the client's efforts and provides suggestions depending on the client's readiness to hear them.

Other Common SF Techniques and Therapist Positions

Normalizing, a common approach in SF therapy, involves letting clients know that their concerns *do not* lie outside the sphere of most of the population. Most often used in the beginning of the session, the therapist normalizes problems that seem to isolate the client and refrains from labeling. For example, when a therapist works with parents, normalizing issues regarding 12 year olds who argue as a normal part of development relieves parents. Teens struggling with issues of intimacy and career choices may find normalizing these issues to be comforting. Insoo Kim Berg, in many of her videos, normalizes with the statement, "Of course." Other therapists may state "That's not unusual for this age," or "I know some others struggling with similar issues."

Reframing, another common technique in SF therapy, helps clients view problems from new, positive, and creative perspectives. For example, normalizing also involves reframing wherein the therapist assists the client in viewing the problem as normal rather than as pathology, thus reducing "shame, isolation, desperation, and support a sense that the [client's] couple's issues/problems/concerns are manageable" (Ziegler & Hiller, 2007, p. 93). Berg and Steiner (2003) discuss reframing as offering different, also credible, ways to view a problem. For example, a mother's constant nagging may be reframed as "caring." The therapist working with a student who seems to be annoyed by another student's constant talking may state, "She really likes talking to you." Reframing puts a positive spin on difficult circumstances.

An important technique in SF therapy involves using language that assumes positive changes will or have taken place. For example, the therapist asks the client "How are things better?" rather than asking "Are things better?" Rather than asking the client "If you make these changes, what will be different?" the therapist asks "When you make these changes, what will be different?" The type of language presumes positive changes will occur, shifting client doubts to more hopeful and future thinking.

The SF therapist asks many "what else" questions instead of assuming the first answer entails the entire client response. For example, after the therapist asks the miracle question regarding what will be different when the problem no longer occurs, the client often responds with one or two items, but the therapist continues to wait and pursue what else is different, by asking, "What else?" Another example is when the client answers the scaling question regarding what will be different when she is a number higher, and the therapist continues to garner details by asking "What else will be different?" In follow-up sessions when the client answers the question "What's better?", the therapist gathers details about what is better, but then continues with, "What else is better?"

Expressive and Creative Approaches Using SF Therapy

Recognizing the need to address different populations of children and adolescents in ways that do not rely on verbal communication, clinicians and researchers continue to employ more expressive and playful approaches in the use of SF therapy. Berg and Steiner (2003) lay out developmental considerations and applications of SF therapy when working with children and adolescents. Selekman (2010) also describes collaborative work using SF therapy with children, parents, and other professionals and the need to be "therapeutically flexible" (Selekman, 2010, p. 16) by incorporating other therapeutic approaches as needed. Selekman's work with difficult adolescents illustrates his ability to use SF therapy creatively and flexibly (Selekman, 1993).

Play

Although Nims (2007) and Leggett (2009, 2017) propose SF play therapy (SFPT), King (2017) provides an in-depth look at SFPT as a direct (versus nondirect) therapeutic approach with young children, incorporating parents and families. Paying attention to developmental concerns and using principles common to other play therapy methods, King focuses her attention on children's strengths using playful language and materials. She states,

> In my twenty-plus years of therapy with children and families, I have found combining playful activity and talking about strengths and abilities sets a powerful expectation that therapy is a place that is helpful and fun (even when it is hard).

(p. 21)

She creatively employs simple materials, such as an abacus, a copy machine, a ruler, and paper and pencil to address children's concerns and find solutions, often externalizing and using metaphors children understand (King, 2017).

Drawing

Leggett and Ybañez (2011) suggest asking the client to draw the problem followed by drawing the miracle. The therapist then asks the client to describe the miracle in detail, asking about exceptions, scaling questions, and relationship questions. Hudak (2003) also discusses the use of drawing as a way to bridge narrative and SF techniques. Cook (2011) suggests creating a book and stitching pages together in which the client writes or collages images representing the answer to the miracle question, giving the book a title, and discussing how the book ends.

Sandtray

Sweeney (2003) proposes the use of three sandtrays in working with children dealing with trauma—one depicting the client's problem, the second depicting life without the trauma, and the third showing how to get from tray one to tray two. Through this process, clients create a new future and the means to achieve it. Taylor (2009, 2015) describes the use of SF sandtray to describe the problem and answer the miracle question, find strengths and solutions, and use relationship and scaling questions through miniatures. She suggests the use of specific miniatures tailored to provide different metaphors for possible strengths and miracles, such as jewels, a wishing well, wizards, a fairy godmother, a treasure chest, and other miniatures that might lead to creating goals and possibilities. King (2013) and Dell (2017) also explore the use of miniatures and other objects as tools to use when scaling in order to enrich descriptions in assessing and setting future goals.

Principles for Combining SF Therapy with Creative and Playful Approaches

By pulling together many of the ideas and techniques researchers and clinicians utilize when incorporating creative and playful approaches into SF therapy, the following principles emerge:

Table 5.1 Solution-focused Sandtray Suggestions

Solution-Focused Questions		Solution-Focused Sandtray Suggestions
Future-focused questions	From the present to the future	• Make a sandtray that shows how things will be better when this problem is solved. • Show me one thing that will be better when you no longer have to come to see me. • If using two sandtrays, clients can make a sandtray of what it looks like right now with the problem and then a second of what it will look like when the problem is solved, and then compare them.
	From the future to the present	• I want you to make a sandtray of what it might look like if next week I came into your classroom and the problem was solved. • Pretend I see you in line at the movies and you are no longer having this problem. Make a sandtray to show me what would be different.
Miracle question		Suppose that today you go home [pause], do what you normally do when you get home [pause], perhaps have something to eat, do some homework, go out and play [pause]. Then, you go to bed. While you are asleep a miracle happens [pause], only you don't know this miracle has happened [pause]. The miracle is that the problem that brought you here is solved [pause]. When you wake up in the morning, what will be the first thing that you will notice that lets you know the problem is solved? The client can then construct the sandtray illustrating the miracle. The miracle can be modified to make it easier to understand, for example, "the wizard raises his magic wand and the problem is gone" or "the fairy sprinkles magic dust over you while you are sleeping and when you wake up the problem is gone."
	Exception questions	• Make a sandtray of what it would look like if you didn't have this problem right now. • Make a sandtray of your day when you don't have this problem.
	Relationship questions	Make a sandtray of . . . • What your [important other] will notice when you are no longer having this problem. • What you will have to do to convince [important other] that you no longer have this problem. • Show me who would notice if things were better. Is there someone missing who might also notice? Find a miniature to represent that person and place him/her in the tray. • Who could you go to for help if you needed it? Who is someone you feel safe with? Who do you like to play with?

(continued)

Table 5.1 (continued)

Solution-Focused Questions	Solution-Focused Sandtray Suggestions

Scaling questions	• Use a sports goal, e.g., goal post, basketball goal, soccer goal, on one end of the sandtray. Ask client:
	
	  ○ This is the ___field, put the miniature that represents you in the sandtray that shows how close you are to getting to your goal, followed by . . .
	  ○ What could you do next to move closer to your goal?
	
	• Ask the scaling question, "On a scale of 1 to 10, where are you right now, with 1 being you have not reached your goal and 10 being you have reached your goal? Create a sandtray that shows what that looks like."
	
	• On one end of the sandtray, make a scene showing where you are right now. On the other end of the sandtray, make a scene that shows where you want to be when you are grown up or no longer in school. Choose some miniatures that represent what you will be doing between now and in the future to get to your goal and place them in the middle.
	
	• Use different miniatures to represent the scaling question. Ask the client, "Choose which miniature represents where you are right now."
	
	• "We are going to make a scale from 1 to 5 with 1 being the worst and 5 being the best. I want you to choose a miniature that would represent each of the numbers on the scale from 1 to 5 and place them in the tray." The client can then use these to answer scaling questions about goals, motivation, confidence, or other notions of current status.

Note: From Taylor, E. R. (2015). Solution-focused sandtray. In H. G. Kaduson & C. E. Schaefer (Eds), *Short-term play therapy for children*, p. 165. New York, NY: Guilford. Copyright 2015 by The Guilford Press.

1   The therapist uses many of the same techniques as other play therapy approaches, that is, tracking, restating content, reflecting feelings, and returning responsibility to the child (see Kottman, 2001).

2   Children communicate through toys, puppets, miniatures, and expressive arts materials that are carefully selected according to personal strengths and abilities, interests, and developmental levels with consideration for and inclusion of different learning differences, cultures, and socioeconomic strata.

3   The therapist realizes children and adolescents live within systems, and systems, as often as possible, should be included. Therefore, whenever

possible, the therapist includes parents or guardians, siblings, and friends in the process.

4 Children possess strengths and resources necessary to solve their problems, resources that may be encouraged and strengthened through developmentally appropriate methods and expressive materials, including, but not limited to, specifically selected toys, sandtray, puppets, games, music, clay, collage, writing, and other creative modalities.

5 Affirming the clients' struggles but also highlighting their strengths provides feedback to children and adolescents regarding their personal strengths and interpersonal resources that may be useful in coping and finding solutions.

Clinicians and researchers continue to research and write about effective ways to modify SF therapy to help children and adolescents maximize their strengths in the face of challenges. They emphasize the need for flexibility and modifications that appeal to and increase engagement of youth in the therapeutic process, expanding the range of possible clients and problems that can be effectively addressed by SF therapy (Franklin, Streeter, Webb & Guz, 2018; King, 2017; Dolan, 2000; Metcalf, 2008; Ratner & Yusuf, 2015; Sklare, 2014). This text builds on the emerging practice of combining concrete and expressive materials in the practice of SF therapy with children and adolescents.

References

Berg, I. K. & de Shazer, S. (1993). Making numbers talk: Language in therapy. In S. Friedman (Ed.), *The new constructive collaboration language in psychotherapy of change*, pp. 5–24. New York, NY: Guilford.

Berg, I. K. & Dolan, Y (2001). *Tales of solutions*. New York, NY: W. W. Norton.

Berg, I. K. & Steiner, T. (2003). *Children's solution work*. New York, NY: W. W. Norton.

Bliss, E. V. & Bray, D. (2009). The smallest solution focused particles: Towards a minimalist definition of when therapy is solution focused. *Journal of Systemic Therapies*, 28(2), 62–74.

Cook, K. (2011). New chapter pamphlet stitch book. In S. Degges-White & N. L. Davis (Eds), *Integrating the expressive arts into counseling practice*, pp. 37–38. New York, NY: Springer.

De Jong, P. & Berg, I. K. (2013). *Interviewing for solutions* (4th Ed.). Belmont, CA: Brooks/Cole.

Dell, K. (2017). Less talk, more action: The integration of small figures in a solution-focused counselling practice with children (unpublished master's thesis). University of Canterbury, Christchurch, NZ.

de Shazer, S. & Dolan, Y. (2007). *More than miracles*. Binghamton, NY: Haworth Press.

Dolan, Y. M. (2000). *One small step: Moving beyond trauma and therapy to a life of joy*. San Jose, CA: Authors Choice Press.

Franklin, C., Streeter, C. L., Webb, L. & Guz, S. (2018). *Solution-focused brief therapy in alternative schools*. New York, NY: Routledge.

Hudak, S. (2003). The solution drawing. In H. G. Kaduson & C. E. Schaefer (Eds), *101 favorite play therapy techniques* (Vol. III), pp. 72–76. New York, NY: Rowan & Littlefield.

Iveson, C. (2002). Solution-focused brief therapy. *Advances in Psychiatric Treatment,* *8*(2), 149–156.

King, P. K. (2013). Solution-focused brief therapy and play scaling. *Journal of Family Psychotherapy, 24,* 312–316.

King, P. K. (2017). *Tools for effective therapy with children and families: A solution-focused approach.* New York, NY: Routledge.

Kottman, T. (2001). *Play therapy: Basics and beyond.* Alexandria, VA: American Counseling Association.

Leggett, E. S. (2009). A creative application of solution-focused counseling: An integration of children's literature and visual arts. *Journal of Creativity in Mental Health,* *4*(2), 191–200.

Leggett, E. S. (2017). Solution-focused play therapy. In E. S. Leggett & J. N. Boswell (Eds), *Directive play therapy approaches,* pp. 59–79. New York, NY: Springer.

Leggett, E. S. & Ybañez, K. (2011). Drawing a solution. In S. Degges-White & N. L. Davis (Eds), *Integrating the expressive arts into counseling practice,* pp. 34–36. New York, NY: Springer.

Lethem, J. (2002). Brief solution focused therapy. *Child and Adolescent Mental Health,* *7*(4), 189–192.

Metcalf, L. (2008). *Counseling toward solutions: A practical solution-focused program for working with students, teachers, and parents.* San Francisco, CA: Jossey-Bass.

Nims, D. R. (2007). Integrating play therapy into solution-focused brief therapy. *International Journal of Play Therapy, 16*(1), 54–68.

Nylund, D. & Corsiglia, V. (1994). Becoming solution-focused forced in brief therapy: Remembering something important we already knew. *Journal of Systemic Therapies,* *13*(1), 5–12.

Ratner, H. & Yusuf, D. (2015). *Brief coaching with children and young people.* New York, NY: Routledge.

Ray, W. A. & Brasher, C. (2010). Brief systemic therapy: Creating our future while embracing our past. *Journal of Systemic Therapies, 29*(4), 17–28.

Selekman, M. D. (1993). *Pathways to change.* New York, NY: Guilford Press.

Selekman, M. D. (2010). *Collaborative brief therapy with children.* New York, NY: Guilford Press.

Sklare, G. (2014). *Brief counseling that works: A solution-focused therapy approach for school counselors and other mental health professionals* (3rd Ed.). Thousand Oaks, CA: Corwin.

Sweeney, D. (2003). Creating a new story with sandtray. In H. G. Kaduson & C. E. Schaefer (Eds), *1001 favorite play therapy techniques* (Vol. III), pp. 298–302. New York, NY: Rowman and Littlefield.

Taylor, E. R. (2009). Sandtray and solution-focused therapy. *International Journal of Play Therapy, 18,* 56–68.

Taylor, E. R. (2015). Solution-focused sandtray for children. In H. G. Kaduson & C. E. Schaeffer (Eds), *Short-term play therapy for children* (3rd Ed.), pp. 150–174. New York, NY: Guilford Press.

Thomas, F. N. & Nelson, T. S. (2007). Assumptions and practices within the solution-focused brief therapy tradition. In T. S. Nelson & F. N. Thomas (Eds), *Handbook of solution-focused therapy: Clinical applications,* pp. 3–24. New York, NY: Haworth Press.

Ziegler, P. & Hiller, T. (2007). Solution-focused therapy with couples. In T. S. Nelson & F. N. Thomas (Eds), *Handbook of solution-focused brief therapy,* pp. 91–115. New York, NY: Haworth Press.

CHAPTER 6

Motivating the Client

Elizabeth R. Taylor

Melanie's mother peeked her head in my room to let me know they had arrived. Melanie, once again, refused to get out of the car. She clung to the door handle, and I crawled in through the other side and sat by her as we talked about the upcoming events of the day, trying to entice her to come in to my class of "emotionally disturbed" children who were waiting as patiently as they could with my assistant. Mom, getting impatient with Melanie, started yelling that she had to get out one way or another because she had to get to work. Her mom peeled Melanie's fingers from the door handle and brought her into the room, kicking and screaming. I closed the outer door to my classroom, and wrapped my arms around Melanie, and her mother left. In her panic, she looked at me with her big watery brown eyes and said, "I'm going to slit your throat."

Gradually she calmed as I hummed whatever music I could think of in the moment, rocked her slowly, and spoke to her softly letting her know I was there for her. As she began to self-regulate, we walked into the other room where the other ten students worked on art projects. She said nothing about what had occurred and didn't have any more problems the rest of the day. The person she was that morning seemed to disappear.

Melanie lived in a trailer with her mother and mother's abusive boyfriend. The separation anxiety that Melanie felt was panic that something might happen to her mother, so when Melanie separated from her mother at school, she went into a full-blown panic attack. After several weeks of working with Melanie and her mother, Melanie gradually let out the secret about the abuse of her mother at home. When the boyfriend was arrested and finally left, Melanie mainstreamed slowly into her regular classroom.

De Jong and Berg (2013) provide three reasons clients might have for attending therapy, closely aligning with Prochaska and DiClemente's (1983) stages of change. They may come because they a) want to be there and believe they have a part in the change process, b) know there is a problem, but it is someone else's fault and they don't feel any need to change themselves, or c) are mandated to come and may not feel there is a problem or feel any need for change. The therapist's goal focuses on finding unique ways to cooperate with clients, see their perspectives, and join them where they are rather than where we think they should be, avoiding getting into a tug of war to "make" them change. Within the first session, the therapist asks questions that give clients control and honors their perspectives of the problem, solutions, and goals. Not surprisingly, within the first session, clients often switch from not wanting to come to therapy to finding the therapy process helpful or at least pleasant.

Regardless of the client's motives for attending therapy, the therapist begins with building the relationship, the most important aspect of engaging clients. Just as Rogers' conditions for therapeutic change state that the client perceives the therapist's unconditional positive regard and empathic understanding (Rogers, 1957), the client-therapist relationship provides the basis for building strengths and solutions and reaching goals (De Jong & Berg, 2013).

I don't know why I am here. I don't have a problem

Often, young clients deny knowing the purpose of their visit or why they were sent. Perhaps they do not trust the therapist or don't want to share their problems, or maybe what appears to be problematic to the person who refers the client is not problematic to client, or maybe the client just doesn't want to come to the therapist's office. Much like the precontemplation stage of change, clients who do not want to come to therapy and feel no value in change often terminate therapy prematurely, find excuses not to attend, or never fully engage in the process (Swift & Greenberg, 2015). They visit the therapist only because someone told them they had to do so or because of the negative consequences that might ensue if they don't attend. In other words, the client is mandated to attend therapy. However, just because clients do not want to come to therapy does not mean the therapist gives up or tries to make them do something they do not want to do. Instead, the therapist takes their side and asks, "What do you need to do so you don't have to come anymore?"

When a child or adolescent attends therapy, he often attends because someone told him that there was a problem. Rather than beginning by focusing on the problem, the therapist focuses on what the client thinks needs to happen so he does not need to come anymore. One way to do this is through relationship questions. For example, the therapist may ask, "What does your mother hope you will do differently after we meet today?" or "What does your teacher say needs to happen so you do not need to come anymore?" The SF therapist accepts the client's perspective and frame of reference by listening carefully and paraphrasing the client's comments, conveying to the client that the therapist is listening.

Another approach to encourage the client who does not want to come to therapy involves using presupposition language. For example, Marco, a junior in high school, does not believe he has a problem with friendships but his mother made an appointment for him to see the therapist. One of the first presuppositional questions the therapist asks might be, "*When* you no longer have to come to therapy, what will be different?" The question assumes the client will eventually not need therapy and that something different will occur. The therapist might also ask, "What are some things going on right now that you want to continue to happen that seem to be helpful?" This question assumes solutions already exist that can help the client solve his problem (de Shazer, 1984). Another presuppositional question the therapist asks might be, "What needs to happen so your mother no longer thinks you need to come to therapy?" In this way, the client assumes responsibility for the goal and its solutions rather than the therapist giving advice. Presuppositional questions encourage internal motivation on the part of the client and facilitate the client–therapist relationship.

Those clients who do not want to come often sit quietly and answer in as few words as possible while the therapist scrambles to engage them. Many therapeutic philosophies regard such clients as "resistant," and therapists and clients get into a battle for control. However, the SF therapist does not view clients as resistant but as cooperating in their own unique ways. The therapist shifts the focus from working against the client to working with the client to "defeat your mutual opponent" (de Shazer, 1984, p. 14). Rather than trying to gain control, SF therapists maximize clients' sense of control without using confrontation (De Jong & Berg, 2013), particularly with children and adolescents, who often feel they have no control. To maximize clients' sense of control, the therapist provides choices and affirms clients' abilities to make decisions by being respectful of their boundaries and fostering a relationship of respect and self-determination (Watts, Cashwell & Schweiger, 2004). By cooperating with clients and working from their perspective, positive changes are more likely to occur.

Using art and other creative activities provides a motivational and engaging venue for working with clients of all ages (Goldstein, Lerner & Winner, 2017). Drawing, painting, music, mixed media, and other creative activities provide an inviting and developmentally appropriate motivation for attending therapy, as well as advantages of alternative approaches to verbal expression. The therapist attempts to provide different media so that clients choose what to use rather than the therapist choosing for them. Children and teens who are reluctant to attend therapy willingly participate in expressive modes of therapy. Similarly, those with disabilities who often feel thwarted in their attempts to be successful in the academic arena find that expressive arts allow them to demonstrate skills that others may overlook. "We cannot afford to ignore such naturalistic activities that involve so many basic phenomenon—attention, engagement, motivation, emotion regulation, understanding of others and so on" (Goldstein, Lerner & Winner, 2017, p. 1505). Using expressive arts allows child clients to cooperate using alternative approaches to communicate, natural approaches more in line with their developmental levels.

Another approach that proves helpful with those who do not wish to attend therapy and are reluctant to talk involves the use of scaling questions. Since scaling questions require only a one-word response, even reluctant clients often respond. Through scaling questions, the therapist gleans an abundance of information regarding how the client perceives the problem. For example, the therapist asks Marco, "On a scale of 0 to 10, with 0 being you don't have any friends and 10 being you have all the friends you need, where do you think you are?" Marco states he is a "4." The therapist might respond with, "A 4! Wow! What makes you a 4 and not a 3 or a 2?" The use of the scaling question also provides many possibilities for nonverbal responses, wherein the client writes, draws, colors, or points to a scale to indicate his answer.

For clients who have not wanted to come to therapy, a shift in context could change client perspectives about working with the therapist. For example, Melanie, mentioned at the beginning of this chapter, continued to find it difficult to come into the room without coaxing and assistance. However, on the fourth day, I changed the schedule so that art became the first activity of the day. Once she realized this, she only required a little encouragement since art provided a nonverbal approach for expressing her thoughts and feelings, while working within the small group lessened the focus on her.

When the therapist finds it difficult to engage the client, taking a walk is often helpful in reducing stress and anxiety. Walking together allows the client to talk about concerns without eye contact and lessens any embarrassment or shame about what is discussed. I prefer to walk outside, as nature seems to provide a natural and calming backdrop to conversations. However, weather limitations may make it important to walk inside, preferably in a place that is neutral for the client.

For reluctant children and adolescents, including a friend in the first session may be helpful as it takes the focus off the client. The friend may be an acquaintance with whom the client feels safe or a best friend. Many of the questions the SF therapist asks may be useful to both the client and the friend, since SF therapy focuses on strengths and goal-setting. For older children and adolescents who increasingly look to peers for support, small groups provide another option for those who seem reluctant to attend therapy. However, small groups do not always provide for the confidential nature of the relationship client and therapist may need to help the client discuss embarrassing or shame-filled challenges.

The therapist might consider logistical issues that may prevent children and adolescents from engaging in therapy. For example, by visiting the school counselor, clients may be missing art, music, or physical education, times in the academic day that they enjoy. Others may go to therapy after school and miss important extracurricular activities, thus preventing clients from fully engaging in the therapeutic process. The therapist should work closely with parents, teachers, and clients and remain flexible as to times favorable for meeting.

It's Not My Problem

Some clients do not mind coming to therapy to discuss the problem and may recognize the problem exists; however, much like clients in the contemplation stage of change, they do not feel the need to change since it is likely someone else's fault. The client tends to view therapy as a place to vent or discuss what is wrong, often with the hope the therapist might change the situation or another person.

For example, Sam, sent by the teacher to the school counselor for angry and tearful outbursts, insisted the problem was Mike. Mike and Sam, both eight years old and in the third grade, constantly argued. When the counselor asked Sam exception questions about when things were better, he stated, "When Mike is absent." When asked the miracle question about what would be different if a miracle occurred, Sam responded that Mike would not be in his class. When asked what he would be doing differently if Mike wasn't there, Sam said he would be able to get help from the teacher and Mike wouldn't tattle on him. Sam felt that when he got in trouble, it was Mike's fault, and that Mike received the positive attention. As he continued to talk it became evident that both boys competed for the teacher's attention; however, the boys did not possess this insight. Sam, who experienced challenges with self-regulation, was often called on for his misbehavior; whereas Mike's problems did not include self-regulation. So how does the therapist proceed, since Sam seemed to think the only solution was for Mike to get out of the classroom? The therapist asks Sam coping questions.

Coping questions shift the focus to the client's strengths and away from outside factors. Therapists often use coping questions to help clients in times of crisis, but they also provide a useful response with clients who do not seem to notice their own power in the situation. The therapist focuses on the client's strengths rather than the problem.

Sam: I wish you could get Mike moved to another class.

Therapist: How would this be helpful?

Sam: He wouldn't be in my business and tattling on me all the time. He is always getting me in trouble with the teacher.

Therapist: So you feel like you are always in trouble because Mike tattles on you. Tell me Sam, how do you cope with this all the time? You have been with Mike in the classroom for three months. How do you do it?

Sam: I don't know. Sometimes, I just put my head down and ignore him. Sometimes, I cry.

Therapist: So you have found that putting your head down is helpful. What else helps you when Mike gets on your nerves?

The therapist asks a coping question and then expands on Sam's positive approach to dealing with Mike to find out what else might be helpful.

I've Got Issues

While working with a former student in her school counseling office, a little seven-year-old girl walked into the office, went up to the counselor, looked

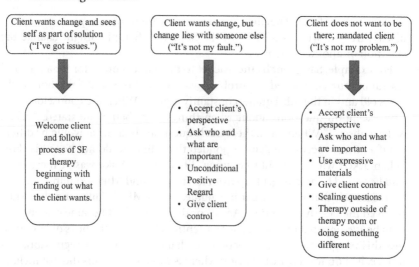

Figure 6.1 Motivations of Client and Possible Therapist Responses.

at me and then back at her counselor and announced, "I'm here cuz I've got issues." Obviously, this child had been in therapy or overheard adults discussing her, but she willingly talked to her therapist about her problems. Within minutes, she engaged in conversation with the therapist about what occurred in her home over the past few days and the goals she had set for herself.

When clients recognize there is a problem and view themselves as part of the solution it is easy to engage them in therapy. Yet, some clients do not necessarily come because of a problem but because going to the therapist offers them the opportunity to be heard, to be given credit for strengths, and to enjoy a safe place away from other areas of life that may not feel safe. However, they still come and willingly participate in the change process, finding participation leads to reaching goals and feelings of self-efficacy. When working with those who willingly come to therapy, we must be on guard to not take therapy sessions with them for granted but to continue to honor them and their perspectives, remaining attentive to those things that motivate them, and humbled by their confidence in us.

Regardless of the client's motivations for coming to therapy, the therapist works to help the client feel respected and empowered by treating the client with unconditional positive regard, regarding the client as the expert, communicating with the client in developmentally appropriate ways, and using playful and creative approaches to encourage the client to find solutions and reach goals.

References

De Jong, P. & Berg, I. K. (2013). *Interviewing for solutions* (4th Ed.). Belmont, CA: Brooks/Cole.
de Shazer, S. (1984). The death of resistance. *Family Process, 23*, 11–17.

Goldstein, T. R., Lerner, M. D. & Winner, E. (2017). The arts as a venue for developmental science: Realizing a latent opportunity. *Child Development, 88*(5), 1505–1512.

Prochaska, J. & Diclemente, C. (1983). Stages and processes of self-change of smoking: Towards an integrated model of change. *Journal of Consulting Clinical Psychology, 51*(3), 390–395.

Rogers, C. R. (1957). The necessary and sufficient conditions of therapeutic personality change. *Journal of Consulting Psychology, 21*(2), 95–103.

Swift, J. K. & Greenberg, R. P. (2015). Enhance motivation for treatment. In J. K. Swift & R. P. Greenberg, *Premature termination in psychotherapy: Strategies for engaging clients and improving outcomes*, pp. 127–135. Washington, DC: American Psychological Association.

Watts, R. H., Cashwell, C. S. & Schweiger, W. K. (2004). Fostering intrinsic motivation in children: A humanistic counseling process. *Journal of Humanistic Counseling, Education, and Development, 43*, 16–24.

CHAPTER 7

Beginnings

Elizabeth R. Taylor, Amanda Allison,
and Becky Southard

Anthony, a 6th-grade student, had been diagnosed with Asperger's in the second grade. Since he was being home-schooled, he had not received services. His parents were in the military, so he moved often from school to school. When he first came in, he had difficulty talking and communicating his thoughts and feelings. Additionally, he had been diagnosed with a speech problem that presented itself with a halted speech pattern. Some interpreted his speech as defiance, but Anthony just needed a longer time to respond verbally. A screener administered at his school also showed he experienced suicidal ideation and depression. Building a positive rapport was the cornerstone to helping him develop trust and become comfortable with the school counselor. To do this, I offered him several different games, but he chose "Get to Know You, Jenga."

For this "Get to Know You, Jenga," I wrote questions on the Jenga playing pieces, so when players chose pieces, they answered the question. I also played with the client, so that the client learned a little about me. By providing Anthony with choices regarding which game to play, he seemed to relax. I asked him what his best hopes were for the session. He replied, "To make friends."

In the first session, the therapist begins developing the therapeutic relationship, finding exceptions, developing goals, and creating solutions. The therapeutic relationship refers to building rapport with the client by showing the client respect, demonstrating a genuine interest in his or her well-being, and treating the client with kindness. Rogers (2007) might refer to this as "unconditional positive regard," that is, "a warm acceptance of each aspect of the client's experience as being a part of that client" with "no conditions of acceptance," and "caring for the client as a separate person, with permission to have his own feelings, his own experiences" (p. 243).

In addition to developing the therapeutic relationship, the therapist begins by focusing on the therapeutic process: 1) the structure of the session, 2) confidentiality, and 3) rapport building. The therapist remains flexible to the order in which these are addressed depending on the client's disposition. Building rapport, for example, occurs throughout the session, not just at the beginning, since the therapist continually monitors the therapist–client relationship.

The limits of confidentiality, however, should come early in the session, since the client may disclose information early that requires the therapist to notify others or enlist outside resources. Finally, by providing the structure of the session, the therapist lessens anxiety, making it easier to build rapport.

Explaining the Process

Merriam-Webster (2017) defines anxiety as "apprehensive uneasiness or nervousness usually over an impending or anticipated ill." Various concerns may run through the minds of children and adolescents before going to therapy. "Who is this person I have been sent to see?" "What am I supposed to do?" "What if I don't know the answer?" "What if he asks about my dad, who drinks and doesn't remember when he beats my mom?" "Can I tell this person that I live in my car?" "What if the counselor doesn't like me?" When a young female counselor in training sat down with one of her first families, the teenage son looked at his anxious mother and said, "You said we were going to the dentist!" Was it worse going to therapy versus the dentist? Clearly this young man felt some anxiety!

Anxiety may result in the fight, flight, freeze response, no matter what the age (Steimer, 2002). This could be played out in the therapist's office as yelling, crying, or cursing at the person bringing the client or at the therapist. Another child might try to run out of the office before getting started. The freeze response, often labeled as resistance, is not unusual with those who have been traumatized; however, it can result in complete silence as the therapist tries to ask questions.

Since it is rare for children and adolescents to just show up for counseling without someone sending or bringing them, they often feel some anxiety about what this experience entails. To relieve anxiety, the counselor provides a general structure of how the session will go.

By providing information about what to expect anxiety lessens and trust increases, so the therapy process can move forward. The process can be simply explained in three short steps: 1) We get to know each other by talking, creating, or doing things together; 2) I may ask you a few strange questions; and 3) We will take a break, and then we will create possible solutions together. Rather than using verbal approaches alone, the therapist provides a list of the sequence using words or pictures. Drawings, emojis, icons, or clip art pictures printed on paper or an index card provide a good visual of the steps or stages of therapy (Figure 7.1).

Figure 7.1 Pictorial Process of Therapy.

Confidentiality

Important in the process of working with children and adolescents is a discussion of confidentiality and its limits. The therapist should examine the state and federal laws regarding releasing records, court testimony, custodial issues, and other areas related to working with minors in order to know the state's specific requirements. The client needs to know the limits of confidentiality, so that if and when a situation arises and the therapist must inform others, the client does not feel betrayed. Needless to say, if the counselor fails to discuss these limitations, the client will disclose abuse or threaten violence. If these issues have been discussed, then the client knows (and can be assured) that help will be solicited from parents or other adults.

Building Rapport

Building rapport involves negotiating the dance between client and therapist: timing, voice tone, body language, eye contact, and facial expressions. Building rapport requires flexibility, understanding, and awareness, that is, following the client's lead, understanding the child's developmental level, and having an awareness of the child's current mood and willingness to engage. Often, what the therapist is feeling in the relationship matches that of the client. This intuitive awareness allows the therapist to move in synch with the child or adolescent, providing conditions that build rapport and enlist the client's willingness to engage in therapy.

Rapport building with a child or adolescent begins with the first glance and most often proceeds to introductions, oftentimes through another adult. When the child is the client, it is important to kneel down to the child's level to gain eye contact. For adolescents, building rapport may include smiling and offering a handshake. How the therapist approaches a child or adolescent depends a great deal on the sensitivity of the therapist to the nuances of the child's personality and situation. The therapist notices whether the client is ready to engage, not forcing the client to speak. If the client does not seem willing to communicate, the therapist may invite the client to work side by side on a puzzle, coloring, or play a simple game. It is helpful to have several games from which the client can choose, so the client feels some control in the situation. Sometimes, reading to young children invokes relaxation and nurtures the relationship, allowing the child time to become comfortable with the therapist and the therapeutic environment.

Some do not believe that getting to know the client or "problem-free talk" is necessary in beginning the therapy process (Ratner, George & Iveson, 2012, p. 32). However, not only can this problem-free talk help in building rapport but also in getting to know the client and identifying important clues as to the client's strengths and talents, important others, and how the client communicates. Asking questions from a stance of curiosity (versus interrogation) sends the message that the therapist is interested in knowing about the client, what the client enjoys doing, what subjects pique his interest, what expertise the client has, and who the client's family and friends are. For example, a child might state that he loves to play football. The response to this client might be, "Wow! What do you do when you play football?" By allowing the client to discuss what is important to him, the therapist begins the process of letting the client know that he is the expert in his problems and their solutions. Getting to know the client requires giving up any preconceived notions acquired from others or demands of adults. It also means remaining sensitive to nuances in the client's feelings, facial expressions, and behaviors, as well as to the client's preferred modes of communication. As the client and therapist gain synchronicity in communication, it becomes easier for the client to become vulnerable and open in the relationship and the power difference between client and therapist lessens.

Relying on verbal curiosity questions, however, does not give the client many options in communicating the dimensions of the client's life. For younger children, who communicate more naturally through play and expressive materials, the use of developmentally appropriate materials sends the message that therapy is for them, not for the therapist; that this space honors their preferred style of communication. With adolescents, we often err on the side of assuming they have reached the stage of formal operations, when in reality they are still cognitively working at the concrete stage of development and may be functioning at immature levels emotionally due to their challenges with self, peers, family, and school. Being able to express themselves without relying on verbal approaches communicates respect for who they are and how they choose to communicate regardless of age or abilities.

Being respectful of the client's developmental age also requires appropriate furnishings and materials that fit the client. Chairs and tables that fit the client demonstrate respect for the client and his/her physical age, as does providing a variety of developmentally appropriate materials, such as blank paper, colors, paints, clay, fidgets, and other items that the child or adolescent can use as modes of expression (see Chapter 1, Table 1.1). For those who have physical disabilities, the therapist ensures that the doorway is accessible to wheelchairs, that writing and drawing materials can be adapted to fit the client's needs, and that materials are at the appropriate height for those in wheelchairs (See Chapter 4).

Creative and Playful Approaches to Build Rapport

Coloring

One of the best activities for building rapport involves sitting side by side and coloring. It does not require eye contact, so anxiety and shame lessen. Children, adolescents, and even adults often find coloring to be relaxing. Research indicates that coloring and drawing increases blood flow to the prefrontal cortex, that part of the brain associated with motivation and rewards, supporting the idea that coloring provides a relaxing and calming effect (Kaimal et al., 2017). Coloring neutralizes emotions in many children and allows space for building trust with the therapist. Bruce Perry (Perry & Szalavitz, 2006) frequently begins his sessions with children who have been traumatized by coloring with them. As they color together, children begin to relax and feel safe, finding assurance that this is a person with whom they can discuss their most difficult, traumatic, and shaming experiences.

For older children and adolescents who may feel that simply coloring is not age-appropriate, the use of the more recently popular "adult" coloring books might be appropriate. Magic markers or pastels provide a good substitute for crayons. Those who wish to employ electronic media might use some of the coloring aps available, such as "Colorfy©," that provide a variety of pictures to color on iPads, iPhones, or other electronic devices. Coloring, of course, is not just limited to the beginning stages of therapy. Sometimes, building rapport is an ongoing process occurring over several sessions, so coloring may be a positive technique for beginning each session.

Ball Games

Young toddlers enjoy rolling a ball back and forth to their parent or guardian. As they do, they learn to trust that the parent will not intentionally push the ball in a wild direction. Similarly, the therapist playing catch with children using a nerf ball teaches them that the therapist can be trusted as she throws the ball in a way that helps them be successful. Playing games such as catch metaphorically connects the adult and child, the child learning to trust the therapist with each toss of the ball.

Children in early and middle childhood also enjoy playing a game of baseball using a nerf ball and bat. Once again, the therapist, whom the child most often determines is the pitcher, tosses the ball over the plate (paper plates make for good bases) in a way that the child is most likely to hit it, so the child builds a sense of mastery but also develops trust in the therapist. Rules of baseball carry metaphorical concepts that provide useful interventions. For example, when the child lands on the base, the therapist states, "You are 'safe'," metaphorically communicating to the client that this is a safe place.

Emily, who had been diagnosed with Acquired Immune Deficiency Syndrome (AIDS) in a time when there was little chance of a cure, laid out the bases using paper plates to play nerf baseball. She then placed base plates in between the bases, so there was little chance of walking between bases without landing on a plate. Each time she hit the ball, she would run from base to base and then stop and wait for me to say, "You're safe!" She desperately needed to hear those words, and what was supposed to be the beginning of our session often lasted for 30 minutes, as she gradually determined she was indeed safe in this place and with me.

Checkers

The checkerboard connects the space between the therapist and client with the game of checkers providing the connection. By using the game as a process of communication, the therapist builds rapport and comments on strengths as the game is played.

A teacher referred Juan, a fourth grader attending elementary school, for counseling. This wiry, dark-haired, Hispanic boy rarely spoke to me (though he was fluent in English) except in one- or two-word sentences. His referral was for disruption in the class and not doing his work. Since he seemed hesitant to talk, we started by playing checkers. I always let him win, although I do not know if he was aware of this fact. I did not want to undermine his competence, but build it, similar to tossing the ball to a child in such a way that he will likely catch it. By doing so, I tried to judge how much to challenge him to win without making it seem too easy, thus building his self-confidence and helping him understand that I was a safe person. One day, after about two weeks, the teacher told me Juan's behavior had much improved. "I don't know what you are doing, but it works!" she said. Unsure of what worked, I would like to think that it was the relationship we built, a relationship of trust, respect, and unconditional positive regard. Over time, he began to talk more, and he seemed to develop more confidence in himself. After seven sessions he had reached his goals and decided he didn't need to come any longer.

I have played checkers with several acting-out youth, focusing on client strengths rather than deficits. By complimenting the client and looking for exceptions, particularly when the client didn't play well, we developed a positive relationship. Although a set goal for therapy was established, the process of therapy often included a great deal of time playing checkers, providing the client with exceptions to the negative and incompetent feelings he often experienced in school. The repeated experiences of a trusting relationship, feelings of competence and success, and learning about personal strengths provided the background in which the child's behaviors improved.

Opening the Session

The beginning of therapy, in most approaches, starts with the first therapist–client meeting. However, in SF therapy, therapy begins with the referral, whether by the mother, teacher, or significant other. The referring person often contacts the therapist with concerns about the client and problems the client is having at school or home. When the referring person makes contact, the therapist might begin solution-building by asking such questions or statements as: "How do you think therapy will be helpful?" "How will you know when therapy is successful?" "Notice those things that are happening that you would like to continue to see happen and we can talk about them when you come in."

Looking for strengths and resources begins the minute the therapist meets the client. It is a mindset—everyone has strengths. It is the filter through which we view the child. However, to jump right in and point out strengths while the client is describing the problem may create an instant barrier between the therapist and client. For clients, their perceptions of the problem need to be heard and validated. To move too quickly tells the client that his or her perceptions are unimportant and lack credibility, resulting in the client doing any one of three things: 1) shutting down and not expressing anything that might seem risky; 2) expressing those things that would seem to please the therapist rather than genuine and personal perceptions; or 3) re-enforcing low self-efficacy and a sense of hopelessness.

Young clients need to know they have been heard, that their perceptions of their problems are important and valid. Bliss (2010) describes this type of attention as "extreme listening" (p. 219). This intentional focus on clients' perceptions requires giving up any preconceived ideas about the problem or its solution, accepting clients totally and fully and with the same spirit as Rogers' unconditional positive regard.

An important beginning involves finding out what the client wants from the session. For example, many SF therapists begin therapy by asking, "What is something that would need to happen today to know that our time together was helpful?" For clients who have problems in receptive or expressive language or who cannot shift to future-focused questions, this type of question could be difficult to understand or answer. For example, asking "How can I help you?" might be a simpler approach. Since many children and adolescents attending counseling have been "sent" rather than making a conscious decision to come on their own, a better question might be "What would the teacher (or referring person) say needs to happen?" or "What would your mother say needs to happen, so you can get off restriction?" This approach conveys to the client that therapist and client are on the same team, that the counselor is there to help the client rectify whatever the problem is.

Following the constructivist perspective that the client creates his or her reality, the therapist provides the conditions and materials that give the client options for communicating their perceptions. The following activities provide alternatives to verbal approaches to help clients talk about themselves and their concerns. During these activities, the therapist acts as a witness to the client's strengths and challenges.

Creative and Play-Based Approaches to Address Current Perceptions

Sandtray

The use of sandtray offers the client a method to convey his world to the therapist without words. The therapist begins by providing a selection of miniatures, the sand, and a sandtray preferably painted blue on the bottom to represent water. The therapist asks the client, "Using these miniatures, make a sandtray of your world." The therapist, without comment or interpretation, steps back and observes. The client speaks through the miniatures, their arrangement in the sand, and even through the sand itself. Most children and adolescents readily participate in sandtray and often externalize their world better through the miniatures than they do through the spoken word alone. Once the client completes the sandtray, the therapist asks the client "Tell me about your sandtray." The therapist asks questions of the client to get a better understanding of the client's world, who and what are important, client resources, as well as how the client perceives the problem.

With adolescents, miniatures can play a vital role in describing families and family events. For example, in working with Adelita, a middle-school Hispanic female, I asked her to "Make a sandtray of your family." Adelita selected a father figure, a mother figure, and two children representing her siblings, as well as a person whom she laid down in the sand, stating that person had died. She explained that her mother had left her father and had a romantic relationship with a female who currently lived with them. And, although the father was not in town, Adelita and her father remained close. But it was the death of her older brother that grieved her, because she had been close to him before he died and felt guilt over comments she made to him before the accident that took his life. Although Adelita was referred for academic problems, through sandtray important events became evident and could be used to help her move forward.

Drawing, Coloring, and Mixed Media

The therapist, using paper and mixed media, uses a similar approach to sandtray by asking the client to "Make a picture of your world." Once again, the therapist does not interpret what the client does but acts as an active observer in the process. When the client finishes, the therapist asks the client to "Tell me about your picture." Similar to the sandtray, the therapist asks curiosity questions to get a better understanding of the client's world and perceptions (Figure 7.2).

Writing

For adolescents, writing poetry allows them to express their feelings, perceptions, and information about areas of interest. Through poetry, an adolescent girl, an accomplished dancer, discusses her feelings and stressors about performing, and her striving for perfection (Figure 7.3).

Journaling and keeping a diary, popular among older children and adolescents, are often enhanced by mixing writing with other forms of creative expression. For example, using a journal, a teen might draw or paste magazine pictures that represent her thoughts and feelings and perhaps add a few words or sentences to further express what the pictures represent.

Life Collage

Clients create collage portraits about themselves using objects. Objects could be things they like or representations of what they like to do. Clients choose to incorporate magazine pictures, drawings, or objects into a collage representing

Figure 7.2 Mixed Media Ballerina.

those things that represent who they are on a large piece of poster board or construction paper. The therapist begins by asking:

- Tell me about what you notice about your creation.
- What does this say about you?
- What are you most proud of in this creation?
- What are some of your challenges?

Post a Secret

Another approach to helping clients express their perceptions is taken from Frank Warren's (2005) "PostSecret," an ongoing community mail art project, created by Frank Warren in 2005, in which people mail their secrets anonymously on a homemade postcard. These secrets are compiled and posted each Sunday (https://postsecret.com). Warren has received and posted thousands of cards from around the world about shame, joy, hope, fears, and all

I Need to Dance

Competition time

My head spins

My stomach turns

I will never give up

I won't, I won't, I won't

Blood, sweat, and tears

And now this moment

Overstretched, over-flexed, over-rehearsed

Each and every position

Again and again

One more time

Hours and hours of hard work

Stumbling, falling, and rolling

Will it pay off?

I hear my name announced

And stare ahead of me

The lights

The stares

The judges

My stomach double backflips

All I can do is breathe

In

Out

In

Out

I dance from my heart

Taking a chance

To be free

To shine

Flying, spinning, swaying

Living in every moment

I cry, scream, laugh, sweat, and bleed

Leaving fears and anger behind

Grasping hopes and dreams from ahead

Complete but not perfect

Free from the outside world

I am a stroke of paint

And a bird flying through the wind

I am not dancing

I am living

The song comes to an end

I can't breathe

Where has my breath gone

But I did it

I knew I could

I made it

I feel so good

May the judges be fair

And everyone proud of me

It felt so good

To fight for myself

To be right where I've always belonged

I exit

I need one more dance.

Figure 7.3 Teenager's Poem.

those things that make us human. His approach offers the therapist a way to help clients to nonverbally express themselves individually or in groups. Although presented as an approach to communicate present ways of being, doing, and feeling, it can also help clients communicate about personal strengths and challenges.

Having postcards or index cards available to the client to write on when he first comes in allows freedom to bring up whatever topic might be concerning or important. Perhaps the adolescent is having difficulties with carrying out his goals due to problems with parents, or maybe he does not want to let you know that he has really accomplished something amazing, because he is embarrassed to draw attention to himself or brag. The client might create the card before coming to or at the beginning of the session to give to the therapist.

Allowing clients to discuss problems does not equate with problem-focused therapy, but does allow the therapist and client to better appreciate what each has to offer—the client's ability to cope and the resources she brings, and the therapist's ability to hear the client's pain, ask good questions, and notice strengths. "To ignore their needs can sometimes have worse consequences than to force the conversation toward positives and the future because of the effect this pressure can have on the emotional climate" (Lipchik, 2002, p. 44).

Who and What are Important

Finding out who and what are important to the client increases awareness for client and therapist of client resources, what activities the client enjoys doing, with whom the client enjoys spending time, influences that may increase or decrease solutions' success, and those relationships that may be enhanced as clients work toward reaching goals. Gaining information about who and what are important often involves just listening to the client, paraphrasing, and asking for more details to gain an understanding of the client's perspectives. However, this information may be better gleaned and increases motivation by using more tangible, visual, and playful techniques.

Who Lives in my House

For children, a picture of a house may help the client tell his or her story about family. A five-year-old, shy, Hispanic girl, born to migrant and seasonal farm workers and who often missed school, found it simpler to discuss her family using a blank picture of a one-story house with windows and a door. The therapist asked the young girl "If I looked in this window, who would I see?" The young girl stated "My mom. She is cooking." This continued as she told the therapist about the eight people living in her home. The therapist gained an understanding of who lived in the home, the client's perceptions of the different individuals, and their roles in the child's life. Subsequently, the child drew each member of the family looking out of the windows and in the front yard of the home.

Genogram

A genogram, described as a "quick gestalt of complex family patterns" (McGoldrick, Gerson & Petry, 2008, p. 2) provides a visual display of the client's family members over generations, their relationships, dynamics, and changes (Figure 7.4). McGoldrick, Gerson and Petry (2008) describe various symbols used to express these different family dynamics; however, the symbols used in constructing genograms can be complicated for children and adolescents, and patterns may not be as obvious to younger generations. Standard genograms may be modified in several ways to provide information to the therapist, as well as young clients, about who is in the family and the client's perceptions of family members.

The first approach, described by Gil, McGoldrick, Gerson, and Petry (2008), uses miniatures to represent family members. The therapist draws the child's basic genogram on a large piece of paper, asks the child to select miniatures that represent each family member, and then directs him to place them in a designated space. Miniatures selected provide the therapist and the child with an externalized view of the family and family functioning. Questions about the genogram might address how the miniature reminds the client of the family member, the member's strengths, and the relationship the client has with the family member.

A second approach to constructing a genogram involves creating a key with symbols to represent positive qualities of family members that may be a resource to the client (Figure 7.4) (Taylor, Clement & Ledet, 2013). The client and therapist create the standard genogram, and, instead of using the usual symbols representing relationships, the client selects symbols from the key that represent the family member and draws them next to the person (Figure 7.5). For example, a picture of a heart may represent love, a picture of an ear represents someone who listens to the client, or a picture of a fork represents someone with whom the client eats. The client may add other symbols, thus creating other possibilities. Those who have the most symbols most often represent those who are most supportive and provide resources for the client (Taylor, Clement, & Ledet, 2013).

The therapist can also create cards with each of the symbols on them and ask clients to place the card next to the family member that possesses the strength on the card. This can be particularly helpful for children who have difficulty with movement due to physical handicaps. If clients are unable to direct their hands to place the card next to the family member, the therapist places the card for them with the clients' directions.

Draw a Family

An approach often used by art therapists to examine family members and their relationships involves asking the client to draw her family. The client's drawings provide a way for the therapist to gain insight into who the client

SF Genogram Symbols

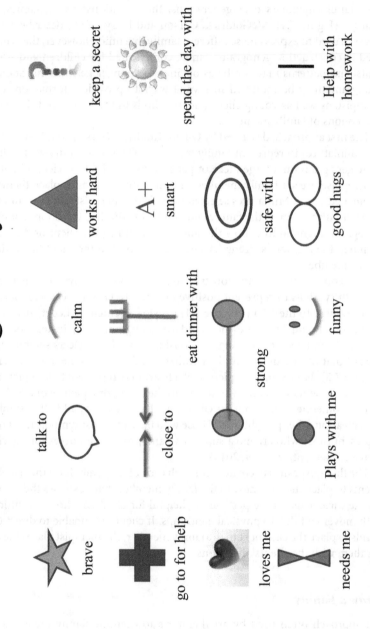

Figure 7.4 Genogram Key.

Note: Adapted from Taylor, E. R., Clement, M. & Ledet, G. (2013). Postmodern and alternative approaches in genogram use with children and adolescents. *Journal of Creativity in Mental Health*, 8, p. 284.

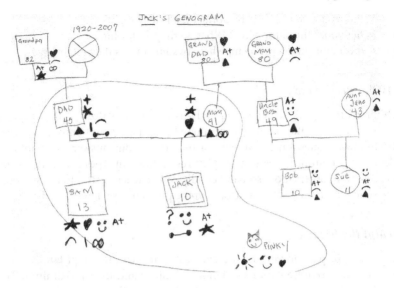

Figure 7.5 Jack's Genogram using Symbols.

Note: Adapted from Taylor, E. R., Clement, M. & Ledet, G. (2013). Postmodern and alternative approaches in genogram use with children and adolescents. *Journal of Creativity in Mental Health, 8,* p. 284.

considers to be part of the family and what the client thinks about family members. Looking at the expression on family members' faces, how close they stand to one another, who is and who is not included in the family picture, and other important aspects of the picture provide cues as to the child's standing in the family but also the child's resources. The therapist asks SF questions that the client can respond to orally or simply by pointing, for example:

- Who is someone you could go to if you were hurt?
- To whom can you tell a secret?
- Who is the person with whom you most like to play or do things?
- Who is someone that makes you smile when you are with them?
- Who is someone that you wish was closer to you?
- Who could you call if you had a big problem?
- Who could you call if you had a small problem?
- With whom do you spend most of your time?
- With whom do you eat dinner?

Sticker Family

Using stickers of robots, animals, or other animated types of pictures, the therapist asks the child to create a picture of their family and then asks questions such as:

- What would your family be doing on a Friday night?
- Where does this family live? What do they do for fun?
- If this family had a problem, what are some things they might try?

My Family is Like . . .

Children often speak in metaphors, and this activity capitalizes on this strength. The therapist asks the client "I want you to think about your family and answer the following question by drawing a picture of your answer. My family is like . . . ." Oftentimes, clients draw pictures of different types of animals, some ferocious and others more soft and cuddly. When teaching this to my students, one stated her family is like a taco, with the protective shell on the outside.

Sculpt the Family

Using clay or play dough, the therapist asks the client to sculpt family members, creating representations of family members and their proximity to one another. These representations provide client and therapist with nonverbal information about the family, closeness and distance, size, and importance. The process of sculpting family members offers a multisensory approach for discussing members and their ability to be a resource to clients.

The Moon

In this activity, the client pretends that he has been selected to go to the moon. Providing a picture of a moon can be helpful in creating the visualization. The therapist states, "You have been selected to go on a mission to the moon. You get to choose what your house looks like, who and what you want to take with you, and what you do while you are there."

1   Draw a picture of what you want your house to look like on the moon.
2   Draw a picture of the people you want to take with you to the moon.
3   Draw a picture of anything else you might like to take with you.
4   Once you get to the moon, what is one of the first things you would like to do?

The therapist asks questions of the client regarding the people and objects the client selects and how they might be useful, as well as questions about what the client hopes to do first on the moon. The experience provides another way for the therapist and client to discuss who and what are important.

Tell a Family Story

"Tell Me a Story" uses art history to explore family stories. The painting *Starry Crown* by John Thomas Biggers shows two women creating a cradle with a string, like games children play. The string represents words spoken by the women as they pass down their traditions from one generation to another. The therapist shows the painting to the client and tells the story of the painting. The therapist then asks the client to talk about her family—the family's history, traditions, traits, and events. For example,

- Who are you most like in your family? What traits did you receive from relatives (hair color, personality, etc.)
- What are some important events that have happened in your family?
- What are some of your family traditions?

Facebook

Most older children and adolescents use or have used Facebook or text messaging. Using a paper copy of a modified Facebook page (see Figure 7.6), the therapist asks the client to write a brief description of the self and then write the names of close others. In the dialogue box, the client shares a thought or concern. Using the list of close others, the client writes the name of the person and what he or she might say in response to the client's concern. This way,

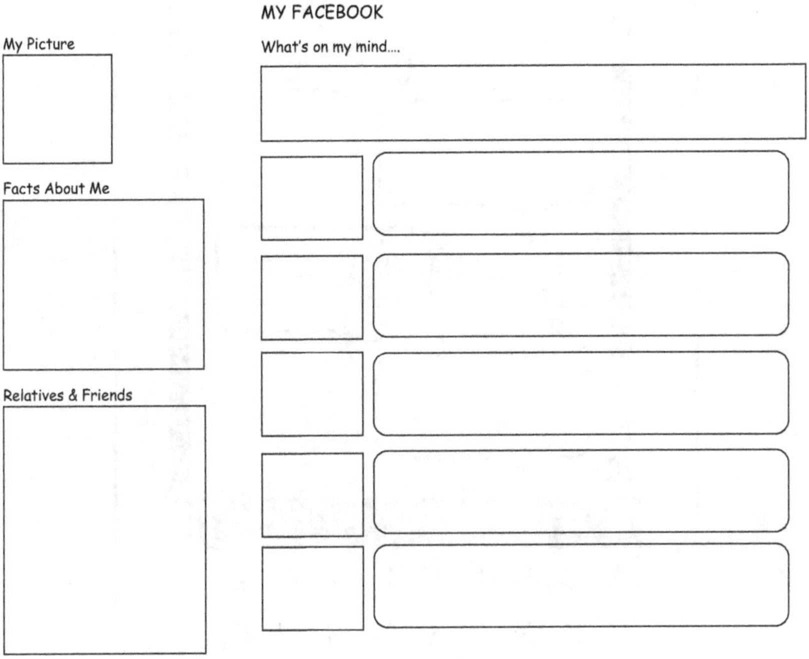

Figure 7.6 Facebook.

Note: Adapted from Taylor, E. R., Clement, M. & Ledet, G. (2013). Postmodern and alternative approaches in genogram use with children and adolescents. *Journal of Creativity in Mental Health, 8,* p. 286.

the therapist gains an understanding of who is important in the client's life, the type of relationship the client might have with the person, and how that person might be helpful (Taylor, Clement & Ledet, 2013). In a similar way, the therapist can use a picture of text messaging on a cell phone. Who the client chooses to text and the content of the text messages provide information regarding how the client interacts and relationships the client enjoys (Taylor, Clement & Ledet, 2013) (see Figure 7.7). Both approaches allow the person to communicate about important information nonverbally through a familiar and popular adaptation of technological communication.

Photographs

The therapist asks the client to bring three or four pictures of her family to share with the therapist. Keeping in mind that photographs provide more

Figure 7.7 Cell Phone.

Figure 7.8 Child's Pictures of What is Important.

information than just the picture of the subject, the therapist begins by asking "Tell me about your picture." Other questions asked out of curiosity may include:

- Who and what are important in this picture?
- Where did you take this picture? What do you like about this place?
- Who took the picture?
- Who else was there? What were they doing when the picture was taken?

Another use of photographs is to ask clients to take pictures of what is important to them at home. Since this requires little skill except in learning to operate the camera, cell phone, or tablet, it provides an amazing adventure for the child and information about who and what are important in this child's life. For example, the following photographs were taken by a six-year-old girl with instructions to "take pictures of what is important to you." She told me the important things for her were her doll, the pumpkins, her swing set, and her dog (Figure 7.8).

The first session, particularly in SF therapy, provides the basis for all other sessions. The therapist begins therapy by preparing the room and materials, addressing the client respectfully and with genuine interest in who and what are important, seeking to identify client strengths, and determining what the client wants from the session. Similarly, if meeting with parents and children, the therapist makes sure that there is enough room and chairs for family members and considers the ages of those attending to create a possible plan for therapy. The therapist explores through various expressive approaches who and what are important and other client resources.

References

Bliss, V. (2010). Extreme listening. In T. S. Nelson (Ed.), *Do something different*, pp. 109–116. New York, NY: Routledge.

Gil, E., McGoldrick, M., Gerson, R. & Petry, S. (2008). Family play genograms. In M. McGoldrick, R. Gerson & P. Suili (Eds), *Genograms: Assessment and intervention*, pp. 257–274. New York, NY: W. W. Norton.

Kaimal, G., Ayaz, H., Herres, J. et al. (2017). Functional near-infrared spectroscopy assessment of reward perception based on visual self-expression: Coloring, doodling, and free drawing. *The Arts in Psychotherapy, 55*, 85–92.

Lipchik, E. (2002). *Beyond technique in solution-focused therapy*. New York: NY: Guildford Press.

McGoldrick, M., Gerson, R., & Petry, S. (2008). *Genograms: Assessment and intervention* (3rd Ed.). New York, NY: Norton & Norton.

Merriam-Webster (2017). Anxiety [definition]. Merriam-Webster's Online Dictionary. Retrieved from: www.merriam-webster.com/dictionary/anxiety.

Perry, B. & Szalavitz, M. (2006). *The boy who was raised as a dog.* New York: NY: Basic Books.

Ratner, H., George, E. & Iveson, C. (2012). *Solution focused brief therapy: 100 key points & techniques.* New York, NY: Routledge.

Rogers, C. (2007). The necessary and sufficient conditions of therapeutic personality change. *Psychotherapy: Theory, Research, Practice, Training, 44*(3), 240–248.

Steimer, T. (2002). The biology of fear and anxiety-related behaviors. *Dialogues in Clinical Neuroscience, 4*(3), 231–249.

Taylor, E. R. (2015). Solution-focused sandtray for children. In H. G. Kaduson & C. E. Schaeffer (Eds), *Short-term play therapy for children* (3rd Ed.), pp. 150–174. New York, NY: Guilford Press.

Taylor, E. R., Clement, M. & Ledet, G. (2013). Postmodern and alternative approaches in genogram use with children and adolescents. *Journal of Creativity in Mental Health, 8*, 278–292.

Warren, F. (2005). *Postsecret: Extraordinary confessions from ordinary lives.* New York, NY: Regan Books.

Winburn, A., King, A. & Burton, E. (2017). Me, my selfie, and I. *Play Therapy Magazine,* March, 6–22.

CHAPTER 8

Digging for Treasure

Elizabeth R. Taylor, Amanda Allison, and
Becky Southard

Sasha is a 13-year-old girl who has a history of emotional dysregulation. As a young child, she was strong-willed and very active. She was adopted at birth and had a younger brother who was adopted into her family when she was five years old. At the age of 11, her adoptive parents divorced, and she lived primarily with her mother and brother. She visited her dad every other weekend in a nearby town.

Sasha began presenting with significant emotional outbursts at home shortly after her parent's divorce. Additionally, she began to experience suicidal ideations along with depression. Her suicidal ideations came to the attention of the school administrator and, after she was hospitalized for treatment of depression and mood swings, she began counseling with her school counselor.

Initially, Sasha did not want to discuss her feelings, thoughts, or behaviors. The counselor realized that she needed to engage Sasha through a more creative approach. Since Sasha enjoyed painting, drawing, and creating, the counselor provided a blank art canvas, paints, and other materials such as feathers, shells, and glitter. She told Sasha she could use the materials to create whatever she wanted. Sasha began by using several bright colors as she painted across the canvas. However, she began to add more black to the color scheme and eventually painted the canvas black. Initially, the canvas looked completely black, however, Sasha had left one small area in the canvas brighter and it showed through the darkness. The therapist stated what she noticed about the canvas with an emphasis on the area that was brighter. Sasha articulated that the black areas were her feelings of depression and sadness, but that the lighter part was hope that she could feel better again. The counselor explored her areas of brightness and asked questions regarding her strengths and exceptions, for example, "When do you notice the hope?" "What is happening when hope appears?" "What will be happening when hope is bigger?" This activity became the cornerstone for future activities that helped her discover her hope even through her depression.

Digging for treasure involves listening for, noticing, and asking about times when problems are not occurring, when things are not so bad, and how the client is coping. The therapist focuses on efforts the client makes in finding solutions, resources the client possesses intrapersonally and interpersonally, and how these help the client in dealing with challenges. As the therapist identifies these treasures, she affirms the client, compliments client efforts, and encourages the client to continue to work towards reaching goals and overcoming challenges.

Exceptions and Differences

One of the main techniques that separates SF therapy from other therapies is the use of exception questions (Lethem, 2002). For example, a therapist might ask, "What's different when your teacher isn't mad at you?" or "When was a time that you and your mother didn't fight?" With adolescents, noting exceptions to the problem early in the session may be beneficial and prevent blaming. Melidonis and Bry (1995), when working with adolescents and their parents, note that finding exceptions interrupts the negative communication cycles involved in blaming one another, since these negative cycles make it difficult to find exceptions. Once the therapist quits focusing on exceptions, blaming returns, so the therapist must be diligent in helping the client to continue to take notice of exceptions times. For example, consider Matthew, age 17, who finds it difficult to manage his academic work due to his outside work schedule. The teacher brings Matthew to the counselor's office because he appears angry and frustrated, though he makes good grades.

Teacher: I am sick of Matthew spouting off at me over the least little thing.

Therapist: I can see you are upset with Matthew. Matthew, how do you see it?

Matthew: I am tired of her always being on my back. I am trying so hard, but I can't get things done (voice grows louder).

Therapist: So, you sound a bit frustrated with trying to get the work done (focuses on the feeling rather than blaming the teacher).

Matthew: I can't even get a good night's sleep. I don't get finished working at the store until 10, and then I try to do homework until midnight and get up at 6 and try to finish up. It's just not good enough. I think you need to move me out of this class and into an easier one.

Teacher: I didn't know you worked after school. Why didn't you tell me this?

Matthew: I figured you would think I am making excuses. That's what you told Sam when he told you about football practice.

Teacher: Give me a chance, Matthew. You are just jumping to conclusions (starts to get upset).

Therapist: I can see that you both really want to work this out. Matthew, when do you and your teacher get along better?

Matthew: When I feel like I am caught up and not so tired. It is just that I am so frustrated.

Teacher:	I am frustrated too, but I get it that you're tired.
Therapist:	Matthew, when have there been times when you might have been frustrated but didn't get upset with your teacher?
Matthew:	When she didn't get so loud. I just get more and more frustrated when she gets loud.
Therapist:	What else was helpful when you didn't get frustrated and angry?
Matthew:	When she talked to me before class. I guess I felt like she was on my side. Then she seemed like she understood, until today when she started getting upset.
Therapist:	So, you feel better when she talks with you a little. You feel like you have an ally.
Matthew:	Yea. I guess she isn't so bad.
Mrs. John:	I am sorry that you feel I am not on your side. I am just worried about you passing your state tests and I want you to do well. This is an advanced class, and you could go to college.

Exception questions vary but normally come after the client has had some time to talk about the problem or express concerns. Because the therapist assumes exceptions exist, she asks, "*Tell* me about a time when this hasn't been such a problem," versus "*Can* you tell me about a time . . .?" However, clients may ignore the question. "Asking clients to forego talk of their concern or aspiration, to discuss solutions implicit in exceptions to what they came to discuss, is arguably an audacious conversational and relational invitation" (Strong & Pyle, 2011, p. 112). If the therapist fails to fully establish the therapeutic relationship, clients do not feel heard and understood. Once clients feel they have had time to express their problematic situations, they often expect and even hope for the therapist to facilitate change.

Since asking exception questions involves an interruption in the flow of the conversation, the therapist might pause or speak with a different tone or inflection to signal this shift. Once the therapist asks an exception question, a period of silence often follows as the client reflects on differences between problem and exception times. The therapist remains cautious in interrupting the silence, as it takes time for some clients to process the question. After 7 to 10 seconds, the therapist might state, "I can tell you are thinking about it." This helps the client who may have difficulty staying on task or who may have forgotten the question.

Wehr (2010) studied the qualitative differences between clients in problem-focused versus SF interventions, and found that focusing on one exception led clients to benefit from the intervention, that is, a small change led to more desired changes. By focusing on exceptions, participants came up with more exceptions leading to more solutions. Overall, participants remembered more exceptions to the problem than the problem itself.

Exceptions and differences may be difficult for younger clients and those with developmental delays to understand. Several ideas presented below may be helpful when asking exception questions.

Creative and Playful Approaches for Finding Exceptions

List It

To validate clients' concerns, the therapist lists the concerns the client expresses about his life in black pen or pencil on the side of a piece of paper. Then, the therapist writes personal observations regarding strengths the client demonstrates on the other side of the paper using a colored writing tool. For example, the client states that he has few friends; the therapist writes "friends are important." If the client states that he has problems in math, the therapist asks about those subjects that the client finds interesting and challenging but not problematic. As the client lists challenges, the therapist reframes the challenge into a strength or inquires about a similar area or topic that does not cause concerns. The therapist continues to ask the client about strengths in extracurricular activities and strengths at home. The therapist also asks the client if the therapist could write down other strengths the therapist has noticed while they talked. If the client agrees, the therapist adds to the list of strengths in the right column, explaining what he specifically noticed about the client's strengths. Looking at the final list, the therapist asks the client which strengths might be helpful in overcoming current challenges, how they might be helpful, and which strengths the client might employ to reach the current goal.

Collage

Using a file folder, the client chooses from a selection of precut pictures from magazines that represent those aspects of themselves they show others and pastes these on the outside. For the inside of the folder, clients choose magazine pictures that represent good and bad aspects that others may not know about them. From these pictures on the inside and outside of the folder, the therapist highlights through questions and conversation those aspects that represent the client's strengths. The client or therapist then highlights these qualities visually and kinesthetically by tracing or decorating the boundaries of the pictures that represent strengths using colored pens, markers, or tactile materials such as glue, colored sand, or glitter. Young clients can trace their strengths while talking about how they use them.

Evidence of Exceptions

The therapist gives the client a small paper bag and asks the client to collect evidence of those things the client would like to continue to happen or that the client enjoys or likes to do (family, nature, animals, etc.). Items collected might include movie tickets, pieces of bark, receipts from a restaurant, photographs, or other physical evidence. When the client returns to therapy, the client talks about each item and what makes it special. The therapist explores with the client each item, asking questions such as:

- How is this helpful to you?
- When are some other times you have done this activity?
- What are some things you can do to make this happen more?
- Who else is there when you are enjoying or doing this activity?
- How could you use this to help you reach your goals?
- If I asked one of your friends about what makes this special, what would she say?

Video

Videoing a client during exception times (when the problem is not occurring) provides a way to point out exceptions or those times the client is doing what is helpful in reaching goals. For example, Murphy and Davis (2005) discuss the use of videoing a client who was deaf and who had decreased his use of sign language. The authors video the client, editing out those times when the client does not use sign language, then they show the client the video of himself using sign language, that is, "video exceptions" (Murphy & Davis, 2005, p. 70). Today, with the development and accessibility of cellular devices, the therapist might ask the client to video herself doing those things she wants to continue to do or those times when the problem should have occurred but didn't. Through video, the client monitors and reinforces herself doing what works in the present moment. Considering positive moments shifts the focus from problem situations to those moments of success and strength. This approach also allows the client to review the video and vicariously experience the exception once again.

Photographs

The use of photography may also be helpful in documenting exceptions. For example, a high school girl who talked about not having friends is asked to photograph those times when she "might" have some friends. Her use of "selfies" showed herself with different people she considered to be friends and discussion ensued regarding the types of friendships she had and reasons that some were closer friends than others.

Sticky Notes

When clients begin to talk about their problems, it is helpful to write each one down on the same colored sticky notes placed on the wall or table. When the therapist asks about exceptions, each exception is written on a different colored sticky note and placed with the others. At the end of the session, the therapist places the sticky notes inside a file folder for the next session. In future sessions, as exceptions continue to be identified, the therapist adds these to the sticky notes in the folder. Eventually, the sticky notes that represent exceptions begin to crowd out the ones that represent problems, giving the client an excellent visual of how strengths overcome challenges.

Masks

Sometimes, people do not show their strengths to others. The use of masks allows clients to identify strengths others may not see. First, using masks purchased or made from heavy stock paper, the therapist asks clients to select pictures from magazines or write words on the outside of the mask that illustrate what others see. The therapist asks clients to consider the positive qualities they possess that most others do not recognize, such as a good work ethic, being helpful to a parent, or the ability to work math problems. Clients choose words or pictures that illustrate these positive qualities and write them or paste them inside the mask. Discussion about the mask centers on what clients want others to know about their strengths, what ways clients could reveal strengths so others would notice, and how the clients' personal strengths can be used to assist others.

Lenses

The following approach highlights the exceptions to the self-critical ways children and adolescents may view themselves. Using a pair of large sunglasses provides an instant prop to help clients consider what they see when they look at themselves through critical lenses or through positive lenses. The therapist states, "These are special glasses. When you look through them, they only see your strengths, talents, and positive qualities. What do people see when they look at you through these glasses?" The therapist explores with the client personal and interpersonal characteristics, strengths and talents, positive personality traits, and possibilities. The therapist discusses with clients how these traits motivate them, how that might be useful or used more often, and how they can replace negative views of themselves.

Relationship Questions

The interactional and systemic influences of family therapy on SF therapy become evident when looking at relationship questions, often used with circular questioning, an approach developed by the Milan Group in family therapy. To gain an understanding of relationships between two family members, the therapist asks a third person about the relationship. For example, if a family comes for family therapy, the therapist asks the teenage son about his view of fighting between his parents. His perspective provides information to the parents who may not realize their conflicts affect their children. Circular questioning includes asking questions about different types of behavior, feelings, beliefs, meaning, and their influences (Brown, 1997). Further, the family members do not need to be present to gain their perspectives. Instead, the therapist asks the client what he thinks the different family members or important others might say in a certain situation.

Relationship questions often consist of three types related to what others notice or see the client doing and what the client does that affects others.

The first relationship question may involve goals, that is what others will see the client doing when the client reaches her goals or who will notice when the client reaches her goals. For example, the therapist asks, "What will your mom see you doing differently when you are doing better in math?" or "What would your mom say you need to be doing so you do better in math?" The second type of relationship question focuses on the client purposely doing something different that would cause others to notice or would convince others that a change occurred. For example, the therapist might ask, "What would you have to do to convince your teacher that you are going to do better in her class?" A third type of relationship question amplifies positive changes, for example, "What did your mom say when you brought home your good grade?"

Asking circular questions, or relationship questions as they are referred to in SF therapy (Nelson, Fleuridas, & Rosenthal, 1986), offers several advantages. First, they lack the judgmental qualities that often accompany linear questions. By asking about someone else's perspective, the client steps back and gains a broader viewpoint. Relationship questions also allow the client to provide information without shame or feelings of guilt. As the therapist asks questions about interactions and their effects on problems and solutions, clients recognize the indirect influence they have on others (Brown, 1997).

When first introduced in family therapy, circular questions served the purpose of locating and hypothesizing about dysfunction in the family system, but, in SF therapy, relationship questions provide a way to address goals and amplify strengths. For example, one child experiencing behavior problems in his elementary classroom while a substitute tried to teach comes to the counselor upset that he had to leave the classroom. Rather than addressing the substitute's complaint, the school counselor asks, "What do you suppose your teacher would say you need to do, so you can return to the classroom?" The child responds without being defensive and states that he needs to not talk so much and stay at his desk.

Relationship questions are particularly valuable in helping clients amplify successes. Consider the following scenario with John, a middle-school adolescent, who has difficulty getting his work done at school and becomes easily distracted by peers.

Counselor: What would be different if you got your work done?
John: I would have more free time after school.
Counselor: What else?
John: I would probably make better grades.
Counselor: If you were making better grades, what do you think your father would say?
John: He would probably say he was proud of me.
Counselor: So your father would be happy about this? What would your mother say?
John: She probably wouldn't say much, but she would cook something I like to eat.

Counselor:	So cooking something you like is a way for your mother to show you she likes what you did. What would this be like for you if your mother and father said and acted this way?
John:	I would be a lot calmer at home. We wouldn't fight so much.
Counselor:	So, if you weren't fighting so much and things were calmer, what would you and your parents be doing?
John:	My dad might take me hunting sometime.

This scenario demonstrates how relationship questions serve to amplify goals and successes and points out the reciprocal influences the client has with others. Once clients realize that their success impacts other relationships rather than just that of the one who sent them, their motivation increases, and the therapist and client become more aware of interpersonal resources.

Relationship questions with children may involve several different types of concrete and creative approaches. By using more concrete materials, clients may view their relationships more objectively and externalize emotional content that may disrupt cognitive processing.

Creative and Playful Approaches for Asking Relationship Questions

Sandtray

Taylor (2009, 2015) discusses the use of sandtray, wherein children select miniatures representing important family members and place them in the sand. When working with children, it is best to have appropriate figures (see suggestions from Homeyer & Sweeney, 2011) from which the child may choose to represent each of the family members, as well as other important people or animals in the child's life. Once the client selects the miniatures, including one that represents the self, the therapist asks SF questions regarding each miniature.

- Who would be the most supportive of you reaching this goal?
- What would this person say to you if you reached your goal?
- What would this person notice you doing differently if you decided to do your school work?
- What would this person say you need to do differently, so that you can get your iPhone back?
- What do you need to do to convince your dad that you can be a responsible person?

With adolescents, miniatures can play a vital role in describing how clients view their support systems. For example, when working with Sam, a young man who had not attended school for several years, I asked him, "Make a sandtray of your family." Sam selected a man, a superhero, and several creatures. He created the sandtray using the entire sandtray but only 6 miniatures. When I asked him about his sandtray, he told me that one of the figures was his father and the others were his siblings, except for the superhero. He pointed to the superhero and said, "That is my counselor. When I am sad or need some place to go, I can always go to Mr. Johnson's office." Sam viewed his counselor as his sole ally at school where he often felt lonely and out of place. Mr. Johnson was his superhero.

Companions and Allies

Some children and adolescents want so badly to be popular that they confuse allies (people they can trust and turn to when needed) and companions (people with whom the client spends time). This activity helps them define who is a companion and who is an ally. Clients begin by listing everyone they know or who they feel is important to them. After defining companions and allies, clients circle in one color everyone they view as an ally. Then, using another color, clients circle those they view as companions. Discussion focuses on what makes an ally and how others important to the client perceive the client, as an ally or as a companion.

Friendship Lifelines

Children and adolescents frequently discuss relationship issues that cause them distress. This activity allows clients to see how there are times when a friend may be difficult but also when being a friend with the same person may be fun or easy, illustrating that friendships do not always stay the same. Using a piece of paper, the therapist draws a straight line across the center and then marks the beginning of the line to represent the beginning of the relationship. The adolescent then places a dot below or above the timeline illustrating when the friendship seems to go well and times when it seems difficult. The client then connects the dots. The therapist explores with the client what is different (the exceptions) when she feels close to her friend.

- What was the client doing differently?
- What about the times when things do not seem to be going well? What is in your control? What seems to be out of your control?
- What would your friend say is different when things are better?

Circles of Support

To examine supportive others in the client's life, the therapist draws three to four circles, from a smaller circle to a larger one nested into one another.

The therapist asks the client to label or draw a representation of the self on the inside of the circle and then circles to represent those from whom she feels the most support in the next circle, then in the next circle those who also support the client but perhaps not directly or as frequently, such as grandparents or friends (Figure 8.1). The therapist asks the client questions to encourage the client to consider resources, such as:

- Who would you go to if you needed help with your homework?
- To whom do you go when you are in trouble?
- To whom do you tell secrets?
- To whom do you go for information about how to do something you don't know how to do at school?
- If you had a serious injury, who would you tell first?
- With whom do you feel you could eat lunch at school?
- If you were going to ask people to do something with you for fun, who might you ask?

Gil et al. (2008) modifies this approach using miniatures. Using larger butcher paper, with the circles drawn on it, the client selects miniatures to

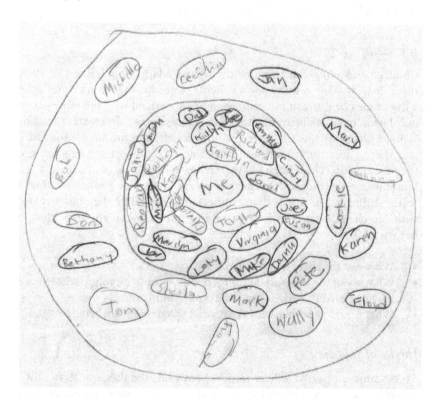

Figure 8.1 Circles of Support.

represent the different levels of influence and support and places them on the different circles.

Facebook and Cell Phone

As therapists look for hidden treasures, using replications of electronic media sources, such as Facebook or text messaging, provide indirect approaches for helping clients talk about their personal strengths. For example, the client states in a Facebook post or text message something that she is good at doing. Then, listing important others, she writes what others say about her strengths (see Figures 7.7 and 7.8).

Complimenting, Encouraging, and Affirming

One of the keys to digging for client treasure involves awakening the client to strengths, positive changes, and resources available (De Jong & Berg, 2013). How we perceive our own strengths and resources often reflects what others notice or have said to us. For example, how does a person know if she is a good singer unless someone tells her or she receives positive feedback? Some strengths and talents may not be so tangible, such as courage and empathy; therefore, the therapist, as she becomes aware of strengths and resources, provides compliments and positive feedback in verbal and nonverbal forms of expression and enthusiasm.

Compliments

The SF therapist uses compliments to: 1) reinforce client strengths, 2) gain more details about these strengths, and 3) focus on what the client sees as important (De Jong & Berg, 2013).

Compliments should be genuine and reality-based, not just offered in efforts to be kind (De Jong & Berg, 2013) or to manipulate behavior. Compliments insincerely offered or given off-handedly result in eroding trust between client and therapist. When the therapist offers a compliment that is sincere by specifically acknowledging the uniqueness of the client, then trust between the client and therapist increases. With children and adolescents, nonverbal approaches to compliments, such as eye contact or closer proximity—or, when working with younger children, a soft touch on the shoulder—may make compliments more effective (Bartholomew, 1993). I have found it can be highly effective when working with a child with disabilities in a classroom to whisper a compliment into the child's ear. In response to this special attention, the child often smiles, but the positive attention also increases the child's status among his peers.

Compliments acknowledge and reinforce clients' strengths, but they also offer an opportunity to gain more information. Not surprisingly, once therapists give a specific compliment, clients most often elaborate on the strength or success, providing important details about how it occurred. De Jong and Berg (2013) group compliments into three types—direct, indirect, and self.

Direct Compliments

Direct compliments tend to be specific, evaluative in nature, focus on what the client can control, and celebrate the child's efforts. For example, Jackson states that he arrived at school on time because he quit playing his video games and got in the car when his mother called him. The therapist states, "That's wonderful! You quit playing, got in the car, and made it to school on time." The therapist, through her voice tone and words, expresses approval of Jackson's success, thus reinforcing it. By complimenting specifically, the therapist also acknowledges the uniqueness of the client and his or her success (De Jong & Berg, 2013).

One of the most problematic direct compliments is, "You are so smart." Although the therapist intends the statement to encourage the client, it may actually discourage the client from trying. After all, if a person is smart, things should come easily, and "being smart" is not necessarily something a person can control. When a "smart" person finds something difficult, she may be quickly discouraged and give up. Instead, the therapist might state, "You worked hard on that project though it was difficult." Another problem with direct compliments is that they can lower motivation. Generic compliments given too frequently may backfire and lead to shorter on-task behaviors, less creative approaches to answering questions, and lower expectations for success (Meyer et al., 1979; Rowe, 1974).

Direct compliments, due to their evaluative nature, tend to carry an undercurrent of obligation, that is, the need to continue to perform the approved behavior or be faced with disapproval by important others. When the therapist uses too much praise or too many direct compliments, they lose their effectiveness or turn intrinsic into extrinsic rewards, so that the individual works only when a direct compliment is given. Over time, the effectiveness of the compliment erodes, and the child's interest in continuing the wanted behavior wanes; therefore, direct compliments should be genuine, focused, and mixed with more effective types of compliments—indirect and self-compliments.

Indirect Compliments

Indirect compliments involve asking questions that give the responsibility for the strength, progress, or talent back to the client. For example, the therapist might ask Jackson, "How did you manage to get to school on time?" This sets the responsibility for success with Jackson, recognizing his personal control and increasing self-efficacy. Further, when the therapist repeats the details of the success, Jackson vicariously practices it once again, thus reinforcing the behavior and making it more likely to reoccur.

Another way to give indirect compliments is through relationship questions. For example, the therapist might ask Jackson, "What did your teacher say about you getting to school on time?" or, "What did your mother think or do when you got into the car right away?" By asking the question from the viewpoint of another person, Jackson sees how his behavior might affect others and gives himself a compliment but from another's perspective. When the therapist asks relationship questions, the client better understands others' perspectives on his strengths, and the therapist gives him permission to talk about his positive qualities without having the social restraints that might consider it "bragging."

Another way to deliver an indirect compliment involves showing interest in clients by asking questions about strengths, coping skills, and resiliencies. By asking children or adolescents about their strengths, they are often eager to tell you about them. However, we must listen intentionally to their answers, paying full attention and asking questions from a not-knowing stance of curiosity, continuing to identify and highlight their strengths.

Another indirect compliment occurs when the counselor says something to the teacher or parent about the client's strengths in the presence of the client. The therapist, sensitive to where and when this occurs, talks about positive things the client does to an important other in the client's life in the presence of the client. This influences the important other to recognize these strengths and hopefully reinforce them as well. By "overhearing" others discuss something positive about the client, the client discovers strengths as perceived by others. Others also begin pairing the compliment with the child, so that the child is perceived by others in a more positive light. However, not all children enjoy being the center of attention, so the therapist must be cautious and sensitive to children who might be upset by being the focus (Bartholomew, 1993).

Self-Compliments

Self-compliments involve questions that emphasize the client's control and allow him to own his successes. For example, the therapist asks Jackson, "What is it about you that you were able to stop playing your video games and get to school on time?" or "What does that say about your ability to do math in that you raised your grade this six weeks?" The child or adolescent learns to identify and apply positive labels for himself and to shake off the negative labels that often diminish self-esteem.

Another approach to helping clients apply self-compliments is to ask the "how" questions, that is, "How were you able to get to school on time?" "How did you make a better grade in math this six weeks?" These questions facilitate discussion of the client's personal actions that lead to success. As the client discusses these successes, the therapist continues the discussion by asking "what else" questions. "What else did you do to make this happen?" Asking "what else" questions allows the client to expand in detail about specific action steps she took to realize the goal.

Compliments in SF therapy are so important that not only are they used throughout the therapy session, but every session ends with a compliment. Compliments encourage the client to take the next step, affirm hard work in the face of challenges, and recognize inherent strengths and possibilities.

Encouragement

Throughout the therapy process, whether it is one session or six sessions, SF therapists encourage. The word "encouragement" stems from the word "heart," meaning that when we encourage we ask the person to "take heart," "to take courage." *Merriam-Webster* (www.merriam-webster.com/dictionary/ encourage) defines encourage as "to inspire with courage, spirit, or hope" or "to spur on." Encouragement fosters hope in the face of challenges, strengthens motivation by recognizing even the smallest step, and focuses on what is possible. Adlerian Therapy makes encouragement a central principle on which it builds its therapeutic process (see Watts & Pietrzak, 2000). Solution-focused therapy involves encouragement within the process of counseling by complimenting the client using direct and indirect compliments, asking the miracle question (which encourages the client to see hoped-for futures), and focusing on solutions using language that implies the problem can be solved (versus "if" the problem can be solved) (Scheel, Davis & Henderson, 2012).

Encouragement can significantly increase children's academic success as well as physical abilities and endurance (Guéguen, Martin & Adrea, 2015). Kelly and Daniels (1997) find that children prefer teachers who encourage rather than just praise them and may see the teacher who praises as manipulative and controlling. This same study indicates that many adolescents prefer encouragement to praise, perhaps due to their developmental age, since this stage of life often finds adolescents disengaging from adults and their requests as they enter the identity formation stage of development.

Affirmation

The most important quality of a relationship is affirmation, defined as "something affirmed: a positive assertion." We affirm others when we pay attention to them, call them by name, and show a personal interest in who they are. Those who affirm us let us know that we are accepted regardless of our problems, insecurities, accomplishments, differences, or challenges. To affirm my niece, I lean over her wheelchair close to her face and speak a kind word. She responds by reaching up and touching my face. For my teenage niece, affirmation means responding to text messages and letting her know I am supporting her.

Our clients, many of whom are dealing with abuse, neglect, and severe challenges, require affirmation first. For those most in need, affirmation may be all that is required to help them feel strong enough to overcome their problems. "Students who need attention may not need encouragement, evaluation, or guidance. Maybe, all we need to do is recognize their existence" (Bartholomew, 1993, p. 41).

Creative and Playful Approaches to Uncover Treasures

Sandtray

Using sandtray and miniatures, the therapist asks clients to select miniatures that represent important others in their lives, including family, friends, pets, and teachers. The therapist asks the client what each miniature would say is one thing that the person likes, admires, or sees as a strength about the client. As the client discusses what each would say, the therapist listens intensely, asks the client details about when and where these strengths occur, and uses similar terms to compliment the client and point out strengths in the future.

Figure 8.2 Arthur's Trophy.

Mining for Treasure

Using small colored gems in a sandtray, the therapist asks the child to search for the "buried treasure." When the child finds it, she describes a personal strength. Buried treasure also includes strengths the client uses or has used in the past, people who befriend or assist the client, and tools that help the client with strengths, such as a computer for doing math, tennis shoes for running, or paper and pencils for drawing.

Trophy or Award

The therapist asks the client to create an award or trophy using paper, pens, colors, markers, and various objects, such as boxes, cans, plastic bottles, rocks, sticks, or other common objects. The therapist relates the following scenario: "You have just won a trophy. You won it because you demonstrated a strength or talent. Create your trophy." The therapist inquires about how the client was able to win the trophy, details that describe the situation(s), who knows about it, and how the client might use that strength again.

Arthur first built a trophy of legos and then drew it. As he drew, he discussed learning about a new technique, "scratchboard," incorporating the skill into his drawing (Figure 8.2).

Body Image

Few feel satisfied with their physical appearance and often judge themselves based on how they look, overlooking positive aspects about themselves. Unfortunately, when we look in the mirror, we tend to screen out the good and see the bad. This exercise is meant to screen out the bad to see the good.

Using butcher paper, trace the child's body. If working with adolescents, you might use a precut generic picture of a body on a piece of paper. Ask the client to draw in whatever details she wishes to draw. Then, as the session continues, the client adds more features. When complete, talk about those areas that the client feels good about by asking questions, such as:

- When someone has given you a compliment, what is it that he or she would mostly likely describe? This compliment does not have to be a physical characteristic but the part of the body that is helpful in using strengths, such as a hand that allows a person to play the piano.
- What part of your body do you use the most, and how is it helpful to you?
- Which part of your body is the strongest? What makes it so strong?
- If your friend/parent/teacher was here, what would he/she say is your best feature?
- Which part(s) of your body helps you the most in school/home/other?
- Which part of your body helps you the most when you are upset?
- Which part of your body do you rely on when you need help?
- Which part(s) of your body show that you are happy?

Photography

Photography appeals to all ages and tends to break down barriers for those with disabilities or severe psychiatric disorders. One of the ways to use photography in therapy is to ask clients to bring pictures of themselves and their families. Pictures might be paper copies or digital copies on their iPhones or iPads. Children or adolescents often respond positively and quickly engage where verbal approaches might not be as effective. Photos also provide a way to look at client strengths and resources. When looking at the picture, the therapist comments on the quality of the picture, for example, "This picture really highlights the colors of the flower," or "I like how you have used lighting to show the colors of his eyes." A second way to use photos as a source of finding treasure involves commenting on the relationship the photographer might have with the client. For example, if the picture shows the client smiling, the therapist might state, "You seem to be happy in this picture." "Who was the photographer? Was she someone you liked?" "What were your thoughts when this picture was taken?" The therapist also encourages the client to bring pictures of himself engaged in some activity or with others, which also provides information about the client's strengths and resources.

Puppets

Puppets can be useful in helping the client to compliment herself and talk about her best qualities. For example, Cici, a five-year-old of a mother who recently gave birth to Cici's baby brother, talks about her frustration but also her strengths through puppets. She selects the pony puppet for herself, the elephant puppet for the therapist, the puppy puppet for her baby brother, and the kangaroo puppet for her mother. Cici and the therapist discuss what it is like with the new baby.

Cici:	My mom has a baby. His name is Juan. This is Juan (holding the puppy puppet).
Therapist:	Tell me about Juan.
Cici:	Juan cries a lot and throws up a lot. Sometimes, Juan makes mom cry. (Uses a kangaroo and shakes it at the puppy stating, "Juan, it's okay. Don't cry.") (Cici tears up.)
Therapist:	It is upsetting to talk about this.
Cici:	Yea, because I can't help mom, because she is upset, so I try to keep Juan from crying, but he doesn't always stop crying.
Therapist:	You try to help mom by helping Juan.
Cici:	Mom doesn't know how to keep Juan from crying. That's why she gets upset. She gets tired.
Therapist:	Mom is tired and gets upset. When mom gets upset, you get a little upset too. How do you handle it when you get upset?

Cici:	I just go to my room, sometimes, to get away from it and play with my dolls.
Therapist:	You found a way to get away from the crying. How is that helpful?
Cici:	I can do something else and then just forget about the crying. Sometimes, when I come out, things are better. I am going to put Juan here (puts the Juan puppet out to the side and then places the mother puppet next to her puppet).
Therapist:	So you figured something to do when Juan cries. You are sitting close to mom now.
Cici:	Yea, I like to sit close to mom, but Juan is always there.
Therapist:	When are sometimes you get to sit close to mom?
Cici:	At church and sometimes at night mom gets in bed and cuddles with me if Juan goes to sleep early.
Therapist:	It sounds like you have a good relationship with mom.
Cici:	Yea, we used to play a lot, but now Juan needs her.
Therapist:	You don't get to play as much with mom because Juan needs her. When are some times you get to play with mom?
Cici:	When Juan takes a nap, mom will sometimes play with me with my doll house. We like to pretend a lot.
Therapist:	So sometimes you and mom get to play with your doll house. It sounds like that is a good time for you.
Cici:	Yea. It is fun.
Therapist:	When are some other times you get to play with your doll house?
Cici:	When my friend, Anna, comes over.
Therapist:	Which of the puppets can be Anna?

As this session continues, the therapist asks Cici about her friendship with Anna, how Anna provides someone else to play with as well as her mother. The therapist compliments Cici on her understanding that the baby requires more of her mother's time and asks how Cici might spend more time with her mother and Juan.

Cici:	I sometimes help my mom rock Juan.
Therapist:	So, you help the baby to relax?
Cici:	Yea, I guess. I sing to him. He likes it when I sing to him.
Therapist:	So when you sing to him, he seems happy.
Cici:	Yea, he smiles. Sometimes, mom and I sing to him when she gives him a bath. It helps him calm down.
Therapist:	It sounds like you are good at singing to him.
Cici:	Yea. I can read to him too. I don't read hard books, but I read little books, you know, for babies. He is too little to read big books to him.
Therapist:	Wow! You sing to him and read to Juan. Show me how that looks with your puppets.
Cici:	(Cici picks up the puppy puppet and holds it like a baby.) It's OK Juan. It's OK.

Therapist: You seem to know just how to hold the baby. How did you learn to
          do that?
Cici: My mom showed me.

Throughout the session, Cici demonstrated understanding of the difficulties
her mother had in taking care of Juan but also found ways to talk about her
personal strengths, so that the therapist recognized her strengths and asked
questions to expand on them. Through indirect compliments and recognition
of strengths, Cici began to recognize ways to spend time with her mother and
use positive behaviors to help her cope with the new baby.

Scaling Questions

In SF therapy, scaling serves several purposes: setting goals, assessment of
progress, and as an intervention to compliment and encourage the client to
continue with changes (de Shazer & Dolan, 2007; Shilts & Gordon, 1996). The
therapist might use scaling to compare different points in time to reinforce
progress (Lethem, 2002). Solution-focused therapy incorporates scaling questions (SQs) into therapy, because clients find SQs make it easier to explain their
progress and perspectives (De Jong & Berg, 2013).

Scaling questions offer several advantages. Through a simple number, the
client communicates an amazing amount of information about his well-being,
success, motivation, coping skills, and other areas of focus, as well as progress.
For example, if a client states he is a 4 on a scale from 0 to 10, then the client
is not a 0, 1, 2, or 3. Therefore, the client must be doing something that makes
him better than any of the lower numbers. If the client states he is a 0, then the
client is using resources (internal and external) to cope, so the therapist asks,
"How have you managed to cope considering how difficult things are right
now?" No matter what the number, the client provides significant information
about himself.

Scaling questions often disarm fears and anxiety, so that more reluctant clients participate. Softas-Nall and Francis (1998) describe the use of scaling as a
way to reach and engage a client contemplating suicide. By answering the SQ,
the client communicates to the therapist perceptions about her challenges, giving the opportunity for the therapist to validate the client and her experiences,
enhancing trust and encouraging further discussion.

Scaling provides a reliable measure of progress and therapy success
(Fischer, 2011). The therapist asks clients SQs to measure motivation, opti-
mism, and effort, and to assess multiple problems and their solutions, and
uses relationship questions to provide different perspectives and priorities for
clients (Iveson, 2002). For example, when clients present several concerns,
the therapist scales their concerns regarding which would be most helpful to
work on first.

Scaling takes place in the context of conversation, making it an interactional
experience between at least two people (Berg & de Shazer, 1993). The objectivity

of SQs and their ability to be defined by the client offer the advantage of allowing clients to relay their perceptions without the therapist imposing his ideas (Strong, Pyle & Sutherland, 2009).

SF therapists find SQs useful with different populations, including individuals, couples, families, and groups; parents and children; and teachers, leaders, and organization members. Since most people easily understand their meaning, they can be crafted to fit most any situation. Medical staff frequently use scaling to assess patients' pain levels, sometimes using pictures for those who are unable to speak English and to help patients have a better idea of what each number means.

In SF therapy, the therapist asks SQs in such a way that the lower number represents the negative aspects and qualities and the higher numbers represent more positive aspects (Iveson, 2002). For example, a middle school counselor asks Paul, "On a scale of 0 to 10, with 0 being you do not think you can bring your grade up at all, and 10 being you are positive you can bring your grade up, where do you see yourself?" Paul answers,

> I think I am a 5. I think I can bring it up if I can just find a good place to study. Sometimes it is easy to study at home, but other times I'm having to watch my brother or the television is on. Sometimes, I just don't want to do my work because I am sick of school.

The counselor responds,

> That's great that you are a 5. I think it is amazing you can find places to study and do your work. I know it's not always easy, but you are making progress. So, when you come back next week, and you say you are a 6, what will you be doing different?

The scale may initially be created by the therapist, but the client should be the one who defines the anchors and points in between. This can be done verbally, concretely, and symbolically. Further, as with the WOWW (Working on What Works) program created by Berg and Shilts (2005), the client can define the meaning of each number rather than just the anchors of the scale. When the client defines each number, the client and therapist know when progress occurs and goals are reached.

One of the main advantages of SQs is their ability to be made concrete, so that the client who may not be as competent in oral or written language might communicate through numbers and their representations. Charlés (2010) describes working with a new mother and her newborn in a war-torn region of Africa where families are not only affected by constant fighting but also by disease and malnutrition. Communication is difficult, since the workers do not have a good command of the native language; however, through the use of a translator and the mother using her fingers to scale, Charlés uses scaling questions as a way to assess whether the mother believes that her child can survive.

Scaling questions offer younger clients the advantage of making what seems abstract more concrete and simple to answer, so that even one word or representation of that word provides a great deal of information about the status of the problem, its solution, client motivation, and other client dispositions. Children, feeling less threatened, can answer with one word or gesture, and provide their perspectives without fear of reprisal. After all, children have a legitimate view of solutions, so, even in the company of adults, SQs provide their viewpoint without focusing on the problem (De Jong & Berg, 2013).

When working with a child, the therapist may assist the client in creating a visual and tangible scale, being sensitive to the client's preference in the type of scale, the client's developmental age in determining how many end points, and how the client perceives progress. For younger children, the scale may only go from 0 to 5; whereas, for older children and adolescents, the scale may go from 0 to 10. Interestingly, the child often starts thinking about the scale even before the session begins. For example, one little first-grade boy ran into the school counselor's office and announced, "I am a 6," obviously having given it some thought on his way down the hall.

Creative and Playful Approaches for Asking Scaling Questions

Sandtray

Using miniatures to scale provides a concrete way to represent each number from the viewpoint of the child or adolescent. Miniatures representative of sports provide a way to scale and measure progress concretely. For example, soccer players moving down the field (sandtray) trying to get their ball to the net on the other side provide an example of progress, who might be able to assist in making progress, and even defining what the goal is. The therapist should have ample miniatures of different sports so the client can choose which sport to represent progress in reaching her goal.

Miniatures, instead of numbers, can be used to scale how children or adolescents view their current status and progress. For example, Taylor (2009) asked an adolescent during his first session to scale where he is now using the miniatures. The young man lays out the miniatures so that the donkey takes the lowest point of the scale, and the batman is the highest point of the scale (Figure 8.3). Dell (2017) finds children to be more honest and talk more about their scale if they use miniatures to answer scaling questions than if they answered verbally.

Personal Scale

Clients can create their personal scales using a variety of materials. For example, Beth, using an arrow template, illustrates what progress means to her (Figure 8.4). The therapist keeps the scale, so that each time she visits, Beth can point out where she is in reaching her goal.

Figure 8.3 Using Sandtray and Miniatures to Scale.

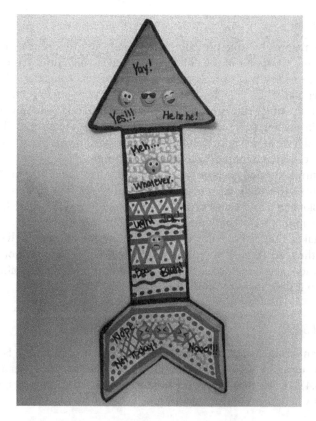

Figure 8.4 Scaling Arrow Created from Template.

Racing

The therapist provides a track drawn on a large piece of butcher paper to illustrate progress toward the goal. The type of race depends on the interest of the client. For example, if the client talks about running, then progress is discussed as the client places a marker for where he is each session as he progresses around the track to reach the finish line. The therapist might use miniature cars or bicycles to represent different types of races. Racing provides an opportunity to discuss obstacles that need to be overcome using the metaphors of the race, such as hurdles (obstacles the client has to jump), climbing up a hill (not easy to reach the goal), or a tire blowing out (events that set the client back). Images provide specific ways for clients to represent themselves and focus on progress, and for the therapist to normalize setbacks as the client progresses.

Faces

This technique provides a way for younger children to express their current feelings about reaching their goals. Commonly, therapists use a standard expression chart and ask children to select which face they are at the end of each session to chart their progress over time. This provides an opportunity to discuss what progress looks like and the role of the client in making the progress happen.

Rather than asking children to identify faces, the therapist asks the client to draw a picture on a paper plate of what her face looks like now and then, using a second paper plate, what her face will look like when she reaches her goal. At the beginning of the following sessions, the therapist assesses the client's progress by asking her to draw a face on another paper plate that represents where she is on her goal. Each time the child returns, the therapist lays out the paper plates and talks about what is different now from the session before and how her current status differs from the first session. The therapist continues to ask questions to gain more details about how these differences occur, if positive, and what will be different when the client returns. The therapist also asks how the face she draws will be different when the client no longer needs to come to therapy and inquires about details of those differences, including what others will notice.

Gingerbread Person

One of the most useful approaches for scaling is the adaptation of Terry Kottman's (1999) use of scaling using gingerbread men. Although she used drawings of gingerbread men to scale children's view of Adler's 4 Cs (capable, courage, count, and connect) (Kottman, 1999), the SF therapist can use gingerbread people to scale different aspects of the client's life at the same time, as well as to set goals. For example, the therapist might ask the client to color in the gingerbread person to represent how well things are going at home and at school. If the client colors in half of the gingerbread person, the therapist asks if the client colored just a little bit more, what the client would be doing differently.

Each gingerbread person represents different aspects of the same goal, such as motivation, confidence, and progress.

Gauge

A gauge offers a unique approach for scaling different types of challenges and successes that may not be amenable to a vertical or horizontal scale. The therapist creates a gauge by attaching a cutout paper arrow using a brad to a half circle (could be paper or a paper plate cut in half) representing the gauge. The gauge measures the client's success by moving from low on one side to high on the other side. Colors may be used to illustrate positive and negative areas of the gauge. A gauge is often useful for measuring dispositions such as joy, anger, anxiety, peace, or fear. The therapist might also use it to create goals and help the client to move the arrow to a manageable level by asking questions, such as "What are you doing when you are closer to the middle of the gauge rather than so far to the right?"

Music

Music scales offer a unique approach for scaling. With lower notes representing less progress and upper notes representing more progress, clients use the notes on the music scale to scale their personal status and progress. Another way to use music in scaling involves the use of volume, where soft sounds represent less progress and louder sounds represent more progress. Normal tones represent status quo. A third approach for using music to scale involves asking clients to select songs that represent different points on the scale. For example, the client might select a song that has happy lyrics or melodic tones to represent progress, such as "Happy" by Pharrell Williams. A list of songs and their lyrics made available to clients allows clients freedom to choose which songs fit for them on that particular day.

Ski Run

A map of a ski run offers an interesting approach to scaling, particularly with adolescents. Ski runs generally start in the same place at the top of the mountain, and use illustrations of different paths, according to difficulty, to get to the bottom. Unlike the typical scaling approaches, getting to the bottom is the goal rather than getting to the top. However, the ski run offers a metaphorical example of the many paths that one can choose to reach the goal, some more difficult and others less challenging. Clients describe the different paths they might take to reach their goal considering advantages and disadvantages of choosing the challenging and less-challenging paths.

Subway Map

A subway map, similar to a map of the ski run, offers different paths for getting to one's destination or the goal. The client creates smaller goals indicated by each stop on the subway, but also uses the subway map to chart progress getting to the goal. Sometimes, riding a subway requires changing subway trains to get to a certain destination. These metaphorically stand for the decisions clients make when obstacles get in the way of reaching goals. The therapist selects from several questions including:

- What choices do you have that might help you reach your destination?
- When you are trying to reach your goal and you find that you cannot go the way you had hoped, what can you do?
- If you get to one of your destinations and find out it isn't going to be helpful to be there, what can you do to change direction? How do you get back on the train and go in a different direction? What might be an advantage of going in another direction?

Nature Walk

The client creates a nature walk using a variety of materials, including markers, watercolors, chalk, and three-dimensional objects that can be glued to complete the picture, such as small pebbles, wood, clay, or grass. The therapist states,

> I want you to pretend you are going for a nature walk. Think about where you are going to start and then where you are going to end. It might be anywhere, at a park, the beach, in a forest, or in the neighborhood. You can use any of the materials we have for your picture.

Once the client completes the picture, the therapist talks about what each part of the walk entails and how it relates to where the client is now in the process of reaching his goals. For example, if the client creates a path through the woods, the therapist asks, "How would you describe this in terms of where you are now in reaching your goal?" "What do you need to do to prepare for the next stop along the path?" "What will it mean when you reach your goal?"

Many other creative and play-based approaches offer different alternatives for scaling, such as the use of a ladder, blocks, rulers, beads, or a thermometer. For example, a counselor in a high school places a large laminated poster of a thermometer on her wall. When a student comes to visit the student places a mark by the number representing her current status. Just by making the mark, the counselor reports that the student tends to engage more readily in counseling. Another more active approach to scaling includes using stairs, where the client walks up and down the stairs and discusses their current and future status. Concrete and expressive approaches to scaling appear to be unlimited and offer a variety of ways for the therapist to adapt scaling to the client's developmental level with consideration for the client's understanding and interests.

Treasure seeking is an ongoing process of asking questions out of genuine interest and a strengths perspective. Through creative and playful approaches, the therapist and client find strengths and resources that enable them to find solutions.

References

Bartholomew, D. (1993). Effective strategies for praising students. *Music Educators Journal, 80*(3), 40–43.

Berg, I. K. & de Shazer, S. (1993). Making numbers talk: Language in therapy. In S. Friedman (Ed.), *The new constructive collaboration language in psychotherapy of change*, pp. 5–24. New York, NY: Guilford.

Berg, I. K. & Shilts, L. (2005). *Classroom solutions: WOWW coaching*. Milwaukee, WI: BFTC Press.

Bronfenbrenner, U. (1979). *The ecology of human development: Experiments by nature and design*. Cambridge, MA: Harvard University Press.

Brown, J. (1997). Circular questioning: An introductory guide. *A.N.Z.J. Family Therapy, 18*(2), 109–114.

Charlés, L. L. (2010). Family therapists as front line mental health providers in war-affected regions: Using reflecting teams, scaling questions, and family members in a hospital in Central Africa. *Journal of Family Therapy, 32*(1), 27–42.

De Jong, P. & Berg, I. K. (2013). *Interviewing for solutions* (4th Ed.). Belmont, CA: Brooks/Cole.

de Shazer, S. & Dolan, Y. (2007). *More than miracles*. Binghamton, NY: Haworth Press.

Dell, K. (2017). *Less talk, more action: The integration of small figures in a solution-focused counselling practice with children* (unpublished master's thesis). University of Canterbury, Christchurch, NZ.

Fischer, R. L. (2011). Assessing client change in individual and family counseling. *Research in Social Work Practice, 14*(2), 102–111.

Fisk, D. L. (1994). A second look: Photography as an experiential and therapeutic tool. *Experiential education: A critical resource for the 21st century*. Proceedings from the Manual of the Annual Interactional Conference of the Association for Experiential Education, Austin, TX. Abstract retrieved from: https://files.eric.ed.gov/fulltext/ED377016.pdf.

Gil, E., McGoldrick, M., Gerson, R. & Suili, P. (2008). Family play genograms. In M. McGoldrick, R. Gerson & P. Suili (Eds), *Genograms: Assessment and intervention*, pp. 257–274. New York, NY: W. W. Norton.

Guéguen, N., Martin, A. & Adrea, C. R. (2015). "I am sure you'll succeed": When a teacher's verbal encouragement of success increases children's academic performance. *Learning and Motivation, 52*, 54–59.

Henry Miller Quotes (n.d.). BrainyQuote.com. Retrieved January 28, 2018, from: BrainyQuote.com.

Homeyer, L. E. & Sweeney, D. S. (2011). *Sandtray therapy* (2nd Ed.). New York, NY: Taylor & Francis.

Iveson, C. (2002). Solution-focused brief therapy. *Advances in Psychiatric Treatment, 8*(2), 149–156.

Kelly, F. D. & Daniels, J. G. (1997). The effects of praise versus encouragement on children's perceptions of teachers. *Individual Psychology, 53*(1), 331–341.

Kottman, T. (1999). Integrating the crucial Cs into Adlerian Play Therapy. *The Journal of Individual Psychology, 55*(2), 288–297.

Lethem, J. (2002). Brief solution focused therapy. *Child and Adolescent Mental Health, 7*(4), 189–192.

Melidonis, G. G. & Bry, B. H. (1995). Effects of therapist exceptions questions on blaming and positive statements in families with adolescent behavior problems. *Journal of Family Psychology, 9*(4), 451–457.

Merriam-Webster (n.d.). Encouragement [definition]. Retrieved from: www.merriam-webster.com/dictionary.

Meyer, W., Bachman, M., Hempelman, M., Ploger, F. & Spiller, H. (1979). The informational value of evaluative behavior: Influence of praise and blame on perceptions of ability. *Journal of Educational Psychology, 71*(2), 259–268.

Murphy, J. J. & Davis, M. W. (2005). Video exceptions: An empirical case study involving a child with developmental disabilities. *Journal of Systemic Therapies, 24*(4), 66–79.

Nelson, T. S., Fleuridas, C. & Rosenthal, D. M. (1986). The evolution of circular questions: Training family therapists. *Journal of Marital and Family Therapy, 12*(2), 113–127.

Rowe, M. (1974). Relation of wait-time and rewards to the development of language, logic and fate control: Part II—Rewards. *Journal of Research in Science Training, 11*(4), 215–224.

Scheel, M. J., Davis, C. K. & Henderson, J. D. (2012). Therapist use of client strengths: A qualitative study of positive processes. *The Counseling Psychologist, 41*(3), 392–427.

Shilts, L. & Gordon, A. B. (1996). What to do after the miracle occurs. *Journal of Family Psychotherapy, 7*(1), 15–22.

Softas-Nall, B. & Francis, P. C. (1998). A solution-focused approach to a family with a suicidal member. *The Family Journal: Counseling and Therapy for Couples and Families, 6*(3), 227–230.

Strong, T. & Pyle, N. R. (2011). Negotiating exceptions to clients' problem discourse in consultation dialogue. *Psychology and Psychotherapy: Theory, Research and Practice, 85*, 100–116.

Strong, T., Pyle, N. R. & Sutherland, O. (2009). Scaling questions: Asking and answering them in counseling. *Counselling Psychology Quarterly, 22*(2), 171–185.

Taylor, E. R. (2009). Sandtray and solution-focused therapy. *International Journal of Play Therapy, 18*, 56–68.

Taylor, E. R. (2015). Solution-focused sandtray for children. In H. G. Kaduson & C. E. Schaeffer (Eds.), *Short-term play therapy for children* (3rd Ed.), pp. 150–174. New York, NY: Guilford Press.

Watts, R. E. & Pietrzak, D. (2000). Aderian "encouragement" and the therapeutic process of solution-focused brief therapy. *Journal of Counseling and Development, 78*(4), 442–447.

Wehr, T. (2010). The phenomenology of exception times: Qualitative differences between problem-focused and solution-focused interventions. *Applied Cognitive Psychology, 24*, 467–480.

CHAPTER 9

The Miracle Question and other Goal-Setting Techniques

Elizabeth R. Taylor, Amanda Allison, and Becky Southard

Jeremy ran into my room followed closely behind by the principal trying to make sure he came in. Jeremy, a 7-year-old, blonde, blue-eyed boy often displayed disruptive behavior in the classroom and on the playground. He demonstrated difficulty following instructions, impulsively striking out at others without warning, and kept everyone on their toes trying to rein him in. He lived at the air base with his father and his third stepmother. Yet, he performed in school at grade level and sometimes above, having excellent handwriting, physical prowess, and reading skills. His math skills were on grade level. His mother seemed kind and demonstrated a willingness to work with me to help him. I never met his father. His behavior became a campus disruption when he threw a rock at a car that caused a minor accident. When I asked what he wanted to be different, he stated that he wanted friends in a way that made me think he had stated this before or heard someone else voice their concerns about him. I asked him again, "What else do you want to be different?" His reply startled me, "I want my dad to quit hitting me and my mom."

The miracle question (MQ), a question unique to SFT, became one of the three main techniques used by SF therapists (Hillyer, 1996) and one used to set the stage for developing client goals. It was conceived when a client of Insoo Kim Berg noted that "maybe only a miracle will help, but I suppose that is too much to expect" (De Jong & Berg, 2013, p. 91). Berg followed up with, "OK, suppose a miracle happened, and the problem that brought you here was solved. What would be different about your life?" (p. 91). The client described a different kind of future than she had been discussing, a realistic future nonetheless. Impressed with what had occurred, de Shazer, who was watching behind the one-way mirror, and Berg developed and formalized the MQ process (De Jong & Berg, 2013).

The MQ serves several purposes; however, the main purpose, providing a goal that can be broken down into small, concrete, and realistic steps, provides the client and therapist with an understanding of what it looks like when the problem is solved (Shilts & Gordon, 1996). As the client answers the MQ and imagines possibilities, he experiences a sense of control over the problem.

The MQ also prepares the client for more exception questions and an opportunity to build a progressive story toward times when things are better rather than a digressive story focusing on problems (Korman, 2006; de Shazer & Dolan, 2007). The MQ provides an approach for working with the client in his or her frame of reference, respecting the client's perceptions of the solution, using the client's language, and giving credit to the client for his or her strengths and resources.

For example, when the therapist asked the MQ of an adolescent referred to the school counselor due to poor grades, he stated, "My parents would not be fighting anymore." Now with new information, the therapist discussed with the client his concerns about his parents and possible solutions. Instead of setting his immediate goals around academics, his primary goal was to talk to his mother about how the fighting affected him at home and how it affected his school work. After role playing how to talk with his mother, he successfully visited with her about his concerns. Later, he worked with the therapist to find resources to help him with academics.

Although the standard approach would be to ask the MQ early in the first session, doing so may not always be appropriate. For example, Bliss and Bray (2009) describe how a mother spent the first three sessions of therapy discussing her 22 years of challenges in raising her son with autism. To focus on strengths and hopes would have invalidated the hard work and difficult circumstances this mother described. Further, by allowing the mother to talk about her challenging life, the therapist better appreciated her struggles but also her strengths.

The therapist asks the MQ any time during the first session but usually rather early in the session (De Jong & Berg, 2013), so that the rest of the session focuses on the details, steps, and strategies of realizing the miracle. The discussion of the miracle becomes an interactional unfolding of a hypothetical situation, involving three phases: a) introducing the MQ, b) asking the MQ, and c) breaking the miracle down into smaller goals.

Phase 1: Introducing the MQ

To introduce the MQ, the therapist prepares the client by starting with some small word, such as "so" or "OK," to help clients make the conversational shift to a different type of question (Strong & Pyle, 2009). Then, the therapist prepares the client by stating something like, "So, Jack, I want to ask you a strange question. Would that be OK with you?" This question provides a further shift in the client's attention from the previous conversation to a new type of interaction. By letting the client know it is a "strange" question, the client mentally prepares for something unusual. Sometimes, I breathe audibly and with a little louder voice state, "We are going to have some fun by using our imaginations! Are you ready?"

For some clients, a better strategy might be to interweave the MQ into the conversation, since they may find it difficult to handle the abrupt shift in the conversation. When working with an adolescent, finally gaining her trust to enter into a conversation seems like a major accomplishment. It may be difficult to gain the trust and respect of the adolescent, so introducing the miracle question with a dramatic flair may appear demeaning or inappropriate for the client's age. Interweaving the miracle into the conversation makes it appear part of a therapeutic process and not something that challenges the client's participation.

Phase 2: Asking the MQ

After the short pause in preparation for the MQ, the therapist presents the MQ to the client slowly, dramatically, and with pauses, so the client processes and experiences the miracle as it unfolds. This new reality, where the problem that brought the client to therapy is solved, becomes a negotiation of language between client and therapist, whether verbally or nonverbally. As the therapist asks the MQ, he watches the client carefully for understanding and receptiveness to see how the client perceives and interprets the question (De Jong & Berg, 2013; Strong & Pyle, 2009).

The therapist tailors the MQ to the client so that the child or adolescent imagines the sequence of events as the therapist asks the question. For this reason, it is important to get to know the client before asking the MQ, particularly with children and adolescents who often are grounded in the concrete and have problems with the "miracle" aspect or with the length of the question. By knowing some details about the child's life, the therapist tailors the first part of the question to the specific client. For example, a child says that he goes home and gets a snack then plays with his dog outside before getting ready for bed. The therapist weaves this information into the MQ, providing a context to which the child can relate. The following example tailors MQ (de Shazer, 1988) to the client (see bracketed text). When personalizing the MQ, it is important to be brief or the client may be unable to follow.

> Now, I want to ask you a strange question. Suppose that [tonight you go home, play with your dog for a while, take a bath, and go to bed and] while you are sleeping tonight and the entire house is quiet, a miracle happens. The miracle is that the problem which brought you here is solved. However, because you are sleeping, you don't know that the miracle has happened. So, when you wake up tomorrow morning, what will be different that will tell you that a miracle has happened and the problem which brought you here is solved?
>
> (de Shazer, 1988, p. 5)

The MQ sets into motion client imagination, motivation, and possibility, allowing the client to experience hope and life without the problem.

However, since the original MQ caters to adults and adolescents, the therapist can choose to shorten and simplify it to make it more effective for children.

So let's pretend that you go home, play with your dog, take a bath, and go to bed and fall asleep. Show me what that looks like when you sleep. OK, you are laying just like that with your eyes closed. While your eyes are closed, a miracle happens, just like that! (finger snap). You wake up and the problem is solved. What is different now that your problem is solved?

An even shorter approach might be:

Let's pretend there's a miracle, and the problem is gone. What's different now that your problem is solved?

This shorter version might be most appropriate when interweaving the MQ into the conversation. Being so much shorter in length, children of younger developmental ages can better follow the question and understand it.

As noted with Jeremy who wanted his father's abuse to stop, when children and adolescents answer the MQ, their answers may not be related to the problem for which they were referred. Since youth are often mandated clients, the referring person often sends the client to therapy for academic or acting out behaviors; yet, that might not be the problem from the client's perspective. Since the MQ does not point to any specific issue, the client often states something surprising.

Since the MQ is somewhat abstract and a shift from normal conversation, the therapist focuses on how the client hears and understands the question. Some children may have difficulty imagining a different future due to cognitive limitations (Bliss & Bray, 2009). If the child or adolescent does not understand after one or two repetitions, the therapist should not continue to try to get the child to answer as this can become frustrating for the client who may feel that he is not pleasing the therapist. Insisting on an answer is not congruent with SF therapy and does not help the child in capitalizing on his or her strengths.

However, the MQ may be asked more concretely using more expressive materials. Having multiple options for using any of the SF techniques allows clients to use their own language, skills, and communication preferences to address what they want to be different. Therapists should remain flexible to alternative wording (de Shazer & Dolan, 2007) but also to other expressive and playful approaches to asking future-focused questions. Keep in mind that the purpose of the MQ is to "build well-formed goals within their frame of reference, to explore an alternative future, affirm those helpful things that clients are already doing, and invite them to amplify their successes" (De Jong & Berg, 2013, p. 107). This calls for the use of developmentally friendly approaches that consider children and adolescents' developmental levels, trauma histories, and interests.

The following (Table 9.1) illustrates the interesting twists that often present themselves when working with younger clients and the need for the therapist to remain flexible. Ariel, age seven, wants her brother to play with her, but, over the course of the session, it becomes evident that although that is what she first states, her desire is for others to play with her as well. She draws her miracle and continues to add to it as we talk, keeping her focused and considering possibilities.

Table 9.1 Ariel's Miracle Question.

Therapist:	Let's suppose that tonight you go home and go to sleep and a miracle happens, only you don't know the miracle happened.
Ariel:	Like Jesus turned water into wine?
Therapist:	Sort of like that.
Ariel:	Like it was a dream?
Therapist:	Right, so when you wake up in the morning the problem that you have is gone. Draw what you will notice is different when this miracle happens. Tell me about your picture.
Ariel:	So, this is Rick and he gets up and he has Candyland, and he says, "Ariel, do you want to play a game with me?"
Therapist:	That's you? So, Rick is going to ask you to play Candyland with him?
Ariel:	(Nods her head.)
Therapist:	How often does that happen?
Ariel:	Not very often.
Therapist:	What's different when that does happen?
Ariel:	I am more happy. If he wants to play a game with me, I would always say yes.
Therapist:	So, you are always ready to play.
Ariel:	I even say, "Hey, Rick do you want to play a game with me?" And he doesn't even respond because of the red tablet.
Therapist:	Tell me more about that.
Ariel:	He's playing with robots and other games on the red tablet. I can't play it. It's too scary.
Therapist:	If Rick played with you and you were real happy, who would notice?
Ariel:	Rick and me.
Therapist:	What would your mom say if Rick was playing with you?
Ariel:	She'd say, "Hey, good. I can have the tablet now."
Therapist:	So, Rick would let her have the red tablet. What would your dad say if Rick started playing with you?
Ariel:	Hey, good! You're playing with your sister.
Therapist:	Your dad would be happy you are playing with Rick. What would you be doing differently if Rick was playing with you?
Ariel:	I don't play with the red tablet that much, but I would probably say, "Hey, Rick, I am going to go play over here," but I would go play with the red tablet.
Therapist:	So, you wouldn't let him know you were playing with the red tablet. You don't want him to get upset, so you would go somewhere he can't see you to play with it. (Number line is drawn on paper and the therapist points to the ends of the scale.) So, on a scale of 0 to 5, 0 being he never plays a game with you and 5 being he plays with you all the time, how much does he play with you?
Ariel:	Sometimes, he plays with me. On rainy days.
Therapist:	So how much would you say he plays with you? (Therapist points to each number) 1 never, 2 just a little bit, 3 a lot of times, 4 most of the time, 5 all of the time.
Ariel:	2

Therapist:	2, so just a little bit. What would be different if it was a 3?
Ariel:	He wouldn't be on the red tablet as often. Maybe one day the red tablet and another day play with me.
Therapist:	So, he would take turns.
Ariel:	Yea.
Therapist:	OK. What would you be doing differently if he was taking turns?
Ariel:	I would just be doing what I usually do.
Therapist:	How do you manage to do that, that is when he wants to play on the red tablet and you want to play a game?
Ariel:	I would tell mom or dad that I want to play on the red tablet and it is my turn, and they just tell him to play with me.
Therapist:	What happens when you get to play games?
Ariel:	We just mix it up. He wants to play superheroes so we play Barbies and they are superheroes.
Therapist:	Oh, so you make it work. You play superheroes with the Barbies.
Ariel:	I actually have one Barbie that is a superhero—Batgirl.
Therapist:	Batgirl is a superhero. So, when you are playing along like that, you get along pretty good. How do you play so good with him? How do you make it happen?
Ariel:	I don't really make it happen. Rick does. I will be watching TV and Rick walks by me and says, "Hey, you want to play something?" And I say, "Sure." Sometimes, I say, "No," because I may be having things to do like cooking.
Therapist:	So, you are usually ready to play.
Ariel:	I am always ready to play.
Therapist:	You are ready to play when he asks you. That is one thing you do. You tell him you are ready to play.
Ariel:	Yea. I try to play with him each time he wants to play so I don't make him sad.
Therapist:	OK. So, you want to make him happy.
Therapist:	So, let's just pretend that tomorrow you decide you want Rick to play with you. What is one thing you could do so that Rick might play with you?
Ariel:	If he says he doesn't want to play, I just get sad and go lay in my bed for a while, and he comes walking upstairs where I am, because he's sad that he made me sad. Then, he plays with me.
Therapist:	Sometimes, you get sad because of him, and sometimes he gets sad because of you. So, it sounds like ya'll really care a lot about each other.
Ariel:	(Nods her head. Looks at her picture.) See this is me walking upstairs and he has a board game. He says do you want to play a board game, and I say, "Sure." So, we play a board game.
Therapist:	OK. Let's pretend you were a 5. What would you be doing then?
Ariel:	Each day I would be doing something.
Therapist:	So, not necessarily with Rick but every day you would be doing something.
Ariel:	(Nods her head.)
Therapist:	So, you are saying it doesn't always have to be with Rick? You just like to play with somebody.

(continued)

Table 9.1 (continued)

Ariel:	(Smiles. Nods her head.) Even sometimes I play cards with my granny.
Therapist:	So, you and your granny play together.
Ariel:	Yea. We play Go Fish.
Therapist:	So how do you make that happen? How do you get to play with your granny or Rick or your other friends?
Ariel:	It's really easy to play with granny. I just walk over to her house, and she just goes, "Oh, look who's here." I just hang out a bit and then I say, "Hey, granny you want to play Go Fish" and she usually says "sure." But if she doesn't say "sure" she says "maybe."
Therapist:	So, at home, you like to play with Rick, and when you over there, you like to play with granny. Where else do you like to play?
Ariel:	I play next door by the house over there, and I go up to Carrie's house and knock on the door or ring the doorbell, but I don't ring the doorbell because Kim might be asleep. She's only three but tomorrow is her birthday. Carrie opens the door, and she usually says "sure," but sometimes she doesn't 'cause she has to do stuff.
Therapist:	Just like you. Sometimes, you have to do stuff and can't play. (The therapist starts writing down the names of people she can play with and she watches carefully.) You have Rick you can play with. You can play with your granny. You and Carrie play.
Ariel:	And Kim.
Therapist:	Carrie and Kim. Who else do you play with? That's four people right there!
Ariel:	And Emily. She is right behind my house.
Therapist:	Wow! You have another person close by. What happens when you play with her?
Ariel:	I never get to play with her, because she always has stuff. Oh, let me see the pen (takes the therapist's pen and draws her own scale).
Therapist:	So, who else do you get to play with?
Ariel:	Anna is another person. It would be a 3 with Anna.
Therapist:	(The therapist writes down Anna's name.) Wow! You have a lot of people you can play with. When Rick doesn't play, you have other people you can play with as well.
Ariel:	Let me look at that.
Therapist:	(They look at the list together, and the therapist goes down the list reading each name slowly.) You have Rick, your granny, Kim, Carrie, and Anna. That's five people to play with.
Ariel:	(Smiles.) Yea! I have more friends, too.

Creative and Playful Approaches for Asking the MQ or Finding Goals

Illustrating the Miracle Sequence

For those clients who have difficulty understanding the MQ or have trouble with sustained attention, the therapist can use a picture sequence of the MQ on notecards, for example, a bed as the illustration of going to sleep, a picture of a

| home | sleeping | miracle | wake up | problem is solved |

Figure 9.1 Illustration of Miracle Question.

fairy or a bright light to illustrate a miracle, and a picture of a child scratching his head to illustrate a problem that the client brought to therapy (Figure 9.1).

Drawing and Painting

The therapist asks the child or adolescent to draw or paint their miracle using different media, such as pencil, crayons, pastels, paints, or a combination. The different approaches used in art media produce differing types of pictures. Color allows children to be more expressive but drawing helps children be more specific and concrete. Each has its value and the child should have the option of which media to use.

Frame It

The therapist asks the client to draw or paint her miracle, similar to the above activity. Using a matte to frame the picture, the client uses colors, magic markers, or other media to write strengths that will be helpful in achieving the miracle on the matte board. The client decorates the matte board using a variety of colors, pictures, or objects.

Collage

The therapist offers to the client a collection of pre-cutout magazine pictures and words or phrases with the following instructions: "Select pictures and words that represent your world right now and paste them on one page." Once the client completes this, the therapist asks the client: "Now, select pictures and words that represent your future when the miracle happens or when the problem that brought you here is solved." The therapist asks the client to describe the new collage in which the problem is solved, gathering details that lead to small goals.

Sandtray

Using two sandtrays or one sandtray divided in half and carefully selected miniatures (see Homeyer & Sweeney, 2011), children or adolescents create a sandtray that represents their current world and then another that represents their world after the miracle occurs. The therapist may also ask clients to select miniatures for the second tray that represent a helper or resource that might assist them in reaching their goals. The therapist explores with clients what is different in the second sandtray, focusing on what clients are doing, the part clients play in the miracle, and what others notice. In asking the suggested questions below, use the miniatures as if they represent real people and things.

- Tell me about your trays.
- What is different about your second tray?
- Who and what are important in the future?
- What does the helper do? How does he/she help you achieve your miracle?
- What happened between the first and second trays? What specific events helped in creating the second tray?
- When the miracle in the second tray happens, who will notice? What will the person notice you doing?
- What will this say about you that you were able to do this?
- What will (person) notice when your miracle happens?

Sports Goals

Many children and adolescents are acquainted with or are involved in a sporting activity. If a client plays or seems interested in a type of sport, the therapist gathers miniatures or objects representing that sport in order to provide a tangible and visual metaphor for discussing goals. (Sports miniatures can often be found among cake decoration supplies or party stores.) For example, using a sandtray, the goal of a session may be reaching the soccer goal. In baseball or kickball, it might be sliding into home plate.

Using team sports as a metaphor, the therapist asks questions to elicit resources the client might use in reaching goals, stating, "When you play soccer, the team helps one another make a goal. Who are some people on your team that might help you reach your goal?" "What are some things you might ask them to do to help you?" "If I was the coach, what would you want me to do to help you?"

Magic Wand

With younger children, the MQ may take other forms. For example, the therapist says, "Let's pretend I can do magic." Then, using a magic wand, the therapist waves it over the space between the child and therapist and states "Abracadabra, this problem is no longer bothering you. What are you doing now that the problem isn't bothering you anymore?"

Allan (2003) suggests another approach with the magic wand. In her approach, she tells the child that the wand has special power and that by holding it, the child can visualize the changes the child would like to have in his life. She also suggests using it as a way to explore how the child wants himself or his relationships to be different.

Faces

Using paper plates, clients draw a picture of what their face looks like now, and then, on the other side, what they want their face to look like when they don't have to come back anymore. The therapist asks, "What are you doing differently when your face looks like this second picture?" "Who notices things are different?"

Treasure Map

Using a treasure map (easily downloaded from a variety of websites), the therapist and client chart a course over land or through rivers and streams to reach the treasure (goal). The therapist tells the client that the treasure represents the miracle or goal. To break goals down into smaller steps, the client marks smaller goals or stops the client may make along the journey to reach the goal.

Wishing Well

A wishing well provides another approach to asking a future-focused question. Using a miniature of a wishing well in the sandtray, the therapist asks,

> Do you know what a wishing well is? Let's start by closing your eyes. Pretend you throw a coin in the wishing well to wish your problems were gone. When you open your eyes, you see that your wish came true. What is different?

Or the therapist might ask "Show me using the miniatures what is different?" "Show me who would be there?" "What is happening?"

Magic Lamp

The therapist uses a Genie lamp that the client can hold while the therapist asks the miracle questions: "Suppose you rubbed the lamp and a genie came out, and the genie said, 'I will give you three wishes, so that your problems are gone.' What would your three wishes be?" "What would be different if your wishes came true and your problems were gone?" The use of three wishes offers options as far as prioritizing which of the three wishes the client wants to work on first.

Gingerbread People

The therapist uses drawings of three gingerbread people for the client to color in as an assessment of where he was before coming to the therapy, where he is now, and where he hopes to be when he reaches his goal. Questions focus on the differences between each figure, amplifying progress by expressions of admiration for the abilities and strengths of the client, using curiosity questions to find out the details of progress now and in the future, direct and indirect compliments, and relationship questions.

Phase 3: Setting Smaller Goals

Once the therapist sets the stage for the MQ and gains details regarding the miracle using developmentally appropriate and engaging materials, the therapist works with the client to set smaller goals, since clients generally describe their miracle or goal in general terms (Lethem, 2002). The client and therapist work collaboratively to create smaller goals by learning more details about the miracle, where and when it might take place, and how the miracle affects the client and others. The therapist asks questions that help the client identify exception times when the miracle is already occurring just a little bit, and then expands on the client's description of this exception. Since most behaviors the client wants to change occur in an interpersonal context, it is helpful to elicit how others might perceive these new behaviors. The therapist works with the client to develop a specific and realistic goal, one that the client forms and is relevant to the client's context. Just a small change can lead to major improvements (de Shazer, 1987), building confidence and motivation for future changes. As noted in the resilience literature, competence in one area often cascades into successes and competence in other areas (Masten, 2014).

Characteristics of Smaller Goals

Smaller goals contain certain characteristics that make them effective. Overall, smaller goals provide for the client a clear and realistic focus that lets the client and therapist know when the goal has been accomplished. Effective goals:

1   Focus on the presence of something, as this provides evidence that demonstrates to the client and therapist that things are better (De Jong & Miller, 1995).
2   Focus on what the client is doing (De Jong & Miller, 1995), for example, "I would be getting good grades." Good grades provide an objective measure of what the child wants. The therapist might ask, "What will you be doing when you are getting good grades?" By focusing on what the client will be doing, the therapist steers the client toward possible goals and prepares the client for taking action.
3   Are specific and concrete (De Jong & Miller, 1995). Getting "good grades" does not provide enough specificity to enable therapist and client to know what the goal is. Does this mean the client will be just barely passing or will be making significant improvement? A better goal would be, "I would be studying 30 minutes every day, so I can move my grade from a 60 to a 70."
4   Are realistic (De Jong & Miller, 1995). The child who says his goal is to stay in his seat the whole time the teacher is talking may be setting an unrealistic goal. It might be better if he sets a goal of raising his hand when he

needs to get up. Letting clients know that reaching the goal may be hard work can be useful, since it saves the child or adolescent any embarrassment if he doesn't reach his goal right away. However, if he does reach his goal, then it calls for a celebration (De Jong & Miller, 1995).

5   Are small (De Jong & Miller, 1995). Moving one's grade from 60 to an 80 may not be realistic. More realistically, the client might select to move his grade from a 60 to a 70.

6   Are important to the client (De Jong & Miller, 1995), not just to the parent, teacher, counselor, or friend. Asking the client what she would be doing differently and then responding using the client's words demonstrates an understanding of the client's perspective and what the client considers to be a priority.

The following (Table 9.2) provides an example of setting specific goals with Kelsey, a 12-year-old girl experiencing problems with some of her peers. Although she is in middle school, Kelsey attends a high school to address her high academic skills. Being personable and sensitive to others, she finds herself among older girls who do not seem to be as friendly as they once were.

Table 9.2 Kelsey's Miracle Question.

Kelsey:	People just talk over me and don't listen, or they just don't listen when I talk.
Therapist:	If they included you in the group what would you be doing?
Kelsey:	Enjoying or having fun.
Therapist:	How many girls are you talking about?
Kelsey:	Six to ten people about.
Therapist:	So, if they were talking to you, you would be adding six to ten people to your friends. About how many friends do you have right now?
Kelsey:	About five.
Therapist:	Wow! You have five friends. So, if you added these people, you would have like 15 to 20 friends. How do you manage to have so many friends?
Kelsey:	I don't know if they are my friends, but they act like they are. I just pass around and get to know people.
Therapist:	OK. What do you consider good friends?
Kelsey:	Somebody who is there when I need them, who can give me friendly advice.
Therapist:	Ah, so friends are people you can count on. Well, I am going to ask you a funny question. Let's suppose tonight you go home, you feed the dog, and you go to sleep, and a miracle happens. The miracle is that the problem that brought you here is gone. What would be the first thing you would notice that would tell you the problem is gone?
Kelsey:	Probably when I go to school in the morning, everyone would just talk to me saying, "Hi, Kelsey, how are you doing?"
Therapist:	What would that be like?

(continued)

Table 9.2 (continued)

Kelsey:	It would be exciting. We would be friends. I wouldn't have to worry about whether they are going to ignore me.
Therapist:	If you could do this, how would it be helpful to you?
Kelsey:	I would have more friends, and I wouldn't feel bad around the others. In some of my classes, the people I know I can count on aren't in there, so it makes it hard. Last year, they sort of included me, but then it started going down at the end of last year.
Therapist:	So, last year for a while, things were going OK and they seemed like friends. What else would be different if these people would talk to you?
Kelsey:	Like if I need help in a class about something I don't understand I could ask them. It could help me if I feel sad. Like we could make each other happy.
Therapist:	When are times just in the past week or so that just a little piece of that miracle happened?
Kelsey:	Maybe in choir and we figured out our parts. When the girls found out I was Glenda, they were like excited and said, "Good for you! We are so happy you got that part."
Therapist:	Wow! So, they were happy that you got that part.
Kelsey:	Yea!
Therapist:	What does that say about your friendship that they were happy?
Kelsey:	Maybe, sometimes I am judgmental. I skip over the good times. But they don't include me sometimes.
Therapist:	So, it sounds like you worry about whether they are going to include you. If you didn't worry about being included, what would be different?
Kelsey:	I wouldn't worry about my attitude towards them. I would have a more positive attitude. I wouldn't worry about if I got to speak and just let them talk.
Therapist:	You have really thought about this, haven't you?
Kelsey:	Yea.
Therapist:	So, what I am hearing you say is that if they are not listening to you, you would like it not to bother you. Is that right?
Therapist:	So, what are some things you have tried that sometimes help?
Kelsey:	Sometimes, you just have to squish your way in.
Therapist:	Tell me a little more about that.
Kelsey:	I have to stay strong no matter what happens. I have to fight against the flow, so I have to push myself in there, so I can get heard.
Therapist:	You would be pushing your way in there to be heard, pushing against the flow.
Therapist:	When are times that you felt a little bit better around the other girls?
Kelsey:	When I sit at their table. I can talk to some of the girls around me instead of trying to squish my way into the conversation.
Therapist:	So, sitting at their table has been helpful because you are with a few of the girls at a time. When are some other times that you have felt a little more comfortable?
Kelsey:	Sometimes in the morning when we are waiting around for school to start. I talk to a few of the girls, and we can get along pretty good then.

To help the client focus on effective goals, the therapist listens intently to the client's answers and then asks questions based on these answers. The table below (Table 9.3) outlines possible ways a child or adolescent client might answer the MQ and suggests follow-up questions leading to more specific and behavioral goals.

Other Future-Focused Questions

Although SF therapy often uses the MQ to gain an understanding of goals for therapy, other future-focused questions provide alternatives to the MQ and may be more appropriate for clients. For example, clients with intellectual difficulties often have difficulty understanding the miracle question. For those firmly entrenched in concrete operations, the miracle question may be difficult to process. For example, consider Ariel's reply to the miracle question—"A miracle? Like Jesus did?"

The miracle question may be inappropriate when the therapist does not have a good relationship with the client and the client feels like his struggles are not taken seriously, as with a mother caring for a handicapped child or

Table 9.3 Possible Client Responses to Miracle Question and Therapist Follow-Up.

Type of Answer	Client Response	Therapist Response	Explanation
Does not want to answer	"I don't believe in miracles."	"If you did believe in miracles, what would be different?"	Focus is on using her imagination to consider other possibilities.
Feeling response	"I would feel happy."	"If you were feeling happy, what would you be doing?"	Shifting the response to a behavioral goal.
Cognitive response	"I would be able to focus on my work."	"If you could focus on your work, what would you be doing?"	Shifting the response to a behavioral goal.
Absence of something	"I wouldn't get in trouble all the time."	"What would you be doing instead?"	Shifting the response to what is present rather than what is absent.
Presence of something	"My mom would be happy with my school work."	"How would you know she was happy with your work?"	Getting observable evidence of mother being happy.
Unrealistic	"My father would come back home."	"If your father did come back, what would you be doing differently?"	Focus is on the child's behavior rather than on someone else's since the child cannot control someone else.

an adolescent who finds himself in despair over grief and loss. For those with intellectual disabilities, immature cognitive development, or who face over-whelming difficulties, practitioners often prefer to ask about preferred futures (see Lloyd & Dallos, 2008).

- What are your best hopes for our time today?
- When we are finished today, how will you know this time together was helpful?
- Suppose I meet you on the street corner a year from now, and we start talking about what you have done since we last met, what would you like to say you accomplished?
- If I ran into your best friend at the store and he said, "Hey, you would not believe how great John is doing!" What would he tell me about you?
- What if I saw your mom next week, and she tells me you are doing better now. What would she tell me is different?
- If I was a fly on the wall and I could see you in your classroom doing better, what would you be doing?
- When things are going better for you, what would be your theme song?
- When I ask you tomorrow how things are better, what three words would you use to describe how things are better?
- Pretend you can see the future after you have reached your best possible self. What are you doing? How is that different? How did you make that happen?
- Suppose we make a video together showing you doing better, what would we see?

Creative and Playful Approaches for Gathering Details about the Miracle or Goal

Miracle Story Board

The therapist asks the client to draw the things that are different when the miracle occurs. The client draws a picture of each event on index cards. Once the client completes the drawings, the therapist asks the client to sort the cards according to which one she would like to work on first, second, and so on. This activity provides a visual of smaller goals that the client may change, prioritize, and re-sort as priorities shift.

Scaling Questions

Scaling questions (SQs) provide an excellent way to develop a series of smaller goals. Once the client defines each ascending number on his scale, each number then becomes a goal, a measure of the client's current standing or record of past goals accomplished. When asking SQs to make smaller goals, the therapist asks questions as if the client has already reached the next number. For example, if the client states that he is a 5 on a scale from 1 to 10, the therapist asks, "What will you be doing when you are a 6?" Many times, new counselors ask future questions such as "What do you have to do to be a 6?" This question implies obligation, foreknowledge, and motivation; whereas, if the therapist asks the question as if the client is in the future doing the desired behavior, the client suspends feelings of doubt and shifts to creatively considering alternatives.

Some of the activities the therapist employs to help the client answer the MQ and SQs may also be helpful in breaking the miracle down into smaller goals. These activities help clients visualize, manipulate, and create specific goals.

- Treasure Map—The client determines what the treasure is (the larger goal) and then marks on the map using markers or stickers what specific goals may need to be reached to reach the larger goal.
- Sports Goals—As noted earlier, sports goals provide a metaphor for looking at the overall goal; however, the path to the goal makes for visual or tangible metaphors of smaller goals, such as the yard lines in football, the bases on a baseball field, or the court in basketball. If using a sandtray, or even just paper and pencil, the client marks where she is on the sport's field to indicate progress made or how sometimes setbacks occur. Conversation then might focus on what the client does when setbacks occur, what can be learned from mistakes, and how to persist toward goals.
- Subway Map—The client uses the subway map to mark the goal and the different smaller goals at the different stops along the way.
- Mountain Climbing—The client draws a mountain and marks the goal as the top of the mountain and then smaller goals are marked as different ledges or stops going up the mountain.
- Hiking—The client draws, paints, or colors a path and different scenery and structures leading to a goal. Different areas are marked and labeled as smaller goals to reach in order to reach the larger goal.
- Building a Tower—The client and therapist build a tower using blocks or other items and the client talks about each block as the next goal and what will be different when she reaches the goal.
- Book—The therapist asks the client to create a title for a book about reaching his goal. The client then creates titles for chapters that represent the different smaller goals that would be reached to complete the book or larger goal. The therapist and client then discuss what might be included in the chapters, such as events that take place, people involved, the client's role, where the events occur, and other details about the specific goal. Each time the client visits, discussion includes looking at the chapters and how they have played out since the last session.

Empowering Children and Adolescents to Reach Goals

Once the client and therapist know what the miracle is and some of the small steps that might be needed to reach the miracle, children and adolescents may feel perplexed or overwhelmed in implementing these steps. The following section outlines techniques that can jumpstart and empower clients to reach their goals, as well as to help them address specific concerns.

Creative and Playful Approaches to Empower Clients to Reach Goals

Role Play

We learn by doing. When practicing behaviors, we build or reinforce neural pathways for those behaviors. The process of performing and using our bodies in learning, or embodied learning, is a highly effective mechanism in learning. Role play provides an excellent way to practice the behaviors the client wants to do. For example, the child would like to be able to ask the teacher for help rather than getting upset. The therapist might ask the child, "Show me what you think would be a good way to ask the teacher for help." The adolescent who feels he has lost face because of misbehavior and truancy might practice pretending he has it together and is not afraid of what others think. The therapist might scale how possible the client thinks it is that he could do it.

ROLE PLAYING THROUGH SANDTRAY

Sandtray with its miniatures provides another way to practice new behaviors and imagine how others might respond. By role playing through sandtray, the child or adolescent rehearses new behaviors and manipulates the miniatures in ways that demonstrate different possibilities. For example, the client creates a scene in which the goal behavior occurs. The scene includes the self and important others, as well as any other necessary miniatures to make it realistic. The client then pretends that the scene is occurring, doing something different that would bring about the desired change. The therapist might ask questions such as:

- What is it like for you to do this?
- Show me what will happen next?
- What does it feel like to be successful in making this happen?
- How do you think [name each person represented] might react?
- How would their response affect you?
- If they don't respond as you would hope, what would be the best thing to do?
- If they do respond the way you would hope, what would be the best thing to do?

ROLE PLAYING THROUGH PHOTOGRAPHY

Several artists illustrate how photography might be a useful approach to role play. Cindy Sherman (Sherman, n.d.), an American artist who popularized performance-style photography and film in the late 1970s, picks a persona, and then dresses up and acts in the style of that persona. She explores through black and white and color photography various roles people play now and in the past, refusing to give names or descriptions to her photographs. She lets the viewer observe, interpret, and develop their own stories about the pictures she creates (art21.org/artist/cindy-sherman).

Creating self-goals can include similar strategies. For example, the client decides how the future self appears once he reaches his goals and then stages the scene of the future self, including furniture, clothing, posture, and facial expression. The therapist or another person takes a picture of this future self as he looks and acts. These pictures are now part of the therapeutic record or they may stay with the client who may choose to refer to them when working toward goals. Similarly, the client who is having difficulty with another person, whether a friend, parent or another relative, can stage a hoped-for future scene using, if possible, the other person. The therapist takes a picture of the scene but also asks questions regarding how things are different in the future scene in comparison with the present and the role the client plays in the solution.

Photographs are useful in reminding the client of goals, modifying or creating future goals, or exploring the reciprocal effects these changes have on others. The therapist can ask:

- What is it like to be this future self?
- How does this future self act, think, and feel differently?
- What does it mean for the future self that these changes have occurred and goals are reached?
- What will others see you doing when you are this future self?

For younger children, Renee Bergeron's Superhero project (www.dailymail. co.uk/femail/article-3057751/Photographer-captures-poignant-portraits-disabled-children-dressed-superheroes-prove-achieve-anything.html) offers another approach to empowering and helping children envision themselves reaching their goals. Bergeron (Bergeron, n.d.) takes pictures of children with disabilities posing in their favorite superhero costume and later adds an appropriate and fitting background. This approach can be accompanied by certain questions, such as:

- Imagine yourself as this superhero conquering your challenges. What is that like for you? How do you do it?
- How do you feel as this superhero? What is it about this superhero that helps you feel this way?
- What powers do you have that can help you? Which powers are the easiest to use?
- When you are using these powers, how are things different at home? At school? With your friends?
- Who might be some of your allies or people that you call in when there is an emergency?

Design a Superhero

The simplest way to design a hero involves asking the client to draw a superhero and to give it qualities the client finds useful. However, Wolf (2014) describes the process of creating a superhero as taking a picture of the client and asking the client to add visual qualities to herself that encompass desired powers and characteristics (Figure 9.2). The client might do this digitally using photo-editing software, or the client might cut out the picture of herself and draw or paint in the added qualities in a multimedia approach. The therapist might ask questions about the superhero to assist the client in describing her superhero powers:

- What does this hero need to be able to do to help you?
- What powers does this superhero have?
- How does the superhero access these powers?
- What does this superhero look like, wear, or use?
- How is this superhero helpful?
- When are times you use some of these powers? How were they helpful?

Power Pose

The therapist simply asks the client to pose as a powerful person. The client talks about what it feels like to be in this pose, what the client can do, and how this pose might be helpful in reaching goals. The therapist takes a picture of the client in the power pose, either to keep and use for the next session or for

Figure 9.2 Design a Superhero—Mind Readers.

the client to keep. By using the client's phone or camera, the client can refer back to the power pose for inspiration. The therapist can also use an instant camera to take a picture that can be given to the client before leaving the session.

Transpose Images of Power

Kehinde Wiley (http://kehindewiley.com), among many other projects, takes popular art history images and exchanges the faces of people who are in positions of power with his picture.

Similarly, the therapist, using copies of paintings, pictures, or superheroes representing people of power, asks the client to choose a picture that represents the powerful person she thinks would help her reach her goals. The therapist, using an instamatic camera, takes a picture of the client and the client cuts out her face and places it on the face of the picture of the powerful person. For example, a child might cut out the face of a picture of herself and place it on top of the face of Wonder Woman. Through this activity, the client focuses on creating a new image of self, one of strength and abilities that meets and conquers challenges. Questions that might follow include:

- What about this new picture of you is helpful?
- What strengths does this person have that might be helpful?
- What about this picture demonstrates power to conquer and overcome challenges?
- What are some things you are doing right now that might be moving you more toward this kind of strength?

Enlist Others for Help

Once children or adolescents set their goals, they may encounter obstacles or disbelief from others that they are making changes. This results in problematic situations in which their reputation precedes them and sets them up for failure. To overcome this, they need adult allies to assist them. In schools, this might involve letting teachers know that the client is working on a specific goal. For example, the therapist asks the teacher to notice and say something to the client about times when the client seems to be working on his goal, such as staying on task, doing his homework, or coming to class on time. By letting the client know that his teacher is noticing him doing something different provides social reinforcement for continuing his positive behavior.

Similarly, the therapist and client ask parents to notice aloud to the client those things the client is doing that are moving the client in the direction of her goals. As with teachers, so asking parents to focus on what is positive interrupts the negative cycle of nagging, complaining, or other negative communication. By offering positive comments, the client's feelings of success hopefully increase, increasing motivation to continue working toward goals.

For example, Marc, a seven-year-old African American boy, was having a great deal of problems with his classmates. Being quite active, he often endured the teacher's barrage of negative comments about his behavior. Gradually, other students began to seem him negatively as well, so he had few friends. I decided to reinforce Marc, but also his classmates, with cookies when Marc had a good day. The good day was defined with the teacher and Marc agreed. I explained to the class what needed to happen for cookies, but I also enlisted their help. The next afternoon I went into the classroom to find out how Marc had done. One of his classmates immediately spoke up and stated that they should all get cookies because Marc had done what the teacher asked him. I was so encouraged that I continued to do this, but only every other day for a week, reducing it to once a week, and eventually not at all. The power of associating positive things with Marc transformed his behavior and increased his friendships in a short period of time.

The Moon Activity

Just as the moon activity mentioned earlier is helpful in getting to know who and what are important to the client, it can also be used to help the client decide who and what might be helpful in reaching goals. For example, the therapist asks,

> Suppose you are going to the moon on a mission. Your mission is to [client's goal]. Who do you think you will need to help you? What are some other things you might need? What would be your plan after you got there?

Managing Time

Many adolescents feel overwhelmed by the many requirements of their daily life. This leaves them anxious and unable to focus their energy to make changes. Using a life balance wheel (Figure 9.3), clients examine where they spend their time and then create art that focuses on what they can do to make wanted changes (for other ideas see: www.morningcoffeewithdee.com/life-balance-wheel). The following outlines this technique.

1   Using a large circle, ask the client to divide the circle into six different pieces according to how much time the client spends each day in the different areas of her life (areas can be changed or deleted according to the needs of the client):

School	Health/wellness
Friends	Extracurricular/after-school activities
Family	Spirituality

2   Ask the client to look at the wheel as an outsider. Ask, "What conclusions can you make about this person's life or activities?"
3   Ask "Now look at your wheel as yourself. What did you learn? Was this what you expected? Since you spend this much time in each of these areas, what does that tell you? What changes might you want to make?"

4   Ask the client to make a piece of art or a collage to show the change they want in their life. "What would life look like with this change?" Add words to the art describing the change.

5   Ask: "Where will you put your art to remind yourself about what you learned?"

Using the life balance wheel, a client created a collage (Figure 9.4) that placed emphasis on exercise, since it seemed to have been crowded out by the many other life activities, to remind herself of what she needed to focus on more in the future.

Best Place

The therapist asks the client to close her eyes and imagine her favorite place, the place where she feels quiet, peaceful, and safe; where she feels no anxiety and perfectly calm. The client, using paper and pens, colors, markers, or other drawing and painting media, creates a picture that represents the likeness of this best place. It might be realistic or only include the most important colors of the scene. The therapist takes a picture of the client using an instant camera and the client places the photograph on the picture. The therapist gives the picture to the client to use as a way to calm the self and relieve anxiety.

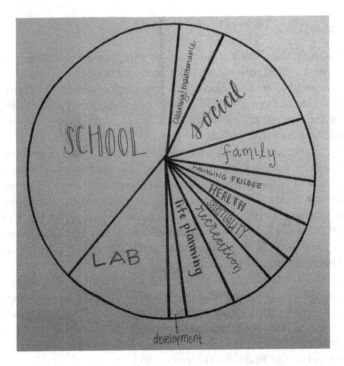

Figure 9.3 Life Balance Wheel.

Figure 9.4 Life Balance Collage.

Square Relaxation

For this activity, the client learns to relax by using square breathing. First, the client draws a square with a dark color or magic marker. For a more tactile square, the outline may be outlined with glue, sand, or glitter. The client decorates the inside of the square with colors or drawings that evoke relaxation. To begin the process, the client traces each side of the square with a finger without letting the finger up from the page. As the client traces the first side of the square, she breathes in for a count of 4, she then traces her finger across the second side and holds her breath for a count of 4, she traces her finger across the third side of the square and lets out the breath for a count of 4, and then traces the fourth side, holding the breath for a count of 4. The client may draw a square that is small enough to fit in a purse or wallet, or, for younger children or those with physical limitations, the square may be larger. If the client practices the process daily, the process becomes internalized and the need for a visual reminder becomes less important.

Many different techniques have been presented here as ways to assist the client in developing goals and ways to reach goals from the client's perspective. The activities presented provide a choice of approaches from which the therapist can select to match the characteristics and preferences of the client. Any of the activities may be and probably should be modified so they are developmentally appropriate and fit the clients' frameworks.

References

Allan, V. B. (2003). The magic wand. In H. G. Kaduson & C. E. Schaefer (Eds), *101 favorite play therapy techniques* (Vol. III), pp. 303–305. New York, NY: Rowman & Littlefield.

Bergeron, R. (n.d.). *The superhero project {Special needs photography}*. http://littleearthlingphotography.com/superhero-project.

Bliss, E. V. & Bray, D. (2009). The smallest solution focused particles: Towards a minimalist definition of when therapy is solution focused. *Journal of Systemic Therapies, 28*(2), 62–74.

De Jong, P. & Berg, I. K. (2013). *Interviewing for solutions* (4th Ed.). Belmont, CA: Brooks/Cole.

De Jong, P. & Miller, S. D. (1995). How to interview for client strengths. *Social Work, 40*(6), 729–736.

de Shazer, S. (1987). Minimal elegance. *Family Therapy Networker, 11*(3), 57–60.

de Shazer, S. (1988). *Clues: Investigating solutions in brief therapy.* New York, NY: Norton.

de Shazer, S. & Dolan, Y. (2007). *More than miracles.* Binghamton, NY: Haworth Press.

Hillyer, D. (1996). Solution-oriented questions: An analysis of a key intervention in solution-focused therapy. *Journal of the American Psychiatric Nurses Association, 2*(1), 3–10.

Homeyer, L. E. & Sweeney, D. S. (2011). *Sandtray therapy* (2nd Ed.). New York, NY: Taylor & Francis.

Korman, H. (2006). Four reasons for asking the miracle question. Retrieved from: harry@sikt.u.

Lethem, J. (2002). Brief solution focused therapy. *Child and Adolescent Mental Health, 7*(4), 189–192.

Lloyd, H. & Dallos, R. (2008). First session solution-focused brief therapy with families who have a child with severe intellectual disabilities: Mothers' experiences and views. *Journal of Family Therapy, 30*(1), 5–28.

Masten, A. S. (2014). *Ordinary magic.* New York, NY: The Guilford Press.

Sherman, C. (n.d.). *Biography.* CindySherman.com. Retrieved from: www.cindysherman.com/biography.shtml.

Shilts, L. & Gordon, A. B. (1996). What to do after the miracle occurs. *Journal of Family Psychotherapy, 7*(1), 15–22.

Strong, T. & Pyle, N. R. (2009). Constructing a conversational "miracle": Examining the "miracle question" as it is used in therapeutic dialogue. *Journal of Constructivist Psychology, 22*(4), 328–353.

Wolf, R. I. (2014). The therapeutic uses of photography in play therapy. In E. J. Green & A. A. Drewes (Eds), *Integrating expressive arts and play therapy with children and adolescents*, pp. 181–203. Hoboken, NY: John Wiley & Sons, Inc.

CHAPTER 10

Ending the Session

Elizabeth R. Taylor

*He was one of the most difficult children I had worked with in special educa-
tion. He was highly intelligent but seemed constantly angry. When I took on
this new classroom for children with emotional disturbances, other teachers
told me to be aware of Mitchell, that he could get violent. Knowing how people
felt about him gave me the motivation to try to win him over. I began by spending a little extra time in the mornings with Mitchell at his desk, visiting about
his family and what he was reading, as he was an avid reader, and ideas he had
about what we could do in art. These little visits helped us to make it through
most days. However, we did have some difficult times—running away, throw-
ing furniture, or hiding my keys on a Friday afternoon.*

*Yet, if there was a crisis, he could take charge. When a child had a seizure, he
quickly responded by getting everyone out of the way. When one of the other students ran away, he ran after him and held him down until I got there. Toward
the end of the semester, I felt like he was ready to try mainstreaming into a
regular classroom for several hours a day, particularly since he was such a good
student. He was a fifth grader and would soon be going to another school, so we
needed to help him assimilate with his peers in a normal environment.*

*One afternoon, I decided to pick him up early from the other class, since
we were going on a field trip. I watched through the window in the door as
the class gathered around the teacher who demonstrated how to do a science
experiment. Mitchell was awkwardly standing around the blackboard and
away from the class, rolling a toy car up and down the chalk tray. Despite
his many strengths, he still lacked the confidence to participate with those
of his own age. We still had work to do. Yet, when I looked back over the year,
he had made great progress—he didn't throw things or run away, he stayed
in the regular classroom for almost half a day doing his work, and he seemed
to be a bit happier.*

Ending the session provides a time for the therapist to give feedback to the
client, reinforcing strengths and providing suggestions based on the client's
frame of reference. The ending of the session also includes an opportunity for
the client to decide if coming to a second session is necessary.

Sometimes, therapists work in teams in which one therapist conducts the session and the other therapists watch behind a one-way mirror. During the break, the therapist confers with the team regarding suggestions; yet, rarely does the therapist enjoy the luxury of working with a team except in training situations. Instead, the therapist takes a "thinking" break to consider feedback to give the client. Feedback takes the form of a compliment, bridge, and suggestion (De Jong & Berg, 2013).

The Break

The break provides the therapist with time to think about the session with some emotional distance and to pull salient ideas together to deliver a message, but it also provides the client with time to reflect and anticipate what the therapist might say. Solution-focused therapists disagree on whether a break is needed (Bliss & Bray, 2009), and those working with children and adolescents may not find it practical or safe to leave the room. So, therapists working with younger clients often take a "thinking break." During this brief break, therapists look over notes or write down thoughts about feedback to give the client (De Jong & Berg, 2013).

Taking a break should not come as a surprise, since in the beginning the therapist outlines how the session will go so the client knows what to expect. When the therapist takes a break, the client also ponders the session. The therapist can suggest that during the break the client thinks about what was discussed and considers whether there is anything to add or perhaps if there is a solution the client might want to try. The break, particularly with a child, should not last more than a few minutes, unless the parents are present, in which case the break may last five to seven minutes (Berg & Steiner, 2003).

Compliment, Bridge, Suggestion

Feedback most often is delivered verbally, but it may be written or given in written and verbal form. The compliment–bridge–suggestion (C–B–S) sequence pulls together in an organized fashion the essence of the session with a focus on client perspectives of solutions. The process affirms the client and the client's strengths and struggles and provides suggestions to help the client reach desired goals. Feedback should be simple, not too wordy, and reflect the client's perspective.

Compliment

The therapist gleans from the session strengths, resiliencies, and successes, with a focus on what the client sees as important, and delivers a compliment that demonstrates the therapist's genuine recognition of these assets and client perspectives. The client may feel like the problem remains bigger than their ability to solve it and need encouragement. By giving a compliment, the therapist "affirms client successes and strengths these successes suggest" (De Jong & Berg, 2013, p. 124). Regardless of why the client attends therapy, every client receives a compliment. The client then leaves with a sense of affirmation and hope (De Jong & Berg, 2013) that encourages the client to engage in therapy and, if appropriate, return for follow-up sessions.

When considering what compliments to give, I often ask myself questions about what I observed in the session, such as:

- What does this child like about school?
- How does she cope with challenges?
- What do others say are his strengths?
- How does she get along with others?
- How does he use his hands?
- How does he use language?
- How hard does she work?
- What particular things did he tell me that were impressive?
- What specific personality traits do I admire about her, for example, courage, helpfulness, honesty, kindness?

Asking these questions provides clues as to what compliments may be meaningful.

Bridge

The bridge links the compliment to the suggestion and should continue to affirm the client's strengths and challenges. By giving a bridge statement, the therapist provides a rationale for the upcoming suggestion. A common phrase to begin the bridge starts with, "I agree with you that . . ." (De Jong & Berg, 2013, p. 124), for example, "I agree with you that focusing on your school work while trying to deal with friend problems can be difficult, but I admire how you manage to get some of your work done despite the problems these girls cause you."

Suggestion

The suggestion should match with the client's perspective and goals. Which suggestion to give depends on: a) the motivation of the client, that is, whether the client by the end of the session recognizes some responsibility in the solution (De Jong & Berg, 2008; b) whether the client identifies exceptions and has clear-formed goals; and c) the client's strengths and resources. Suggestions generally fall into three categories: 1) no suggestion; 2) an observation; or 3) a behavior (De Jong & Berg, 2013). The therapist bases the behavioral suggestions on the principles of SF therapy: "If it's not working, do something different," and "If it works, do more of it" (de Shazer & Dolan, 2007, p. 2).

Suggestions often take the form of "observe something that is working or that you want to continue to happen," "keep doing what you are doing," or "do something different."

If the client continues as a mandated client, does not want to be there, or does not view himself as part of the problem, the therapist provides a compliment but without a suggestion. If the client recognizes a problem but does not think he plays a role in its solution, the therapist provides a compliment and perhaps an observing suggestion. If the client sees himself as part of the problem and its solution, the therapist may provide a behavioral suggestion (De Jong & Berg, 2013).

To formulate a suggestion, the therapist considers the perspective of the client:

- What does the client want to be different?
- What are the client's strengths?
- How capable and motivated is the client in overcoming and coping with challenges presented?
- What are the client's resources, including parents, teachers, team leaders, friends?
- What has the client tried that is helpful or is currently working?
- What is the client's motivational status? Does the client want to be there and feel that she has a role in the solution? Does the client view the problem as someone else's but doesn't mind coming to therapy? Does the client not view the problem as a problem or feel no stake in solutions?

Behavioral Suggestions

When the therapist delivers a behavioral suggestion, it must be delivered in a way that the client accepts. One approach might be to frame it as an experiment. For example, the therapist asks, "I wonder if you would like to try an experiment. Next time you feel like you are about to explode you close your eyes and take two deep breaths." By framing it as an experiment, then if it doesn't work, it just becomes information and does not diminish anything about the client. If it does work, then the therapist gives the client the credit. Another experiment might be to try something different, something the client chooses. "I wonder if the next time you feel like your mom is on your case that you do say something totally off the topic."

The client may reject the message, may only accept a part of the message, or may fully agree with the message, depending on the therapist's ability to deliver a message meaningful to the client, the client–therapist relationship, and the client's motivation for attending therapy.

The C–B–S process, when delivered genuinely, simply, and with a focus on the client, leaves the client with a sense of hope and options. However, verbal messages may be lost once the client leaves. For this reason, the therapist might consider ways to give the message, or part of the message, to the client in a concrete format. Providing the client with a reminder of the compliment or

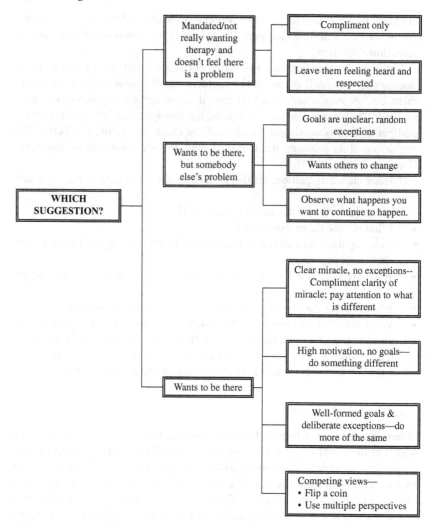

Figure 10.1 Decision Tree for Providing Suggestions.

the compliment and suggestion gives the client a transitional cue to carry over until the next session.

Creative and Playful Approaches to End the Session

Sticky Notes

Sticky notes provide excellent ways to write down a message to give to the client. Many school counselors see students only briefly, so time to create tangible messages may be limited. However, a compliment written on a sticky note or piece of paper for the client to take with her provides a positive reminder of her strengths and the awareness that another person (the therapist) recognizes their strengths.

Pictures

Berg and Steiner (2003) state

> that pictures are a very good way to remind children of what is good about their lives. The use of pictures also helps children focus on making their visual images more vivid through pictures so that they can be reminded of their own dreams and hopes for themselves.
>
> (p. 75)

The therapist can employ different types of pictures to remind clients of compliments and suggestions.

One way to use pictures is to have clients take photographs or use magazine pictures pasted to index cards that can act as bookmarks, reminding clients of the suggestion. The picture may be of the actual suggestion but may also be a representation or symbol. For example, the client might select a picture of hands to represent his ability to help people, to help him remember a suggestion to help a friend rather than fighting with a bully, or a picture of an animal to remind him that his favorite way to relax is to pet his cat to use in those times when he feels anxious. Actual photographs of people that provide support might be helpful reminders for those who struggle with loneliness or feelings of alienation. The child can also use some of the photographs or art representations of her as a superhero to remind herself of her strengths.

Drawings

Clients draw their solutions in the session, but then take the drawings with them to remind them of solutions to try. The client might redraw a picture onto a smaller card or piece of paper so that it can be put in his pocket or wallet.

Numbers

Rather than using a picture, the client might write a number from the scaling questions that represents his goal. For example, the child or adolescent might write or draw the number "5" to represent what the client stated as the next small goal, i.e., as a cue to take a short break and breathe deeply when he begins to feel upset.

Objects

Tangible objects used in therapy or created specifically for the C–B–S provide symbolic approaches to remind the client of strengths and solutions. For example, the therapist might write on a popsicle stick words that remind the client of his strengths, which the client can take with him and use as a bookmark. A piece of wood decorated to remind the client of different ways he might relax when feeling stressed provides an object the client might place on his desk or bureau at home.

Follow-Up

Since most youth are made to attend therapy, they may have little choice about when therapy is over. However, it is important in SF therapy to give choices to the client about coming back. For those who are mandated and still seem to be visitors to the counseling session, the best approach is to give the client a choice about when to come back. For example, the therapist asks, "When do you think the best time is to come back, in five days or in ten days?" By collaborating even on the smaller things, the client often feels empowered and recognized for the ability to decide. It may be helpful to use an actual 30-day calendar and mark the days of the counseling sessions, so the client sees the time and has a physical reminder. Even if a parent accompanies the child, giving both a reminder of the appointment reinforces the collaborative relationship between the therapist and client(s).

Ending the session provides an opportunity to instill hope, motivation, and expectancy for change. The compliment-bridge-suggestion sequence should be used thoughtfully with consideration of the client's perspective, motivation, and strengths.

References

Bannink, F. (2006). *1001 solution-focused* questions (2nd Ed.). New York, NY: W. W. Norton.

Berg, I. K. & Steiner, T. (2003). Children's solution work. New York, NY: W. W. Norton.

Bliss, E. V. & Bray, D. (2009). The smallest solution focused particles: Towards a minimalist definition of when therapy is solution focused. *Journal of Systemic Therapies*, 28(2), 62–74.

De Jong, P. & Berg, I. K. (2013). *Interviewing for solutions* (4th Ed.). Belmont, CA: Brooks/Cole.

de Shazer, S. & Dolan, Y. (2007). *More than miracles*. Binghamton, NY: Haworth Press.

CHAPTER 11

Follow-Up Sessions

Elizabeth R. Taylor

I heard him running down the hall of the elementary school. As always, he was early, hot and sweaty, and eager. He was my prize customer type of client. At seven years of age, Joe was full of energy and highly intelligent, but his self-regulation skills lacked what he needed to be successful in school. Therefore, he frequently visited my office, sometimes as part of his regular schedule and sometimes just to say "hi." Today, however, was his regular time. He quickly popped in the doorway and said, "Guess what's better?" He proceeded to tell me about his new kitten and how it snuggled up with him on the couch, how his parents had found the kitten and decided to keep it, and how he was the envy of his friend Josh.

The second and subsequent SF sessions follow-up the first session by continuing to focus on exceptions and progress toward goals. The therapist begins with "What's better?" and amplifies, reinforces, and asks again, "What's better?" The therapist continues to remain confident in the client's abilities and competence (De Jong & Berg, 2013).

Eliciting Exceptions, Amplifying, Reinforcing, Starting Over (EARS)

What's Better?

When the client answers the question "What's better?" the therapist amplifies the client's comment by asking questions about the exception, when and where it occurred, who noticed, how the client made it happen, and other details about how the exception occurred. The therapist reinforces the exception by paying attention to what the client says, complimenting directly and indirectly as appropriate, and reflecting pleasure in the client's strengths and successes. The therapist then continues with "What else is better?" (De Jong & Berg, 2013).

The client may not answer the "What's better" question right away, but the therapist remains patient and gives the client time to process the question and consider the time that has elapsed since the last session. If the client does not seem to be able to come up with an answer right away, it is sometimes useful to ask questions such as:

- "What is even a little bit better?"
- "What would your mother say is a bit better?"
- "When during the week were things better than other days?"
- "When were things better at home versus school?"

Sometimes, the client begins by talking about the therapist's suggestion from the first session and if it was successful. However, the therapist does not initiate the inquiry for several reasons: 1) it puts the client on the defensive if the suggestion was not followed; 2) by asking about it, the therapist implies the client should have followed the suggestion; 3) the client may do more than the suggestion required; and 4) perhaps other events overshadowed the importance of the suggestion (De Jong & Berg, 2013), such as an accident, an illness, or celebration. Therefore, rather than asking about completed suggestions, the therapist begins with "What's better?" which implies the therapist remains confident in the client's abilities and competence (De Jong & Berg, 2013).

The following scenario illustrates the follow-up session with Joe.

Therapist:	Hey, Joe! What's better?
Joe:	I have a new friend. He's new at school.
Therapist:	You do! Tell me about him.
Joe:	He is really fast. We raced, and he can beat me! His name is Joshua.
Therapist:	Joshua can beat you at running? Wow! He must be fast.
Joe:	Yea. He was kind of scared at first, because his mom left him at school.
Therapist:	So, he was scared of being at a new school?
Joe:	Yea, so I went up to him to tell him it would be OK. I thought the teacher was going to be mad, but I think she thought it was OK since he was scared.
Therapist:	So, you helped him feel better.
Joe:	Yea.
Therapist:	Show me how you did that.
Joe:	(Gets out of his seat and comes next to the therapist and says, "It's OK.") That's what I did.
Therapist:	What did Joshua do?
Joe:	He stopped crying.
Therapist:	I am so impressed with you noticing Joshua having problems and then helped him out. How did you know to do that?
Joe:	I don't know. I just felt bad for him.
Therapist:	It sounds like you knew what to say, and it helped him feel better. So, Joe, What else is better?

Joe visited the therapist twice a week. Each time he visited the therapist asked, "What's better?"(E). He often answered the question with a focus on his friendships, since his goal entailed making friends. They talked about his friendships and the therapist amplified (A) his efforts using comments such as "Wow! I am impressed." After he replied, the therapist asked him questions to gain as many details as possible about his perspective on how these positive events took place and who noticed, intensely listening and paraphrasing his comments. Using indirect compliments such as "How did you know to do that?" helped Joe recognize his personal efficacy in making friends. The therapist continued to reinforce (R) his strengths and the significance of his progress by using more indirect compliments such as "What did you do to make that happen?" and showing interest in Joe's positive behaviors. Then, to continue with a focus on progress, the therapist started over (S) by asking "What else is better?" By the third visit, Joe had learned the routine, in that each time he entered the therapist's office, the therapist asked "What's better?" By eliciting this exception, he began thinking about his progress and strengths before coming into the therapist's office. (Figure 11.1.)

Once the client seems to exhaust answers to "What's better", the therapist assesses progress by asking a scaling question. The scaling question also provides a way to develop the next small goal (De Jong & Berg, 2013).

Therapist: (Using a number line created by Joe that has a picture of him taped above the number 5.) This is where you were last week, so let's look at it this week. On a scale of 0 to 10, with 0 being you have no friends at all, and 10 being you have as many friends as you want, where are you now? (Joe looks carefully at his picture and then places it above the number 6.)

Therapist: What makes you a 6 this week?

Joe: I got a new friend, Joshua, and we like to play the same things. We play *Minecraft* and we run outside at recess. I am going to see if he can come to my house this week and play. Mrs. Schmidt (teacher) says I am doing better too.

Therapist: So your teacher noticed you are doing better. What does she notice you doing that is better?

Joe: I don't get out of my seat as much. She told me if I wouldn't jump out of my seat so much she would let me work at the computer with my friends.

Therapist: So you managed to stay in your seat. I am so impressed. Then, you got to go to the computer and play with your friends.

Joe: Yep!

Therapist: So, Joe, you are a 6, right? (Joe nods.) What will you be doing when you are a 7?

Joe: I will probably be making more friends. I already got five friends.

Therapist: You have five friends! That's amazing. Tell me again who your friends are.

Joe:	(He puts up his left hand and names them as he points to each finger.) Joshua, Marty, Sam, Sheila, Cindy, Damon.
Therapist:	So, you have five friends. How many friends do you need before you do not need to come see me anymore?
Joe:	Maybe, seven.
Therapist:	So if you have maybe seven friends, you wouldn't need to come see me anymore.
Joe:	Yea. Maybe, if I was doing a little better in school.
Therapist:	What does that mean, if you were doing a little better in school?
Joe:	Like I would turn in my homework and keep my hands to myself.
Therapist:	You would turn in your homework and not get into other people's things. So, Joe, what will you be doing next week that will tell us that you are a 7?
Joe:	I would have more friends.
Therapist:	OK. You would have more friends. What else?
Joe:	I would turn in my homework more times.

After the client answers the scaling question, the therapist asks about the next number on the scale. This sets in place the next small goal. The therapist then gives the client a compliment-bridge-suggestion, as she did at the end of the first session. If the client seems to be making progress, as in this scenario, the suggestion might be to continue doing what is working.

Therapist:	I am so impressed, Joe, with how you are doing better in school. When you first came, you told me you were a 2 on the scale, and now you are a 6! You are using your power to stay in your seat, turning in your work, and making friends. I know it has been hard, but you are taking control of yourself. I wonder if you might turn in your homework three times before I see you next time. How does that sound to you?

What if Things Aren't Better?

The process of EARS seems simple enough, but what happens when the client states that nothing is better or the situation seems worse? For example, Malik, age 15, states that things are the same since his father died and he still has trouble sleeping, that he frequently awakens to dreams and nightmares surrounding the cancer that took his father three months earlier. By listening and accepting Malik, the therapist validates his feelings of loss and the associated difficulties he experiences. She then asks Malik a coping question, "How do you manage to come to school and still get your work done?" The coping question allows Malik to identify his strengths and his positive self-talk: "I just think to myself, 'I have to go to school. My dad was proud of me, so I have to keep going.' It's just hard, especially when I can't sleep." The therapist compliments Malik on making it to school and his ability to motivate himself even

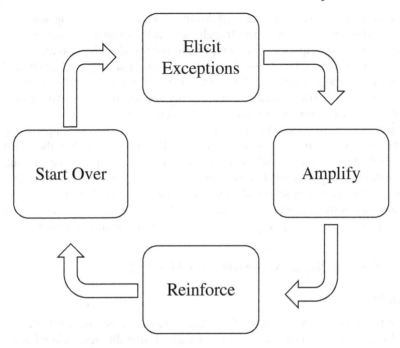

Figure 11.1 Process of EARS.

when he experiences problems sleeping. As the therapist continues talking with Malik, she addresses his sleeping concerns by asking "When are there times you sleep just a little better?" Together, Malik and the therapist create a new and specific goal that addresses his sleeping concerns by asking about what he knows regarding how to get a better night's sleep and things he has tried that were helpful.

When the client states that things are the same, it is the therapist's opportunity to affirm the client's ability to maintain his current status, focusing on the strengths the client demonstrates or discusses. Examples of the therapist's response to no change might be: "How do you manage to keep going to class?" "How come things aren't worse?" "What strengths do you use to keep yourself at this current level?" Similarly, the therapist uses an indirect compliment by asking, "How do you do it?" The indirect compliment shifts his focus from talking about how he isn't making any progress to talking about his personal strengths.

If the client states that things are worse, the therapist's first questions might be "How are you managing to deal with things even though they are worse?" or "How do you get here every day in spite of these difficulties?" "How do you manage to cope?" By asking coping questions, the therapist continues to elicit the strengths and resources the client utilizes and then amplifies and compliments the client on his strengths.

When clients become discouraged due to a lack of progress or ongoing challenges, it is helpful to normalize struggles and let the client know that relapses and struggles are expected. The therapist can reframe the relapse as an opportunity to learn by asking "What did you learn from what happened this time?" The therapist works with the client to problem-solve how to deal with future obstacles or concerns (Bannink, 2006). Using a sandtray or role playing provides an excellent way to problem-solve different scenarios.

If the client continues to find it difficult to make progress, empathizing with the client using statements such as "I know it's hard" lets the client know the therapist hears the client and recognizes the situation to be difficult. Sometimes the goal needs to be revisited to determine if it is an appropriate goal, and if the goal is achievable, realistic, small, and important to the client. If any one of these is missing, the client may be trying to achieve something that does not reflect a good goal or that is no longer relevant. (Figure 11.2.)

Creative and Playful Approaches to EARS

Scaling

The therapist uses a scale from the first or previous sessions with the client to look at what is better since the last session. Using different colored pens, markers, or stickers to mark the scale assists the client in recognizing progress. To maintain consistence, the therapist should use the same scale, as long as it is effective.

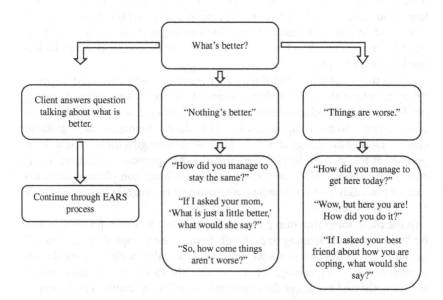

Figure 11.2 Client and Therapist Responses to "What's Better?"

Drawing

The therapist asks the client to draw three pictures that represent where the client was at the last session, where the client is today, and where the client will be when he no longer needs to come to therapy. This allows the client to remember his goal but also to reconsider the goal and whether it still represents the client's hopes for the future.

Show Me

The therapist asks the client to show her what he did differently by acting it out physically, using the sandtray and its miniatures, role playing, or using puppets. By repeating successful behaviors, the client further cements new ways of being and doing. The therapist amplifies what the client demonstrates by asking questions such as:

- "How did you know to do that?"
- "What was it like when you did that? How did you feel?"
- "What are you thinking about when you are showing me what you did?"
- "How did others react to what you did?"
- "How did you get the courage to try that?"

Recording Successes

One of the most reinforcing approaches for continuing successes involves the client keeping a tangible record of each success. Creative approaches for recording successes take different forms depending on the client's developmental age.

Writing a Story or Poem

The client writes the beginning of the story and continues to add to it to reflect her progress. Even if the client isn't making the progress she hopes, writing the story can be cathartic, but may also reveal other options in terms of goals or behaviors to reach goals. Similarly, the client might write a stanza of a poem at each session, reflecting progress made. If the client reaches her goals, she writes an appropriate ending to the story or poem. The client's writing documents each step of progress toward reaching the miracle goal.

Drawing or Painting a Picture

The client draws a part of a picture each time he comes to therapy. Each part that he draws marks a step toward the miracle goal. When the client accomplishes the goal, he draws a completed picture. With a younger child, coloring parts of a pre-drawn page that represents each success allows the child to view the continued progress toward his goal. The picture should represent something meaningful to the child's goal.

Create a Book

Using a journal or blank paper, the client draws, paints, or creates a collage that illustrates progress made since the last session. When the client reaches his goal, the therapist puts the pages together to create a book. The client creates a name for the book, decorates the cover, and draws a picture illustrating what it is like to reach the goal.

Conclusion

The EARS process assures the client that the focus of the session continues to address strengths rather than pathology. Clients often expect therapists to focus on what the client did wrong rather than on client strengths. One session does not necessarily mean the client trusts the therapist; however, when the client experiences even small amounts of success and discusses successes with a therapist who focuses on strengths and demonstrates respect for the client's perspectives, trust grows. Ironically, as clients trust that the therapist will see their strengths, clients feel they can risk sharing their concerns and doubts, as well as experiences of shame and rejection, knowing that the therapist continues to view them through lenses that focus on strengths and valuing their perspectives.

References

Bannink, F. (2006). *1001 solution-focused questions* (2nd Ed.). New York, NY: W. W. Norton.

De Jong, P. & Berg, I. K. (2013). *Interviewing for solutions* (4th Ed.). Belmont, CA: Brooks/Cole.

Duckworth, A. (2016). *Grit: The power of passion and perseverance.* New York, NY: Scribner.

CHAPTER 12

Solution-Focused Group Approaches

Elizabeth R. Taylor, Amanda Allison, and Becky Southard

Sam, a rather energetic, blonde, nine-year-old boy, has been referred for being a constant disruption in class, out of his seat, excessive talking, and interrupting the teacher and others, often exasperating school staff. Sam did not have an official diagnosis, but his teacher called him her "ADHD child." Sam's mother, a single professional woman, stated that he was quite active at home, but she set boundaries that he could not talk to her for an hour after dinner, so she could get some of the household chores done. During this hour, he could work on homework, and, if he had completed it, he could watch television or play his computer game.

After being referred to me, I saw him individually for two sessions. During this time he drew a picture of his family—his mother, his grandparents, an aunt, and a cousin. He talked about the times they went to one another's houses and how they celebrated Christmas at his grandparents' home. He seemed sad at times but eagerly told his stories in great detail. His verbal skills indicated his intelligence to be at least above average, but his behavior prevented him from demonstrating this in class. I decided that adding a child to our counseling sessions might help him practice his social skills, sitting in his seat, and listening.

Marco, a nine-year-old Hispanic male, referred for not doing his work, off-task behavior, and occasional arguing, provided a good fit for our little group of two. The referral stated that Marco might be depressed, finding it difficult to reconcile the idea that his parents recently divorced. For the first few sessions, Marco, Sam, and I played UNO. Immediately, in the first session, Sam grabbed the cards and spread them over the table, so I wrapped my arms around the table to prevent the cards from flying everywhere and quickly pulled the cards together and shuffled them. Marco sat in stunned silence. We had decided on a few rules before the group started, so I reminded them of the rules when it seemed appropriate. One rule was that the person playing could not talk, but the other person had the floor and could talk about whatever was of interest to him. Marco and Sam quickly picked up the idea, and over time they both improved, Marco talking more, Sam talking less, and both acting calmer. I used the talking time as a space to hear their concerns, reflecting thoughts and feelings, and paraphrasing what they said. I used indirect and direct compliments for any hint of strengths, such as having a good idea, problem-solving in a certain situation, or just wait-ing their turn. Having played UNO with other children, I knew this game could last a long time, and it did! For a full 45 minutes we played UNO over three consecutive sessions.

This small group learned to wait, take turns, and sit in their seats, but Sam learned that if he played without talking he could focus better and amazed him-self at his ability to stick with the game. They also learned losing did not mean the end of the world, and that they could play again if they kept the cards on the table and continued to take turns. These sessions also allowed me to spend time with Sam and Marco without focusing on them, that is, they said whatever they wanted but without the scrutiny of eye contact, since we focused on the game.

Although I am the first to admit that playing the same game repeatedly proved to be quite tedious and downright boring, the repetition of practicing appro-priate behaviors repeatedly taught the young boys skills they needed for better behavior in the classroom. However, by the fourth session, both boys needed to do something different, so we painted pictures and talked about them, we did group sandtray, and we sat on the floor in a circle talking about our day using a talking stick to continue practice taking turns. After about seven sessions, Sam played with Marco outside of class, both worked better in school, and we decided to terminate therapy with the agreement that we would get together if either one felt he needed to do so. Even in a small group, we accomplished our goals: Sam listened to his teacher more and did not have any major discipline referrals, and Marco learned to focus on his work in school and turn it in to the teacher thus resulting in better grades.

Why Group?

Group therapy often gets a bad rap—"It's not as good as individual." "You can't make progress as fast." "I don't want other people finding out about my problems and judging me." "It could be embarrassing to talk about my problems." The list goes on, but researchers find that group can be just as effective as individual therapy, and cost-effective (Bastien, Morin, Ouellet, Blais & Bouchard, 2004; McCrone et al., 2005; van Rijn & Wild, 2016; Stalker & Fry, 1999; Weiss, Jaffee, Menil & Cogley, 2004; Westbury & Tutty, 1999; Zettle, Haflich & Reynolds, 1992). Many problems that bring children and adolescents to the therapist's office originate in the social milieu—making and keeping friends, problems with family members, social skills, social anxi-ety, and bullying—all making the list of interpersonal issues that can be more effectively addressed in groups. Through special techniques and group-oriented approaches, clients recognize and play out issues in a group of peers, trying on new behaviors, practicing them, and then experimenting with their new behaviors outside of group.

Solution-focused group therapy (SFGT) provides a short-term but effec-tive approach for children and adolescents. "Brief therapy does not mean 'less of the same' but therapy with its own structure and process that differs from long term" (O'Connell, 1998, p. 6). Solution-focused group therapy builds on strengths and resiliencies of the individual members and of the group. Therapists find these strength-based groups helpful with children experiencing low academic performance, emotional difficulties, and learning disabilities, as well as children of alcoholics, survivors of sexual abuse, homeless adolescents, and adolescent probationers (Arman, 2002; Daki & Savage, 2010; LaFountain, Garner & Eliason, 1996; Kress & Hoffman, 2008; McNair & Arman, 2000; Newsome & Kelly, 2004; Newsome, 2005; Shin, 2009; Walker, 2008). Since prepubescent children and adolescents often learn best from one another, the group interactions enhance new ways of handling interpersonal challenges (Pérusse, Goodenough & Lee, 2009).

How groups are conducted with different populations varies according to developmental ages, challenges and concerns, and personal strengths and abilities. For some concerns, a combination of individual and group therapy works best, and for others, such as those who have histories of abuse or trauma, individual therapy provides a better approach until the individual has worked through the trauma and feels safe enough to participate in group. Some children and adolescents do not have the social hunger to be effective group members and may not be appropriate for group. Older children tend to exhibit this social hunger more intensely than those at ages four or five, but social hunger should be a consideration for inclusion in groups at all ages (Ray, 2011).

When forming groups, short-term groups work better if homogeneous, that is, if they focus on a common theme or problem, such as academic progress, grief and loss, self-regulation, and others. The therapist conducting SFGT works in the present rather than spending time hashing over past problems, addressing interpersonal rather than intrapersonal issues, and focuses on reaching goals rather than making personality changes. Solution-focused groups meet anywhere from 6 to 12 sessions and are generally closed groups (Sharry, 2007), providing a practical approach in working with children and adolescents in schools or community settings due to limited time, insurance benefits, and financial resources.

However, as noted earlier, SF therapy does not always allow for those who have difficulty expressing themselves, particularly those with physical and cognitive learning differences and those whose command of the language precludes them from being able to use words that more appropriately express their thoughts and feelings. In group therapy, other challenges exist as well, such as working with children whose dispositions tend to be quiet, shy, or guarded, and those whose social skills keep them from understanding or using language appropriately, such as those with a diagnosis of autism or impulsive disorders. Using creative and playful approaches in groups provides an avenue that allows for intense expressions of emotions such as grief, fear, anxiety, and loss (Finn, 2003). Additionally, more expressive modes of communication allow group members to express ideas and emotions with less verbalization, focusing on the here-and-now, while gaining understanding that they are not alone in their difficulties (Waller, 2011). Additionally, groups conducted for such issues as grief and loss or trauma benefit from using creative and expressive approaches to allow for communication of intense feelings, such as fear, anxiety, and loss (Finn, 2003).

Forming Groups

Working with children of younger ages or those who have severe cognitive deficits requires less structured group approaches, as developmentally younger children (ages two to three) tend to work in parallel, that is, playing beside others but not with others. Around the ages of five and six, children begin to engage in cooperative play and most often with the same gender. For those at the upper end of this stage, games, expressive art techniques, and more structured SFGT approaches may be appropriate and effective. Younger children and those who have immature emotional development often require more of the therapist's time in forming attachments, making it difficult to give equal attention to each child, necessitating smaller groups.

Goals for children and adolescents in small groups focus on interpersonal challenges, such as friendships, social skills, bullying, appropriate intimacy, anger and conflict, and familial concerns that may interfere with academic progress or impede healthy mental and social development. Preferably, children and adolescents work collaboratively with the therapist to set their goals, though adults often refer them for general issues such as grief and loss, difficulty making friends, or isolation. Once clients attend a pregroup meeting or the first group, asking them what they want to get from group allows them to talk about their personal hopes and goals.

A good rule of thumb for small groups is that the younger the age, the smaller the group. That is, groups for elementary-school children should be limited to three or four members, whereas groups for adolescents may include up to eight members (Cooley, 2009; Corey, Corey & Corey, 2010). Older children and adolescents often look to one another for approval and have more intimate relationships with their peers than those at younger ages. Enlisting one or two more group members than the ideal group size provides for dropouts, extended absences, or other interruptions that may preclude clients from attending group. For groups with highly active children or those who tend to be shy, restricting the group to two or three members allows for better participation and increased cohesiveness.

Forming SF groups involves coordinating the schedules of multiple people, and, when dealing with children, requires working with family schedules as well as school schedules. Conducting groups in the summer presents challenges, as people go on vacation, may be involved in summer camps (day or week-long camps), and have other activities that take them away from home and prevent regular attendance in a group, even a short-term group. After-school groups can also be problematic, but not impossible. Adolescents often do not want more things to do after school, and many cannot participate due to their own responsibilities, involvement in sports, clubs, and other extracurricular activities. Some are responsible for taking care of younger children or have after-school jobs. Yet, many districts offer after-school programs to parents who work, particularly for elementary and middle school students. These after-school programs provide help with homework, extracurricular activities, and enrichment programs, and may be willing to offer intervention services, thus providing an opportunity for group therapy.

Small group counseling most often occurs in schools with school counselors and community agencies providing the group intervention services. Since youth attend school for at least 30 weeks of the year, more opportunities exist for bringing them together to address their concerns without the family schedules and outside forces interfering with the school day. Yet, schools have their own scheduling challenges, such as holidays, testing, and special events. Further, teachers, though aware that youth need help, are often reluctant to let students leave the classroom because the student misses class instruction, which may impact performance on standardized testing. School counselors must be advocates for the needs of students with a focus on the impact counseling can have on students' motivation and performance while addressing personal issues and concerns the child brings from home.

Selecting Group Members

Composing a therapy group differs according to the developmental ages of group members and the context of the group. To determine which clients might benefit from group and make good group members, the therapist often selects clients from a list of referrals from teachers or parents or those attending individual therapy. Although clients may be the same developmental age, they may not be appropriate for the group. To determine the appropriateness of group for younger children, the therapist might observe them in a natural setting, such as the classroom or playground, to determine which children fit best together. The therapist might interview parents and teachers about the client's strengths and challenges, particularly regarding interpersonal relationships. Although group therapy provides an excellent context for helping children with interpersonal skills, placing several children who exhibit problems in self-control or aggressiveness in the same group often creates a disruptive atmosphere that keeps the group members from participating effectively. Much like Marco and Sam mentioned at the beginning of this chapter, matching group members in a way that they complement one another allows the group to function more effectively.

In schools, one of the most effective approaches for selecting group members involves first distributing a general needs assessment to teachers and staff, as well as making a survey available for students, to determine the types of groups that might be needed. The purpose of the needs assessment is to gain an overall understanding of possible concerns to be addressed in small groups, such as anxiety, death and loss, friendship challenges, study skills, youth of incarcerated parents, youth of parents experiencing divorce, problems with substance use, body image concerns, and other issues that affect youth. The school counselor then creates a second survey of the groups needed and asks teachers to identify students who might need to be in one of the groups. The counselor also creates a list of groups offered and makes it available to students in the counselor's office or in other convenient locations, so students need only to write their names and check which group is of interest to them.

Pre-Group Meetings

Although not always possible, conducting a pre-group meeting individually or in groups to talk about the purpose and process of group provides the therapist with important information about the clients' concerns, challenges, strengths, and interpersonal skills. Pre-group meetings offer benefits to the clients as well, since this time provides an opportunity for the therapist to provide information about how groups work, expectations, and how to get the most out of being a part of the group. Yalom and Leszcz (2005) state that "there is highly persuasive evidence that pre-group preparation expedites the course of group therapy" (p. 294).

The pre-group meeting addresses: 1) how the group can be helpful, 2) goal setting, 3) confidentiality, 4) specific information about the group, 5) questions and concerns, and 6) the group contract between the group members and the therapist. In the pre-group meeting, the therapist provides information about how groups can be helpful and an overall picture of the way groups work, including techniques the therapist might use, such as art and music. The group therapist explains that group offers a special time to talk with others who share similar challenges, to set goals, and to discover solutions together.

A second area to address in the pre-group meeting involves setting goals. The SF group therapist asks members to consider what they would like to be different when the group is over and what potential positive outcomes they foresee by participating. Asking clients to consider their possible goals sets in motion the strength-based focus of the group, and, although effective goals may not be set during the pre-group meeting, the clients can begin thinking about the goal in order to define it by the end of the first session.

A third area of discussion in the pre-group meeting involves confidentiality. The limits of confidentiality address several topics: a) the inability to prevent group members from talking about what occurs in group with others outside of group, b) parents retaining the right to information about their children, c) the need to provide counseling records should a judge subpoena them, and d) the need to get help from adults outside the group should clients discuss hurting themselves or others. The therapist should also emphasize to potential group members that they should refrain from talking to their friends about what others say in group.

Other topics for the pre-group meeting include specific information about how the group will be conducted, activities, and the time and place the group convenes. Importantly, the therapist allows time for the potential group members to ask questions and express any fears and concerns to reduce indecision and anxiety about being in the group. If the pre-group meeting occurs individually, the potential group members more readily discuss their questions and concerns. On the other hand, conducting pre-group meetings in groups offers several advantages in that: a) clients gain the opportunity to hear others' concerns and questions, b) clients get to know who other group members are, c) members get to experience their first group process, and d) pre-group meetings are more time efficient than individually meeting with each potential member.

The therapist should consider working with group members to develop and sign contracts that include expectations of group members and of the group therapist. The following requirements for the group therapist might include:

1   responsibility for convening the group each week;
2   keeping confidential what is said in group except when someone might be hurt or harmed, when a parent asks for information, or in the case of an order from a judge;
3   creating a safe place for the child or adolescent to talk; and
4   supporting the client in reaching his or her goals.

The following requirements for the client might include:

1   attending the group and being on time;
2   supporting other group members; and
3   not talking about what others say to friends outside the group.

When client and therapist sign the contract, it sends the message that the therapist, as well as the client, have a responsibility in making the group successful.

Therapeutic Factors

Many of the positive and negative experiences in group provide experiences that help individual members to learn new ways to interact, tap undiscovered strengths and resources, and provide a sense of community. Although group therapists employ various theories and techniques, certain therapeutic factors consistently allow for healing and growth across contexts, cultures, and populations. After researching which therapeutic factors rise to the top in terms of their effectiveness with adult populations, Yalom and Leszcz (2005) propose 11 different factors that comprise effective groups: instillation of hope, universality, group cohesiveness, catharsis, imparting of information, interpersonal learning, development of socializing techniques, imitative behavior, corrective recapitulation of the primary family group, altruism, and existential factors (death, freedom, isolation, and meaning). Sharry (2007), when describing SFGT, does not include existential factors but replaces them with group empowerment. However, it can be argued that existential factors play a role in all groups, since all must deal with existential issues in life, such as the loss of friends, death of a loved one, freedom to choose thoughts and behaviors, and even the "why" we need to behave in certain ways. Depending on the type of group, each of these factors plays a role but to varying degrees. Above all, "instillation of hope" is the match that lights the fire for the other factors. However, once the fire is lit, cohesiveness and universality play major roles in the success and process of the group, particularly with children and adolescents.

Therapeutic factors differ with children and adolescent groups from those with adults. Overall, the main therapeutic factors that seem most applicable to groups for children and adolescents include cohesiveness, universality, instillation of hope, imitative behavior, socializing techniques, and interpersonal learning. With adolescents, catharsis may also play an important role as members share difficult and challenging experiences. Overall, when group members feel that they matter to the group, that they have something to contribute and to gain from being a part of the group, they find the community of group members a welcomed place away from the demands of social and academic forces that often contribute to lower self-esteem, hopelessness, and feelings of isolation. When two, three, or more children or adolescents come together regularly for group, they begin to develop a sense that they are in this together and that they have similar concerns. Over time, their shared space begins to feel like a small community, and when one group member is missing, others notice. Cohesiveness develops as they learn to share the space, the therapist, and experiences together. Imitative behavior occurs as they observe, role play, and learn from one another and from the therapist. Socializing techniques and interpersonal learning, usually the main goals for counseling with youth, encompass many of the goals of children and adolescents.

Process of Group

Solution-focused group therapy views all clients and the group as having strengths and resources, so that the therapist uses SF techniques to help clients uncover their personal resources and find solutions to solve their problems. However, the group becomes the focus, not necessarily the individual client. Keys to effective group process involve: 1) setting norms, 2) working in the here and now, 3) focusing on the client's experience, and 4) encouraging group members to communicate with one another rather than with just the therapist.

Setting Norms

One of the most important jobs of the group therapist, regardless of theoretical orientation, involves setting group norms. Group norms provide the boundaries and expectations of how group members work with one another (Corey, Corey & Corey, 2014). The group leader establishes two types of norms—procedural and process. Procedural norms might include being on time, not eating or drinking during group, and allowing others time to talk. The SF therapist works with group members to develop these norms by asking, "What do you think will help this group be a good group?" "What do we need to do to help each other reach our goals?"

Process norms involve staying in the here and now, listening to others, talking directly to group members rather than through the therapist, and focusing on client strengths. Norms become more explicit as clients listen to and emulate the group leader who models and directs behaviors. Although it may be necessary to remind clients of the norms, they gradually become automatic (Corey, Corey & Corey, 2014).

Working in the Here and Now

In SFGT, the therapist focuses the group on the here and now rather than the past, unless the past provides insight into clients' strengths and how they overcame past challenges. Since SFGT remains a brief approach, exploring past problems and concerns takes up valuable time that might be better spent on addressing current challenges and strengths. However, when clients bring up past problems the therapist should not ignore the discussion but validate their struggles. Sometimes the discussion of past problems allows clients to appreciate one another's struggles, recognize they are not alone, and creates a more cohesive group (Sharry, 2007; Yalom & Leszcz, 2005). The SF group therapist focuses on exceptions to the problem, strengths the client uses to solve problems, and how the client copes when no solution seems apparent. Whenever clients bring up the past, the therapist brings the clients back into the present.

Therapist:	What's better since we last met? (Focusing the client toward what is going better rather than problem talk.)
Jake:	My mom is not so bossy.
Therapist:	Your mom is different. What are you doing when she is not so bossy? (Returning credit for change back to the client as an indirect compliment.)
Jake:	I am doing my homework.
Therapist:	That's great! You're doing your homework, and so your mom isn't bugging you so much. (Direct compliment and rephrasing what client said to reinforce the change.)
Therapist:	(Turning to the rest of the group.) What else is better since we last met?
Sam:	I haven't gotten in trouble with my teacher.
Therapist:	I am glad to hear you aren't getting in trouble with her. Tell me how you are managing to do that. (Reinforcing client and using an indirect compliment to return credit to the client for the change.)
Sam:	I am trying to stay in my seat more.
Therapist:	You are staying in your seat more, so now you aren't having to worry about getting in trouble. (Paraphrase and reinforcing

	change.) So, Jake and Sam are making some progress and getting along better with others. (Linking similarities.)
Sam:	I still got in trouble on the playground, though. It is just like last year when my teacher was mad at me all the time. She constantly yelled. My mom had to go up and tell her to get off my back.
Jake:	I don't like it when my mom goes and talks to the teacher, because then I get in more trouble with the teacher.
Sam:	Last year, they moved me because my mom really told the teacher off.
	(Jake sits quietly, unsure about Sam's comments.)
Therapist:	So, Sam, it sounds like things were difficult last year, but now you are doing better in school and getting along with your teacher because you are working hard at doing better in class by sitting in your seat. (Paraphrasing with an emphasis on current successes rather than difficulties in the past.)
Sam:	Yea, this teacher is nice.
Therapist:	Tell me what you mean when you say she is nice.

The focus of this conversation shifts from the past to the present and from problems to solutions. The therapist capitalizes on Sam's successes rather than focusing on past problems.

Focus on the Client's Experience

Often, when someone talks about a problem, the person listening tries to provide advice. Although it is well-intentioned, advice-giving most often proves ineffective. This does not mean that it should be stifled, since it demonstrates altruism and a sense of caring. However, the therapist offers a more effective approach by asking clients to speak from their own experience rather than giving advice.

Tyler:	Mike is always bugging me. When he talks to me I can't get my work done.
Jack:	Why don't you just tell the teacher?
Tyler:	I have, but it doesn't work. She just tells me to get back to work.
Jack:	Why don't you tell your mom, and she can talk to the teacher?
Tyler:	I tried to, but mom doesn't want to come to school one more time.
Therapist:	Tyler, it sounds like you have tried some things that weren't very helpful. Jack, could you talk about a time when someone bothered you, and you did something that helped. (Stops the advice-giving and acknowledges Tyler's efforts. To bring the group back to the here and now, the therapist asks Jack to speak from his own experience rather than giving advice.)
Jack:	I just tell him to wait until I get my work done.
Therapist:	How has that worked?

Jack: When someone bothers me, I just say to wait until I get my work done.

Therapist: So, telling him to wait has been helpful. (Turning to the rest of the group.) What are some other things you have done that have been helpful?

Once Tyler expresses his concerns, Jack quickly jumps in with a solution to Tyler's problem, but each time it is met with how the solution would not work. Rather than continuing to pursue this line of questioning, the therapist redirects Jack to his own personal experience about what has been helpful and then asks other group members for their experiences. Not only does this help Tyler, but it also empowers the group and encourages group members to participate.

Encouraging Group Members to Communicate with One Another

By encouraging group members to speak to one another, the therapist expands on the resources of group members, often resulting in friendships that continue once group ends. In the beginning, however, group members tend to speak directly to the group leader, much like in individual therapy. This proves to be inefficient and defeats the purposes of the group experience. The therapist employs several approaches to create more interaction among group members and increase cohesion.

1   When a group member asks a question to the group leader, the leader turns to the group and states, "That sounds like a good question. What do you think?"
2   When a group member talks about another group member, the therapist redirects the member to speak directly to the other person. For example, "Sam, look at Marco and tell him directly what you want to say."
3   When group members continue to talk about their personal experiences, the therapist asks the group, "Who else has had some similar experiences, and how did you handle them?"
4   When group members discuss similar experiences, interests, or strengths, the therapist links them together. For example, "Sam, Marco and Juan have found ways to handle their stress. Sam likes to listen to music. Marco likes to run. And Juan talks to some of his friends." Then, turning to the group, the therapist asks, "What other ways have you found to handle stress?"

Group Stages

By knowing the stages of group process the therapist gains a better understanding of group behaviors, the therapeutic factors that might be at stake, and what interventions might be most appropriate for effective group movement. Group stages involve the process of getting to know one another, first by gaining information about one another, understanding commonalities and differences, appreciating challenges, and uncovering what clients want to be different.

The Coreys (2014) divide group phases into four stages: initial, transition, working, and termination. The initial stage, characterized by getting oriented to the process of group, developing personal and group goals, and tentativeness about how much to share and participate, centers on helping members develop a sense of safety in the group. In the transition stage, group members often take risks and share personal stories and fears but may also challenge group members and the leader, as trust and intimacy continue to grow. The third stage, the working stage, finds members continuing to trust one another more, less afraid of challenging one another, becoming more hopeful that change can occur, and recognizing their internal strengths and possibilities. In the termination stage, members struggle with their bittersweet thoughts and feelings as they recognize that group is coming to an end, review what they learned in group, and consider how to continue to apply what they learned in group to their lives once group ends (Corey, Corey & Corey, 2014).

Creative and play-based approaches offer ways to encourage the therapeutic factors and move clients through the tasks of each stage. In creating SF group approaches, the therapist considers if the interventions:

1   focus on strengths and positive aspects of the members and the group collectively;
2   are developmentally appropriate for the ages and concerns of group members;
3   are appropriate for the stage of group;
4   maintain or increase the cohesiveness of the group; and
5   address goals of the group and its individual members.

Initial Stage

During the initial stage, the SF therapist focuses on helping group members feel welcome; getting to know one another; building hope, cohesiveness, and universality; and setting individual and group goals. The group leader finds ways to compliment the individual and the group and takes a mental note of strengths of each group member. I sometimes keep notecards on each group member, on which I list the client's strengths, resiliencies, and resources, and then after each session I add new observations to my list. This offers several advantages. First, by taking note of client strengths and resiliencies, I remind myself that the client has resources despite the challenges. Second, patterns emerge that I might later share with the group members. For example, one person might be encouraging to others, always saying positive things about them. Stating this aloud at an appropriate time during the group not only helps the individual, but it also raises the member's status among other group members.

Just like first stages of building relationships, the main goal of the initial stage is to build trust (Corey, Corey & Corey, 2014). The therapist facilitates these feelings of trust by being encouraging, genuine, and predictable in terms of kindness, consideration of each member, and looking out for the good of the group. Trust and mistrust are openly discussed, and limits of confidentiality are emphasized. If these issues are addressed openly and honestly, group members realize they have some degree of safety and can share without fear of being shamed or embarrassed.

In the first session, the therapist works collaboratively with group members to set realistic and obtainable goals within the time frame of the group. Goals include individual goals but also group goals. Group goals provide direction, as well as safety, by focusing on how members share information about themselves. To help adolescents set goals in their group, the therapist might ask, "How would you like this group to look at the end of the six weeks?" "When group is over, what will be some of the strengths you want to remember about this group?" The following illustrate examples of group goals: "We can be honest with each other." "We support each other." "We listen to each other." "We trust one another." To help younger children set group goals, the therapist might ask, "How can this group be a good group?" "What do you want this group to be like?" Answers vary but could include: "We can talk about our problems." "We can be friends." "We can do things together." Group members often state group goals in general terms and somewhat simplistically, but group goals enhance cohesiveness and possibilities for a positive group experience.

The therapist also aids group members in defining effective individual goals, realistic goals that can be accomplished in the time frame allowed, defined specifically so that group members know when goals are accomplished. Although group members often state goals that appear to be individual endeavors, most goals involve interpersonal struggles and relational support. Solution-focused group therapy enlists the basic principles of SF therapy—that all have resources and abilities to address challenges and, by expanding on exceptions to problems and client strengths, challenges can be successfully addressed, and goals accomplished.

In the beginning stages, group activities should address increasing the comfort level of the group, diminishing anxiety, and helping clients to get to know one another better. Activities should also focus on goal development and empowering the group members to reach their goals by the end of group.

Activities for Beginning Stages

Pass the Hat

This activity addresses fears clients might have about being in the group while increasing a sense of universality. Depending on the familiarity of the group members with one another, it can be done early in the group or after one or two sessions. Clients write down their fears anonymously on small pieces of paper, fold them, and place them in a hat or container. The therapist then selects randomly from the hat and reads each of the fears. As the fears are read, the therapist asks the group who might have similar fears (without asking who wrote it).

Collective Strengths

The purpose of this activity is to increase a sense of universality, hope, and cohesiveness in the group members. The therapist provides three 3 × 5 cards to each member and asks them to draw something on each card that represents something they are good at doing. Once clients complete their drawings, the cards of all group members are taped or placed together in a square to demonstrate the many talents and strengths of the group. Clients are invited to talk about their strengths and how they are helpful. The therapist might ask, "What are some similarities of our group members?" "How can these strengths help us as a group?" "What are some strengths of other group members that might be helpful to you?" The therapist asks the client about what has been helpful and links clients who have similar strengths and coping strategies.

Collage

The purpose of this collage activity is to help students get to know one another better and develop cohesiveness. Members select two pictures from a selection of precut magazine pictures, one that represents the self and then one that represents their relationships, and pastes these on a poster board in a collage. The therapist asks the group: "What commonalities do you notice between pictures?" "What is unique and different about the pictures you chose?" "What does this picture say about your strengths?"

Collages can also be useful in helping clients discuss goals. Group members select pictures from the collage box of precut magazines that represent their preferred futures. The therapist asks questions that help clients to narrow down the larger goals into more effective goals. For example:

- "When is a time that just a little of this preferred future occurred?"
- "If you were to scale where you are in terms of reaching this goal, with 1 representing you have not reached it all and 10 representing that you have reached your goal, where are you now?"
- "What would your (important other) say will be different when you reach your goal?"
- "What will your (important other) notice you are doing differently when you reach this goal?"

Puzzle

Creating a puzzle and putting it together builds a sense of cohesiveness and increases interpersonal learning. For this activity, the therapist uses a plain cutout puzzle (can be purchased at craft stores), provides a puzzle piece to each group member, and asks each person to write one of their strengths on it. Placing the pieces back together, the therapist reflects on how the group members bring together many strengths, linking together commonalities.

A puzzle for adolescents can also be created by using teen magazine pictures mounted to poster board and then cut into different pieces. Each member of the group then writes a strength on the back of the poster piece. Once the pieces are together, they can be glued together so that the completed picture hangs on the wall to remind them of the strengths they bring to the group.

Sandtray

When working with group sandtray in the beginning stages of group, questions that address group members' strengths and assets may be helpful. For example, clients might be asked to select a miniature that represents their strengths. As these are placed in the tray, members talk about them, where they use their strengths, and a time when they were helpful. At the end of this process, the therapist asks questions regarding how the group may be able to help one another by using their strengths.

Word Cards

An approach often effective with older children and adolescents focuses on creating personal goals and building universality and cohesiveness. This activity requires a large deck of differently colored index cards with different words written on them. Words include as many parts of speech as possible, i.e., nouns, verbs, adjectives, adverbs, pronouns, and indefinite articles ("a," "the," etc.), as well as several blank cards that group members use to fill in words or phrases not included in the deck. The group sits around a table, or, preferably, on the floor, with the words placed in the middle. The therapist begins by asking group members, "Pick five to ten words and create a saying or poem that reflects your personal goal for the group." Members select their words from a pile of cards, creating a type of cohesiveness as they look through the pile together, sometimes asking one another about certain words. Members attach their words to the wall and share them with other group members. This activity, introduced by Dr. Poppy Moon (www.poppymoon.com) at a national counseling conference as an approach appealing to adolescents, provides time for adolescents to reflect on their goals.

Instead of using word cards, the therapist might use magnetic words that attach to a small magnetic board. The therapist can also use a large magnetic board and ask group members collectively to work together to create a poem about the goals of their group.

Globe

Using a flat map of the globe, group members choose a color or marker and place a dot on each of the places where they have lived. The therapist asks questions eliciting commonalities and strengths, as well as building connections between group members.

- "What was it like to live in this place?"
- "What did you learn while living there that maybe others don't know?"
- "What is one thing you didn't like about living in this place?"
- "What were the people like who lived there?" "Who was one person you particular liked?"

General discussions regarding places they have lived might center on how these places are similar (houses, places to go, things to do, people) and different. For those who have lived in many places and those who have not moved, the therapist asks questions about advantages and disadvantages of moving to new places (new friends, creating a new reputation versus having a history in a place where people know you, understanding of the community and its resources).

Journaling

The therapist provides small spiral-bound journals to group members to illustrate and write about what they hope to get from group and what they hope to contribute. This supports group members as they set individual and group goals. Journaling can be accompanied by drawings, magazine pictures, or doodles that illustrate their goals. Although journaling has value when done individually, when done collectively members gain a sense of universality and cohesiveness, building a sense of community.

Sports Goals

Using a picture or drawing of a football field or soccer field on large butcher paper, clients discuss what they hope to accomplish individually or as a group. Group goals and individual goals are written or illustrated on the goal line. Progress on the field can be measured by breaking the goals up into manageable parts with specific steps for reaching the goal. The large butcher paper provides a way for individuals to mark their progress each week using colored tape, dots, or colored pencils that illustrate each step of each group member. Members may also create personal illustrations to use as a reminder of their goal and progress made.

Group Story

Using the group as the subject of a story, the therapist asks the group to come up with a story that illustrates what they hope occurs in the group, thus setting group goals. Children and adolescents enjoy creating stories, allowing them to use their imaginations.

The therapist, using a white board or large butcher paper, begins the story with, "Once upon a time there was a group that met together each week. They were a really good group, because . . . ."

Stories may also be used as metaphors in creating group goals. For example, the therapist asks the group to come up with their own metaphor for what the group is like, that is, "This group is like. . . ." The therapist then creates a story around what the group members say about the group and how it operates effectively. Creating stories increases cohesiveness but also provides a way for the group to evaluate themselves at the end of group to see how their group has changed over time.

Group Murals

Murals provide a way to bring individual members together to illustrate similarities and differences among group members. Some therapists use the final group murals as a type of assessment, but, since the group is constantly evolving, diagnosing the group is not helpful except to note its cohesion. Rather, the therapeutic aspects of creating group murals lie in the process of creating them (Rubin & Rosenblum, 1977).

Group murals generally require white butcher paper that can be laid on the table or posted on the wall, and markers, colors, chalk, or pens. How the therapist introduces the group mural depends on the stage of the group and the ages of group members. For younger members or those in the initial stages of therapy, the request should take a more structured approach. For example, the therapist asks clients, "Draw a picture of yourself as an animal on a farm (or a fish in the ocean)." Once clients complete the drawing, discussion centers around the particular animal or fish, qualities the group member likes about the selection, as well as the roles, strengths, and vulnerabilities of the animal or fish. For those who have handicapping conditions that make it difficult to draw, group members can use photographs or magazine pictures. If clients have difficulty placing them on the mural, the therapist asks clients where they would like to place the animal or fish, and the therapist places the picture for them. The therapist might also ask clients to draw in other parts of the mural (or find pictures) that might also be important, such as trees, ponds, grass, houses, or other characteristics. This activity addresses how clients see themselves and their potential, diversity, and ability to live in the same environment.

Transition Stage

According to the Coreys (2014), the transition stage encompasses a critical period for the group, as members test other members, the leader, and the group process. Members often feel anxiety, fear, and tentativeness as they decide whether to trust the group and participate at a meaningful level. Although group members want to participate, they may fear rejection, judgment, or losing emotional control.

A common concern at this stage involves conflict and confrontations. Just like any normal relationship, as differences arise and members realize their sense of vulnerability, conflicts erupt, but these difficult experiences also lead to growth and deeper understanding. Confrontations often center on misunderstandings a group member has of another's intentions or behaviors because of different cultural, familial, or relational experiences. The most effective ways to handle such confrontations involve asking for more information, using reflective listening, and asking others for their perspectives. The Coreys (2014) state, ". . . the key is to be able to facilitate exploration of the topic and the emotions around it without judging or condemning members" (p. 229). This requires the therapist to encourage members to truly listen to one another and share their understandings. The therapist should keep in mind that challenges to the therapist or other group members are part of the group process and not take challenges personally. Challenges are often about the anxiety and fears of group members as they develop deeper relationships with one another. Conflict allows group members to see that their relationships in the group do not always have to be harmonious and that group is a safe place to disagree and openly discuss topics that provoke anxiety. The therapist compliments clients for their courage to share, letting others know that speaking up even when disapproving may be worth the risk. By not becoming defensive in the face of challenges, the group leader models openness and a willingness to hear others, behaviors important for group members to feel safe.

Working Stage

As the group continues to develop, more members take risks and relationships deepen. Members become more cohesive and hopeful as they make progress on their goals. Others may still be anxious about the intensity of the group and withdraw or hold back for fear of losing control or being rejected. However, considering the group's time spent together, the therapist might challenge more reluctant members to talk about what they are feeling, their fears and anxieties. Those who continue to struggle with making progress in reaching their goals are encouraged to ask others in the group for their input. Overall, group members at this stage encourage and support one another and members feel a sense of community and hope as they begin to make progress toward their goals.

During the working stage, group members who may have been reluctant to share due to their lack of trust may now disclose information regarding their challenges and goals. The therapist must continually be on guard against making the group session an individual session or getting too caught up in the problem and forgetting to focus on strengths. For example, an adolescent girl, Lara, whose goal is to make good grades so she can go to college, reveals that she spends much of her time taking care of her mother and her siblings because her mother is often inebriated. The therapist may be tempted to find out more details about Lara and her situation to help her find outside help. However, in group therapy, the therapist encourages group members to provide support and ask questions that facilitate Lara's solution-building. The leader's actions should focus on validating Lara's difficulties and asking others to comment on their own experiences and coping skills. In this way, the leader empowers the group to work together and assist one another. The SF therapist's role continues to be one of nudging the group toward focusing on the here and now, solution building, and recognizing the strengths of the individual and the group. If the group leader needs more information to help Lara with outside resources, the subject is best addressed individually with Lara outside of group.

Activities for Transition and Working Stages

Mandala

Creating a mandala, using a large pie-shaped circle divided into parts for each group member to design and then placing the pieces back together, metaphorically demonstrates the unity of the group and the way their individual contributions add to the overall group. We provide different ideas for using the mandala as part of the SF therapy approach below.

- Members write individual strengths on their slices of the circle and then decorate them.
- Using magazine pictures, members decorate their slices of the circle to tell others something they want others to know about them.
- Using different media, such as watercolor, pastels, pencil, colors, or paints, group members decorate their pieces of the mandala to represent their motivation for reaching their goals.

Miniatures

With or without the sandtray, miniatures provide metaphors to express progress and process of group therapy. The following are ideas for using miniatures with group members to motivate and assess goals.

- The client selects a miniature that represents the client's goal and then a miniature that represents empowerment for reaching the goal.
- The client selects a miniature that represents where he is now and another to represent where the client hopes to be by the next session.
- The client selects a miniature that represents the client's possible self. Discussion centers on what that possible self does and when the client demonstrates some of those qualities now.

Word Cards

In the transition and working stages of group, word cards can be used to help group members describe their progress and encourage other group members. For example,

- The client selects words that describe the problem and selects another word to represent a strength or resources for overcoming the challenge.
- The client selects words to create a rhyme that sounds like a cheer to help a group member reach her goal.
- The client draws a word from the group of words and creates a phrase to go with the word that describes the positive qualities of another group member.
- The client draws a word and creates a sentence using the word that includes what the client is doing now to reach her goals.

Deck of Cards

A deck of playing cards offers several approaches to help clients identify their own strengths. The therapist creates a key in which questions regarding strengths, coping skills, and resources match with the numbers and face cards in the deck. The therapist and client then take turns drawing from the deck and answer questions identifying their strengths. For example, if the group member draws a "3," the matching question might be, "Who are three people you can go to when you need to talk about your problems?" A "4" might state, "Name four ways you can deal with anxiety when it seems overwhelming." Using the deck of cards offers ways in which you can change the key according to the ages and topics of the group.

Facebook and Other Social Media

Just as introduced in Chapter 8, a blank paper copy of a Facebook page or a dialogue box used for text messaging can be helpful in gaining updates on client progress. The therapist might write a message at the top that asks, "What's better?" The client fills in the first box, and then lists what friends and family might say in the other boxes. The therapist can then ask different group members what they would say in response to the client's comment about what is better.

Emojis are useful in several ways. Using cards with emojis on them, the therapist asks group members:

- Selects the emoji that most identifies your progress since we last met.
- Tell us about the emoji you selected.
- What does this emoji say about you?
- What emoji do you hope to select next week that would indicate you made progress?

Masks

Oftentimes we tend to hide our strengths from those around us for fear we are bragging. With teens especially, it can be helpful to have them consider the qualities they feel others see and those positive qualities that maybe others do not know about. To do this, the therapist purchases ready-made plain white masks or makes masks from heavy stock paper. The client uses pictures or words to illustrate the outside of the mask regarding what others see and then the inside of the mask regarding what others might not know. Discussion about the masks involves questions about what they would like others to know about their strengths, how the client could reveal these so others would notice, and how their strengths can be useful. Once the client has shared, the therapist asks the group about other strengths they recognize in the client.

Ending Stage

The ending stage provides an opportunity for group members to celebrate their strengths and successes, to reinforce learning, and to take note of their new relationships. The therapist encourages children and adolescents to continue to see one another as resources and support once the group is over. School counselors and others who have continued contact with those in group might let members know that the therapist continues to be available if future support is needed. The therapist also addresses confidentiality, reminding group members that they should continue to keep what was said in group to themselves and not discuss what group members shared with their peers (Corey, Corey & Corey, 2010).

Not surprisingly, grief and loss become issues for some group members. Endings, as common life experiences, can be experienced in healthy ways. Often, asking clients what they will miss allows them to express their feelings of loss, perhaps for the first time. By having this opportunity, old experiences of invalidation regarding loss are replaced with acceptance and kindness. Sometimes, asking clients what they will not miss about group provides an opportunity to talk about growth that comes from loss and new beginnings (Corey, Corey & Corey, 2010).

During this final stage of group, expressive activities focus on celebrating successes, remembering relationships built, and continuing progress as the formal group ends. These activities enlist members to recall their important history of being a part of this group experience, what part they played in the group, and significant learning that took place.

Ending Stage Activities

Wizard

In the movie *The Wizard of Oz* Dorothy and her three friends uncover the wizard for the man he is and ask him about those things that were promised to them. The wizard then provides metaphorical gifts representing those things they thought they needed—the diploma for scarecrow who wants a brain, the ticking clock shaped like a heart representing a testimonial for the tin man, and an award of heroic service to represent courage for the lion. The four-minute scene at the end of the movie provides a catalyst to focus group members on recognizing and reinforcing one another for their accomplishments and strengths. The therapist should make available different materials for the group members to use in the activity, including a) objects, such as cans, sticks, blocks, paper plates, string, paper towel tubes, and other common items; b) glue, masking tape, scotch tape; c) construction paper or typing paper; and d) drawing instruments, such as pens, markers, and chalk. The following outlines the procedures of the "Wizard of Oz" activity.

1   The group leader plays the four-minute scene from the *Wizard of Oz* (available for download from YouTube) when the wizard gives the awards to Dorothy and her friends.
2   The therapist then asks group members to write their names on small pieces of paper and put them in a container (can or hat).
3   After each person draws a name from the container, they are told to create an award like that created by the wizard for the person whose name they drew. The award they create should represent a strength or an accomplishment of the person in group. They can use any of the materials available. It is important for the therapist to set a time limit. Members should not tell anyone whose name they have drawn until they present the award to the other person.
4   After an appropriate amount of time, each person presents the other group member with their award, stating what the award represents.

(Optional.) If the therapist does not want to use many different materials, the member can create a diploma or certificate for the person whose name they drew.

Create a Trophy

The therapist gathers a variety of materials for the group members, such as different types of tape, foil, markers, stickers, toilet paper and paper towel holders, plastic cups or bottles, pipe cleaners, construction paper and tagboard, toothpicks, and tin or aluminum cans. The therapist instructs the group to create a trophy that represents their progress and experience in the group. First, members work individually to create a personal trophy and then come together to combine their trophies into one trophy. The therapist then asks group members: "Tell me about this trophy." "What do you notice now that might not have been there in the beginning?" "What strengths does this trophy represent?" The therapist takes a picture of the trophy and gives each member a copy to remind them of their experience and to continue to work on their goals. Younger clients need some assistance in combining their trophies, but older youth find ways to put their trophies together in amazingly creative ways.

Portfolio of Progress

The therapist may elect to keep expressive art work or pictures of their work throughout the process of group in a portfolio. In the closing session, the therapist provides the portfolio to the group members and asks them to reflect on their different projects by asking questions such as:

- "What is your favorite project?"
- "How are your first projects different now than your last projects?"
- "If your (teacher, mother, friends, etc.) looked at the progress you made, what would he or she see as different?"

Creating a CD

Before the end of the group, the therapist collects names of songs that group members find empowering or encouraging. The therapist prints out the words to the songs and records each of the songs to make a CD for each member. In the last session the leader provides each member with their copy of the CD and the words to the songs they selected. In the background, the therapist plays the CD while the group talks about what the lyrics mean to them. Clients now have a collection of songs that they can use to motivate themselves and encourage progress.

Strengths of Group Members

The therapist takes a picture of each group member with an instant camera. Each member tapes the picture to a sheet of construction paper. The therapist hangs each of the pictures on construction paper on the wall. Group members walk around to each picture and write a word that describes a strength of the person whose picture is on the paper.

Getting off the Bus

This exercise involves group members pretending they are riding a bus together. A chair is set aside facing the wall away from the group. Members take turns getting off the bus, that is, the person goes and sits in the chair off to the side facing away from the group. For two minutes the rest of the group discusses what it was like to be in group with this member and what this member contributed to group. After the time is up, the member returns to the group and talks about what it is like to hear the group members' comments.

Creating a Dance

Before the end of the group, the members select one song that they find motivating. The therapist brings the song to the last group meeting and asks the group to create their own dance to celebrate their progress. Since the group has been together for at least six sessions, they have little trouble coming up with their dance. In one group I conducted, a group of fifth-grade boys created their own dance to Michael Jackson's "Thriller" by using what they had seen on television. They performed their dance for the Parent Teachers Association monthly meeting.

Cheerleaders

If the clients use a sports metaphor to track their progress in reaching their goals, then the use of cheerleaders provides a wonderful way to celebrate successes. Cheerleaders, defined as those who support and encourage the client, may include teachers, parents, peers, or even pets. The therapist asks clients to create their cheerleaders on blank paper using fingerprints. The client creates fingerprints by placing the thumb on a print pad and then touching it to the blank paper. Using several colors creates an interesting and attractive picture. The client then draws in the face, hair, hands, and feet. Since cheerleaders tend to be in formation, the therapist might ask the client to put the head cheerleader in front, and then others in order of their importance, some being on the same line, others may be on the shoulders of others, and still others in the back. Regardless of how many cheerleaders the client draws, each one should be celebrated for the support he lends to the client.

Letter to Self

A common approach to motivate individuals to continue to make progress is to write a letter from one's future self. The therapist asks group members, "Write a letter from your future self and talk about what you have done since group was over and how you have managed to continue your goals." In this way, clients imagine themselves in the future and accomplishing their goals. The letter also provides a plan for members to use to continue to strive toward their goals and maintain them. If appropriate, each member reads the letter to the group. If the member is too embarrassed or does not want to read the letter, the therapist can ask the client to talk about what he wrote and how it might help him reach his goals.

Timeline

The therapist provides a timeline drawn on a large piece of butcher paper. Each group member draws a picture or uses a word on the timeline illustrating their past, present, and future. Discussion centers on the progress group members have made, not whether they achieved their goals, though these should be celebrated as well. Amplifying their progress by using compliments, relationship questions, and asking questions about their accomplishments encourages members to continue toward their goals.

Reunion

Using a sandtray, clients select a miniature that represents themselves in the future and pretend they come together for a visit. Having these miniatures placed in the sand in a circle metaphorically provides a sense of unity and support. The therapist asks clients to speak from the perspective of their miniatures in the future and discuss what is different since their last group, what goals they have reached, and how they have done this. The therapist asks questions that help group members to break the larger goals down into smaller ones, for example, "What was the first thing you did that helped you reach your goal?" "What else did you do that was helpful?" "Who helped you in helping you to reach your goal?"

Summary

Solution-focused group therapy offers an effective and efficient approach to therapy, particularly when working with interpersonal challenges. By working together, children and adolescents learn new ways to communicate, develop supportive relationships, and recognize that they are not alone in their struggles. By using a SF approach in a group setting, clients also learn that they have resources to enlist in helping them reach goals and recognize personal strengths and resiliencies in themselves and others. The SF therapist compliments the group as well as group members on their interpersonal skills and asks carefully constructed questions to help group members reach their goals. Group members often learn they can rely on one another throughout the duration of the group and hopefully once the group ends.

References

Arman, J. F. (2002). A brief group counseling model to increase resiliency of students with mild disabilities. *Journal of Humanistic Counseling, Education, and Development, 4*(2), 120–128.

Bastien, C. H., Morin, C. M., Ouellet, M. C., Blais, F. C. & Bouchard, S. (2004). Cognitive-behavioral therapy for insomnia: Comparison of individual therapy, group therapy, and telephone consultations. *Journal of Consulting and Clinical Psychology, 72*(4), 653–659.

Cooley, L. (2009). *The power of groups*. Thousand Oaks, CA: Corwin Press.

Corey, M. S., Corey, G. & Corey, C. (2014). *Groups: Process and practice* (9th Ed.). Belmont, CA: Brooks/Cole.

Daki, J. & Savage, R. S. (2010). Solution-focused brief therapy: Impact on academic and emotional difficulties. *The Journal of Educational Research, 103*(5), 309–326.

Finn, C. A. (2003). Helping students cope with loss: Incorporating art into group counseling. *Journal of Specialists in Group Work, 28*(2), 155–165.

Kress, V. E. & Hoffman, R. M. (2008). Empowering adolescent survivors of sexual abuse: Application of a solution-focused Ericksonian counseling group. *Journal of Humanistic Counseling, Education and Development, 47*(2), 172–183.

Lafountain, R. M., Garner, N. E. & Eliason, G. T. (1996). Solution-focused counseling groups: A key for school counselors. *The School Counselor, 43*(4), 256–267.

McCrone, P., Weeramanthri, T., Knapp, K., Rushton, A., Trowells, J., Miles, G. & Kolvin, I. (2005). Cost-effectiveness of individual versus group psychotherapy for sexually abused girls. *Child and Adolescent Mental Health, 10*(1), 26–31.

McNair, R. A. & Arman, J. F. (2000). A small group model for working with elementary school children of alcoholics. *Professional School Counseling, 3*(4), 1096–2049.

Newsome, W. S. (2005). The impact of solution-focused brief therapy with junior high school students. *Children and Schools, 27*(2), 83–90.

Newsome, W. S. & Kelly, M. (2004). Grandparents raising grandchildren: A solution-focused brief therapy approach in school settings. *Social Work with Groups, 27*(4), 65–84.

O'Connell, B. (1998). *Solution-focused therapy*. Thousand Oaks, CA: Sage Publications.

Pérusse, R., Goodenough, G. E. & Lee, V. V. (2009). Group counseling in the schools. *Psychology in the Schools, 46*(3), 225–231.

Ray, D. C. (2011). *Advanced play therapy*. New York, NY: Routledge.

Rubin, J. A. & Rosenblum, N. (1977). Group art and group dynamics: An experimental study. *Art Psychotherapy, 4*, 185–193.

Sharry, J. (2007). *Solution-focused groupwork* (2nd Ed.). Los Angeles, CA: Sage.

Shin, S. K. (2009). Effects of a solution-focused program on the reduction of aggressive-ness and the improvement of social readjustment for Korean youth probationers. *Journal of Social Service Research, 25*(3), 274–284.

Stalker, C. A. & Fry, R. (1999). Comparison of short-term group and individual therapy for sexually abused women. *Canadian Journal of Psychiatry, 44*(2), 168–174.

van Rijn, B. & Wild, C. (2016). Comparison of transactional analysis group and indi-vidual psychotherapy in the treatment of depression and anxiety: Routine outcomes evaluation in community clinics. *Transactional Analysis Journal, 46*(1), 63–74.

Walker, L. (2008). Waikiki youth circles: Homeless youth learn goal setting skills. *Journal of Family Psychotherapy, 19*(1), 85–91.

Waller, D. (2011). Group art therapy: An interactive approach. In C. A. Machioldi (Ed.) *Handbook of art therapy* (2nd Ed.), 353–367. New York, NY: Guilford.

Weiss, R. D., Jaffee, W. B., de Menil, V. P. & Cogley, C. B. (2004). Group for substance abuse disorders: What do we know? *Harvard Review Psychiatry, 12*(6), 339–350.

Westbury, E. & Tutty, L. M. (1999). The efficacy of group treatment for survivors of child abuse. *Child Abuse & Neglect, 23*(1), 31–44.

Yalom, I. & Leszcz, M. (2005). *The theory and practice of group psychotherapy* (5th Ed.). New York, NY: Basic Books.

Zettle, R. D., Haflich, J. L. & Reynolds, R. A. (1992). Responsivity to cognitive therapy as a function of treatment format and client personality dimensions. *Journal of Clinical Psychology, 48*(6), 787–797.

Appendix

Table of Activities and Materials.

Chapter	Topic	SF Technique	Activity	Materials
7	Beginnings			
		Rapport Building	Coloring	Colors, markers, coloring books, digital coloring aps
			Ball Games	Small nerf balls and bats, small soccer balls of soft materials
			Games	Checkers, Jenga, Operation, cards
		Understanding and Perceptions	Sandtray	Sandtray box and miniatures (see Homeyer and Sweeney, 2011)
			Drawing, Coloring, Mixed Media	Drawing and coloring materials, paper, precut magazine pictures
			Writing	Paper, pencil, and/or journal
			Life Collage	Magazine pictures, pencils, colors, markers, pens, chalk, glue, poster board or tagboard
			Post a Secret	4 x 6 index cards, markers and pencils, magazine pictures, glue
		Who & What are Important	Who Lives in My House	Picture of a house
			Genogram 1	Sandtray and miniatures
			Genogram 2	Key with symbols, paper and pencil, colors
			Draw a Family	Paper and pencils, pens, colors
			Animal or Robot Stickers	Animal or robot stickers
			My Family is Like	Paper and pencils, colors, markers
			Sculpt a Family	Clay or play dough
			The Moon	Picture of the moon, paper, pencil, pens, and markers

			Tell a Family Story	Picture of *Starry Crown* by John Biggers
			Facebook and Cell Phone	Blank pictures of Facebook and cell phone
			Photographs and Selfies	Client's photographs from home, Kodak camera or cell-phone camera
8	Digging for Treasure			
		Exceptions	Frame It	Picture matte, paper, pencils, markers
			Collage	Pictures from magazines, glue
			Video	Cell phone
			Photographs	Cell phone or instamatic camera
			Sticky Notes	Different colored sticky notes and file folder
			Masks	Masks from heavy stock paper or commercial blank masks
			Lens	Large pair of sunglasses, paper and pencil
			Circles of Support	Three or four embedded circles on a piece of paper and pencils; optional miniatures
		Looking for Strengths	Sandtray	Sandtray and miniatures
			Mining for Treasure	Sandtray and colored gems
			Trophy	Different materials, such as cans, toilet paper or paper towel tubes, masking tape, duct tape, glue, construction paper, tin foil, etc.
			Body Image	Butcher paper, pens and paper

(continued)

			Photography	Digital or printed pictures of client and others
			Puppets	Bought or homemade puppets
		Relationship Questions	Sandtray	Sandtray and miniatures
			Companions and Allies	Paper and pencil
			Friendship Lifelines	Paper and pencil
			Facebook/Texting	Paper copies of Facebook or text message
		Scaling Questions	Sandtray	Miniatures and sandtray (optional)
			Racetrack	Racetrack drawn on large piece of paper
			Faces	Paper plates and pencils/markers
			Gingerbread Person	Copies of gingerbread people and colors or markers
			Gauge	Copy of a gauge as seen in a car
			Music	Keyboard or guitar; list of songs to represent different levels to scale success
			Ski Run	Copy of a ski run map
			Subway	Copy of a subway map
9	Setting Goals	Asking the Miracle Question		
			Drawing or Painting	Paper and pens, colors, markers, paints
			Frame It	Matte frame, paper, pens, colors, markers, or other media, tape
			Collage	Magazine pictures, tagboard, glue

			Sandtray	Miniatures and sandtray
				Miniatures and two sandtrays
			Sports Goals	Sports miniatures representing different sports and sandtray (optional)
			Magic Wand	Magic wand
			Faces	Paper plates, colors, markers
			Treasure Map	Treasure map and markers, stickers, or pen
			Wishing Well	Miniature of wishing well and sandtray (optional)
			Magic Lamp	Genie's lamp
			Gingerbread People	Copy of three gingerbread people and colors or markers
		Setting Smaller Goals		
			Miracle Story Board	Index cards, markers, pencils, colors, markers
			Treasure Map	Treasure map, markers or stickers
			Sports Fields	Sandtray or pictures of relevant sports field
			Subway Map	Copy of a subway map
			Mountain Climbing	Paper and pencil, markers, water colors, colors, chalk
			Hiking	Paper, pencil, water colors, markers, colored chalk
			Building a Tower	Blocks, cardboard boxes, or other possible materials for building a tower
		Empower Client		
			Sandtray	Sandtray and miniatures

(continued)

				Photography	Instant camera or cell phone, props, costumes
					Superhero costumes
				Power Pose	Instant camera or cell phone
				Superhero	Paper, pencil, colors or markers, colored chalk
				Transpose Images of Power	Pictures of powerful people, people in paintings, superheroes, and instant camera
				The Moon	Picture of moon and pencil, paper, markers
				Managing Time	Pictures of life balance wheel; paper, pens, markers, magazine pictures, and other objects
				Puzzle	Plain cutout puzzle or teen magazine picture cover glued and cutout into a puzzle
				Sandtray	Sandtray and miniatures
				Word Cards	200 or more word cards with various nouns, verbs, adjectives, adverbs, pronouns, indefinite articles, and blank cards
				Globe or Map	Markers or small stickers
				Journaling	Small spiral journals, pens, markers, magazine pictures, patterned paper like in scrapbooks
				Sports Goals	Drawn picture of selected sports field, markers, colored dots, stickers
				Group Story	Large poster writing paper or white board and markers
				Group Mural	Long butcher paper, markers, colors, crayons

		Transition Stage	Mandala	Large mandala cut into pieces for each group member, magazine pictures, pens, markers, and other instruments
			Miniatures	Miniatures and sandtray (optional)
			Word Cards	Same as above
			Deck of Cards	Deck of cards with key
			Facebook Page	Facebook page for each member with "What's better" written in the first box
			Emojis	Copies of emojis
			Masks	Cardboard or commercial masks; markers, magazine pictures
		Ending Stage		
			Wizard	Clip of *Wizard of Oz*, different materials (tin foil, small boxes, cans, string, yarn, glue, magazine pictures, paints, colored chalk, markers, construction paper, decorations, magazine pictures
			Create a Trophy	Various materials, such as markers, stickers, toilet or paper towel holders, pipe cleaners, tagboard, string or yarn, plastic bottles, cups, cans, duct tape or masking tape
			Portfolio of Progress	Collection of client materials in folder or box
			CD	CD with copies of songs and words to songs
			Group Member Strengths	Pictures of group members (Kodak camera), construction paper, markers, tape

(continued)

(continued)

			Getting off the Bus	Chairs, numbers printed on small pieces of paper
			Create a Dance	Music selected by clients
			Cheerleader Fingerprints	Paper, pens, different colors of ink pads
			Letter to Self	Paper and pencil or pens
			Reunion	Miniatures of people and sandtray

Index